D1252553

c.1 ●

Ball, Jeff.
  The self-sufficient suburban garden
/ by Jeff Ball. -- Emmaus, Pa. :
Rodale Press, c1983.
  xiv, 236 p. : ill. ; 25 cm.

  Bibliography: p. 219-223.
  Includes index.
  ISBN 0-87857-457-3 : $14.95

  1. Vegetable gardening. 2.
Gardening. I. Title. II. Title:
Suburban garden. III. Title: Backyard
food production.

THE
SELF-SUFFICIENT
SUBURBAN
GARDEN

THE
SELF-SUFFICIENT
SUBURBAN
GARDEN

by Jeff Ball

Rodale Press, Emmaus, Pennsylvania

Art direction by Karen A. Schell
Book design by John E. Pepper
Illustrations by Brian Swisher
Photographs by John P. Hamel, except for the following: Patti Seip, pp. 98, 100, and 146; Carl Doney, pp. 111 and 113.

Library of Congress Cataloging in Publication Data

Ball, Jeff
     The self-sufficient suburban garden.

     Bibliography: p.
     Includes index.
     1. Vegetable gardening.   I. Title.   II. Title:
Suburban garden.   III. Title: Backyard food production.
SB321.B25   1983   635   82-23102
ISBN 0-87857-457-3 hardcover

2 4 6 8 10 9 7 5 3   hardcover

Contents

CONTENTS

THE
SELF-SUFFICIENT
SUBURBAN
GARDEN

by Jeff Ball

Rodale Press, Emmaus, Pennsylvania

Art direction by Karen A. Schell
Book design by John E. Pepper
Illustrations by Brian Swisher
Photographs by John P. Hamel, except for the following: Patti Seip, pp. 98, 100, and 146; Carl Doney, pp. 111 and 113.

Library of Congress Cataloging in Publication Data

Ball, Jeff
    The self-sufficient suburban garden.

    Bibliography: p.
    Includes index.
    1. Vegetable gardening. I. Title. II. Title:
Suburban garden. III. Title: Backyard food production.
SB321.B25 1983   635   82-23102
ISBN 0-87857-457-3 hardcover

2 4 6 8 10 9 7 5 3   hardcover

Acknowledgments

In 1974 I had not planted a seed or picked a vegetable for over 20 years. But in 1974 I was ready to garden again, and it was my friend Bob Lollo who was instrumental in moving me toward organic growing methods. Bob's enthusiasm for the organic vegetable garden was very contagious, and his wisdom and advice were critical in helping me get through those first difficult years of battling acid soil and the bugs.

Writing a book can get difficult at times. The words do not necessarily flow easily every day you sit down at the word processor. Without the support, encouragement, and critical acclaim given me by my wife, Liz, this book would not exist. I thank her especially for being the loving but hard-nosed editor that only an experienced high school English teacher can be. I am a much-improved writer because of her very professional assistance. Turning from being a "normal" person into a suburban homesteader has not been a smooth and uncomplicated transition for me. Through it all, Liz has given me the strength, help, and love that has made these years productive and terribly exciting.

I received help and encouragement in writing this book from all quarters. I have acquired an enormous amount of wisdom and gained some valuable skills from my editor, Anne Halpin, at Rodale Press. In the early days, especially, my best cheerleader was my very able typist, Lois Murray. Suggestions from friends, loving encouragement from parents and in-laws, and ideas from students and fellow homesteaders all made significant contributions to this effort.

I also want to thank my teenage son, Ted. When he was ten and totally socialized to living on junk food and "normal" cooking, his father and mother went "organic" and turned his suburban childhood upside down. Through these past years he has been my reality tester. He brings me back to earth when I forget that most people are not into compost and cold zucchini soup. What I very much appreciate is that his critiques have always been constructive and offered with love and respect for what I believe in.

In the final analysis, this book is the product of several families rather than of the one individual who gets credit as an author. My parents and grandparents helped me learn the values of self-reliance and good food. My own family, Liz and Ted, helped me understand how moving toward more self-reliance in one's own food production can be satisfying and successful when the whole family participates and supports the idea. So to my whole extended family, I say a heartfelt thank-you.

Introduction

Few Americans appreciate what an enormous economic force backyard food production has become in this country. A recent Gallup survey (conducted for Gardens for All, The National Association for Gardening, in 1981) found that some 38 million American households—47 percent of all the households in the United States—had backyard gardens in 1981. In addition, 7 million households, many of them in cities, grew some vegetables in containers. The total production of these 45 million households was worth a staggering sum of over $15 billion! The survey also found that there were another 17 million households having space for a garden but not choosing to have one and 14 million households not having the space but wishing they could have a garden.

One other statistic is astounding: If half of the 38 million gardeners used what is called the intensive method for growing their vegetables, the total output of backyard vegetable gardens in this country would satisfy 100 percent of the nation's need for vegetables! For now, this is only a theoretical proposition, but it suggests a fascinating and exciting prospect. Can backyard food production be developed to the point where home growers could supply maybe 75 percent of our country's vegetable needs and perhaps 25 percent of our meat needs in the next few decades? I think it can, and I believe that such a goal is worth pursuing.

The Ball family has been learning about food production for over six years. All 12 months of the year we are reaping the rewards of our experience in the form of fresh vegetables, which are supplemented by frozen homegrown peas, broccoli, and green and wax beans; root-cellar-stored carrots, beets, and parsnips; and many kinds of processed foods, including pickles and sauerkraut. With the canning, freezing, and root-cellaring, we are close to producing our entire year's supply of most of these vegetables, and we saved over $800 on our food bills this past year. What's special about our food production effort is that we're doing all this on an average

As you can see from this photo, my garden is attractive and productive, despite the limitations created by restricted space and shade from nearby trees.

80 by 150-foot suburban property with a backyard garden of about 800 square feet. We are growing our own food on a quarter of an acre in the suburbs while both my wife and I work full time.

How the System Works

Our system is so simple and logical that it can be followed by just about anyone, and I'm going to show you how it can work for you as it has for us here in southeastern Pennsylvania. By following the five-stage program outlined in this book, you will be able to turn your plain lawn into a productive, efficient food production system.

The plan takes you through five years. You'll begin with a small, simple garden, and each year you will add a bit more to it. In the first year, most of your time will be devoted to learning some planning and management concepts that will enable you to figure out just how much food you need to grow, and whether you have enough space and time to produce all of your vegetable supply at home. You'll start to apply these concepts to your small garden.

In the second year, you'll expand the garden to produce your entire fresh vegetable supply during the growing season, with a little left over to can or freeze. The third stage incorporates intensive growing techniques and season-extending techniques such as using a cold frame. In this stage you'll increase productivity; you'll learn more about using every bit of space efficiently, and you'll start to plant fruit trees, nuts, and berries.

In the fourth year, you'll be growing food all year round, by using a solar grow frame, greenhouse, or sunny areas of your house. Your winter crops will be supplemented by vegetables you've stored or put up from the outdoor garden. In the final, fifth stage, your food production system will incorporate chickens or rabbits, bees, and fish, and you'll have reached a high level of self-sufficiency.

Of course, if you don't want to go as far as chickens and bees, you can stop before you get there. In fact, you can follow this plan to whatever stage meets your needs and degree of interest, and simply maintain that level of productivity. You can leave the chickens to your more ambitious neighbors. On the other hand, if you're already an experienced gardener, you'll probably be able, after reading through the first two chapters, to start right off with stage two or three.

Learning from Experience

My family and I consider ourselves suburban homesteaders. We try to apply all the principles of self-reliance to a suburban setting, while still maintaining on our property the neat appearance that's so beloved in American suburban communities. We heat our home with a wood stove. Our kitchen has a recycling center for bottles and paper. We have a fair-size garden using intensive beds and succession-planting techniques. With our solar greenhouse, cold frames, and root cellar, we are producing food every month of the year. Our future plans include fruit trees, chickens or rabbits, bees, and fish. To date we may not have made every mistake in the book, but we've certainly made our share. Throughout these pages, I'll share with you some of the mistakes we made, partly because they're amusing to look back on, but mostly in the hope that I can spare you a few of the pitfalls we fell into. Inevitably you'll go out and make some of your own mistakes, too.

One of the problems with producing food, especially in the beginning, is that it's all too easy to make mistakes. The amount of knowledge a successful gardener has to apply even to the simplest of backyard gardens is impressive, and in the beginning we don't always know everything we need to know. And lack of planning can be the source of as many mistakes as lack of knowledge. Most of my problems were caused by trying to do too many things at once. I didn't appreciate the differences between assorted varieties of the same vegetable. I figured that a tomato is a tomato is a tomato, right? Wrong. My enthusiasm for trying lots of new ideas often served to reduce our harvest rather than increase it. But in spite of all that my garden survived, and today we are getting a very nice return in most of our vegetables and see ourselves saving more money as each year goes by.

Looking Ahead

I'm convinced that we will continue to learn new skills and have new ideas about food production for the next 20 years. The anticipation of that personal growth is satisfying. Sharing that growth with each other is even more satisfying. All that and saving money as well—it's not a bad arrangement. Successful food production definitely requires knowledge and skill, but it also requires a plan, a philosophy, and considerable patience. This book is about all those things.

How to Use This Book

Throughout this book, important ideas and concepts appear in **boldface** type. You can page through the book reading just the parts in **boldface** and get an outline of what the backyard food production system is all about. This will also help you later on, when you want to locate a specific idea in the book and reread the explanation to refresh your memory.

At the opening of each chapter, you'll find a Game Plan which states the goal of this particular stage of the system and presents a summary of the steps you'll take in order to reach that goal. These steps are explained within the chapter. The game plan is also intended to help you locate particular bits of information more quickly.

At the back of the book, you'll find an appendix of charts that provide you with instant information on just about every aspect of planting, growing, harvesting, and storing food. This section will be of great help to you in calculating how much you need to grow, and it also provides you with a quick reference to gardening techniques and troubleshooting.

Finally, I've provided an annotated bibliography listing the best, most helpful books and periodicals I've found, for further information.

1

Why Produce Your Own Food?

THE GAME PLAN

The Goal: Your first move in becoming a backyard food producer is to decide to make the switch from gardening to serious food production, and learn the basics of what's involved.

The Strategy:

1. Learn the concept of how backyard food production is different from gardening.

2. Change your thinking—start to look at your backyard in terms of "system" and "savings."

3. Learn what's possible in your backyard—how much food you can grow, how much money you can save, how much nutritional value is attainable.

4. Learn how to calculate your investment costs, maintenance costs, and savings.

5. Assess your eating habits to determine whether the food you produce will form a significant part of your diet.

The question of whether or not to grow some of your own food is becoming more and more of a basic economic issue. The pressures of inflation and a tight economy are making all of us take a hard look at where we're spending our money. Food is a basic necessity, and its cost is soaring; it's taking a bigger cut of our paychecks. If producing some of our own food in our own backyards will save us money, then it is an attractive option to consider.

Gardening vs. Backyard Food Production

Most of us who grow vegetables think of ourselves as "gardeners." We generally don't think of ourselves as "food producers." The "producer" usually is thought to be the commercial farmer who grows food for a living. Since the victory gardens of World War II, gardeners have not been as concerned about the volume as we have about quality and variety of the vegetables that we grow. We've always thought of our gardens as a supplement to the family diet—a source of fresh and tasty vegetables in the summer. But today more and more of us are starting to look at our gardens as one of our primary year-round food sources. We are starting to think in terms of food production, almost like the pioneers did 100 years ago. Food production systems are being developed in suburban backyards all across the nation. But instead of "40 acres and a mule," our rallying cry is more like "a quarter of an acre and a cat."

The garden gives us a measure of control over our lives that nongardeners don't have. We can grow what we want to eat, avoid the use of toxic pesticides and additives used in processing, and save money at the same time. People who produce some of their own food in the backyard are no longer totally dependent on farmers, trucks, and supermarkets for their nourishment.

One problem we have that the pioneers didn't have is limited space. Our forefathers had almost unlimited space in which to grow their food, but most of us live in small towns or suburbs. When we look out our back door we don't see the rolling prairie or the virgin forest, we see someone else's backyard fence only 80 feet away. As a result, backyard gardens are now being designed and managed to produce the maximum amount of food possible in a limited space and in a limited growing period. Research is going on at research centers and in backyards all across the country, and it's proving an enormous help in learning how to get more food out of less space. I'll be mentioning the work at some of these research facilities throughout the book. It helps to know that other people are looking for—and finding—the same answers you're seeking.

You Can Raise More than Just Vegetables and Fruit

Another fairly recent development in backyard food systems is the addition of what had been solely rural kinds of activities such as raising small livestock. A well-publicized research project called the Integral Urban House in Berkeley, California, proves that the backyard doesn't have to be limited just to growing vegetables. You can also produce meat from rabbits and chickens, you can have eggs from those same chickens, and you can even raise fish. Fruit trees, berries, beehives, and nut trees are all possible in the urban and suburban backyard. There are now over a dozen such demonstrations of this integrated approach to food production throughout the United States and Canada. There's a directory of these integral house projects in the Appendix—you may find you want to learn more about them. All of them have materials they can send you, and some publish newsletters to which you can subscribe. These demonstration projects are proving that backyard food production systems can become a major source of food for more and more Americans in the coming decades.

There is no question now that each of us can save a good bit of money by producing more and more of our own food. It's not only feasible, but it can be taken on by almost anyone who has the interest. It doesn't look like our problems with high energy costs, diminishing natural resources, and a sluggish economy are going to go away in the near future. Consequently, it makes more and more sense to take the plunge and start producing at least some of our own food at home.

Changing Your Thinking

When you make the shift from gardening to food production, you will find yourself thinking about your backyard in a very different way. You will begin to think "system," and you'll think "savings." **Food production involves the integration of a number of activities. Not only will you be growing as much of your food as you can, but you will also be processing some of it; you'll be storing some of it; you'll be cooking some of it; and you'll be recycling the by-products in a compost heap to go back into the earth to nourish future crops.** It is planning for the interrelationship of all of these activities that helps you get maximum benefit from your backyard food production system.

In addition, you'll be analyzing your production in terms of the money savings that can accrue. How can you produce the greatest savings? **You must consider at least four issues in weighing production against savings. The cost of setting up and managing your garden, the value of the produce, the space you have available, and the time you are able to spend all contribute to how much money you can save from backyard food production.** All these issues will be thoroughly reviewed in the next few chapters.

Food Production—An Economic Issue

Anyone who does the weekly food shopping is painfully aware that for the past few years the cost of food has been rising at an alarming rate. Whether to buy peanut butter becomes a decision almost as important as deciding whether to take a trip on your vacation. In April of 1981 a family of four with an income of $23,000 spent an average of $5,571 a year for food. That is 24 percent of their income! With inflation running at about 11 percent in 1981, they would have had to spend another $600 in 1982 just to keep up. While every family varies in how much of their diet is made up of vegetables, a reasonable estimate of the range of the cost of vegetables is 17 to 30 percent, excluding potatoes. This means that, in 1982, the average family probably spent between $1,000 and $2,000 on vegetables, most of which could be grown in a backyard food production system.

Looking again at the value of vegetables grown in gardens across the whole country, we learn that about 40 percent of all the vegetables (excluding potatoes) eaten in the country in 1980 were grown in backyard gardens and containers on apartment balconies. As we noted before, this represents more than $15 billion worth of food. **Many variables come into play when we try to figure out how much our own backyard garden produces in terms of dollar value. Nevertheless, I think it is a fair estimate to say that a modest 20 by 30-foot garden can produce $500 to $600 worth of vegetables in the second year of operation. After a few years' experience, and by using intensive methods, that value can be increased to $1,000 or more.** Some vegetables are worth more than others, but among the best values are tomatoes, onions, leaf lettuce, summer squash, and green beans. These are the most popular and generally are easiest to grow.

Before we start to add up all these wonderful savings, we must not forget first to subtract the cost of setting up and maintaining that garden. If you go out and buy a $600 tiller, a $450 shredder, a $300 sprinkler, and a $70 cowboy hat, you have just blown all your savings and more. Obviously, capital expenditures will vary according to your income, the size of the garden, and how much fancy equipment you feel you need. The Gallup survey mentioned in the Introduction showed that once you have whatever tools and equipment you need, seeds, fertilizer, and other supplies for an average garden of about 20 by 30 feet cost approximately $20. Of course, that figure doesn't include the very latest gadget for doubling your tomato crop; that costs $10 more.

To be realistic, I have to admit that I think the $20 estimate is a bit low. While I have a garden that's about twice the size of the national average, I spend $50 to $75 a year on it, and I don't use much fertilizer (compost instead) or insecticide. In addition to seeds and plants, there always seems to be that new pair of gloves, or the watering can that needs replacing, some seed-starting trays that look really neat, and other essential odds and ends that I just can't do without when I see them on sale at the garden store. But even with all that, a $50 investment for a $500 return is attractive in anybody's ledger book.

Food Preferences and Practices

There is a rather critical qualification that must be made very clear in any discussion about how to save money by growing your own food—you have to like to eat what you grow. When you think about it, you realize that American food preferences and practices in many ways dictate *against* backyard food production. Our life-style has many of us eating outside the home a great deal, and although our habits as a nation are starting to change, many of us still have an almost religious dedication to meat, which is difficult, though not impossible (see chapter 7), to grow in the backyard.

Meat is still our primary food in this country. We eat meat at almost every meal. The average American consumes over 260 pounds of it, including fish and poultry, each year—that's far more than we need for our daily protein intake. Meat just happens to be what we like to eat. Many restaurants organize their menus around meat dishes; vegetables just come along for the ride or don't appear in the menu at all. Ask someone what he had for supper last night and his answer will probably be the meat portion of the meal. Cookbooks, too, are organized around the various types of meat; vegetables usually are thrown together in a single group. My own recipe card file had only one category for vegetables and seven for various meats. That changed when my vegetable section got so thick I realized I had to set up some vegetable categories such as legumes, green vegetables, yellow vegetables, and salads. Think for a minute about the sandwich, that great American passion. Quickly, a name a sandwich that does not have meat or cheese in it. I do like a cold baked bean sandwich, but I've never even considered a broccoli sandwich. Another important point to consider here is that meat has a higher unit cost and a lower per unit nutritional value than most vegetables.

However, there is one new phenomenon in America that bodes well for our interest in backyard food production. That is the introduction and popularity of the salad bar, especially in the fast food chains. Salads are becoming interesting again. The variety in a salad bar offers nearly everyone just those things they like to eat, and usually in large quantities. In our family the salad bar is using leftovers creatively combined into a monster salad. Inasmuch as salads are becoming a more common component of American meals, we can talk some more about backyard food production and real savings in your food bill.

What about *Your* Eating Habits?

No matter how you approach it, you have to review certain aspects of your life-style before you can launch yourself into any serious food production effort. **If you are going to save any significant money with backyard food production, at least four things must be considered:**

1. **You must like to eat what you are able to grow.**
2. **The food you produce must represent a significant percentage of your diet. (This is particularly critical for those families with two adults who work out of the home and carry their lunch.)**

   3. You must be able and willing to process and store produce that you can't
      eat fresh.
   4. Your cooking practices must be compatible with the rhythm of the gar-
      den's shifting production schedules.

I will talk in much more detail about all these issues as I get into the planning
process for developing your food production operation.

The Nutritional Value of Homegrown Produce

In recent years, our family has become far more conscious of the nutritional value
of what we eat. Books like *Diet for a Small Planet* by Frances Moore Lappé, and
The Supermarket Handbook by Nikki and David Goldbeck (see the Bibliography),
have had significant influence on our ideas. Magazines, newspapers, and friends
have also contributed to our heightened awareness of what we eat. It's true that
many people have developed increased nutritional awareness in recent years. However, I believe it's also fair to say that the American diet in general can still stand
improvement.

    While the government bends over backward to avoid seriously offending the
food industry, we find ourselves wondering if there is *anything* we can eat and feel
sure it doesn't cause cancer. Now that infectious disease has been replaced by degenerative disease as the most common cause of death in this country, dietary defi-
ciencies have become an important variable in determining which degenerative disease will finally cause our demise. Conversely, diet can have a major influence on
which diseases we *don't* get. My sense of logic encourages me to assume that a
good diet means a longer life as well.

    Technically, what we need to survive and especially, to be healthy, are five
different classes of nutrients that come from our food. We need carbohydrates, pro-
teins, and fats to provide the calories of energy we need to function. In addition,
that energy cannot be effectively produced without the proper amounts of vitamins
and minerals. We have recently learned that the fiber we find in food sources of
complex carbohydrates is also critical to maintaining good health, because it ab-
sorbs water, acids, and bacteria and moves them out of our system.

    But how do we figure out what is a "good" diet, whether it be for weight loss
or simply for maintaining good health? With a new fad diet coming out every year,
it's difficult to know who is right and who is just exploiting us to make some money.
I'm not about to suggest what's best for anyone else. But in my own diet, I try
to achieve a nutrient ratio of 55 to 65 percent carbohydrates, 20 to 30 percent fats,
and roughly 10 to 15 percent protein. At the same time, I'm absolutely convinced
that to assure a healthy diet, it's far more important to observe the principles of
variety and moderation than to worry about these ratios.

Fresh vegetables are an important part of a healthy diet, and homegrown produce that's raised organically and picked at the peak of ripeness assures you of the highest nutritional quality. In addition, as a gardener you have access to high-vitamin varieties that are not grown commercially and can't be bought in the supermarket.

The Ball family members have been slowly changing their food habits over the past few years, and we anticipate still more changes. We now eat less meat and more fruit and vegetables than we did in years past. We are much more conscious of the minerals and vitamins we're getting than we were before. Changing food habits or diet is one of the hardest things to do. I quit smoking after 20 years and cut out hard liquor after 15 years, and I've found those two habits much easier (and they were not easy) to kick than all my favorite little bad food habits.

People are funny about their food preferences. In this country we seem to select as our favorite foods all the foods that aren't good for us. This applies to vegetables, too, for the seeming minority of us who admit to liking vegetables. A fascinating study conducted in 1980 by M. A. Stevens of the University of California
at Davis showed that most of the fruits and vegetables with the highest food value
were nowhere to be found on the list of fruits and vegetables most preferred by
Americans. How do your preferences match up with the chart titled Fruits and
Vegetables Ranked by Nutritional Value and Preference?

Fruits and Vegetables Ranked by Nutritional Value and Preference

Highest Nutrition	Favorite to Eat
Broccoli	Tomatoes
Spinach	Oranges
Brussels sprouts	Potatoes
Lima beans	Lettuce
Peas	Sweet corn
Asparagus	Bananas
Artichoke	Carrots
Cauliflower	Cabbage
Sweet potatoes	Onions
Carrots	Sweet potatoes

In the final analysis, we will eat what we enjoy eating. But you may well find
that growing your own vegetables will help you develop preferences for some foods
that you might not have enjoyed previously.

How Nutritious Is *Your* Backyard?
It is possible to grow all kinds of food, including animals, in a backyard system.
However, most beginners start with vegetables, and then if they wish to expand
their production they can get into the other areas as they develop skills. Most of
this book focuses on the development of the vegetable side of the production system. Consequently, we're talking mostly about producing food that provides carbohydrates, vitamins, minerals, and lots of fiber. The protein and fats must come from
other sources, at least in the beginning. The chart titled Nutritional Content of
Foods, in the Appendix, gives you a clear idea of how all the vegetables rate in
terms of nutritional content. Certainly, though, you should concentrate your first
efforts at backyard food production on those things you most like to eat and that
are easiest to grow. The nutritional balancing can come later.

How Long Will It Take?

It takes three to five years to begin to feel that you know what you are doing in a vegetable garden. But even after that, there will always be something new to learn. One of the fascinations of gardening is that you are always learning something new, no matter how long you've been doing it. In addition, there's considerable research activity dealing with home gardening, which is producing new information and insights into increasing your production. I'll refer to some of this research throughout this book.

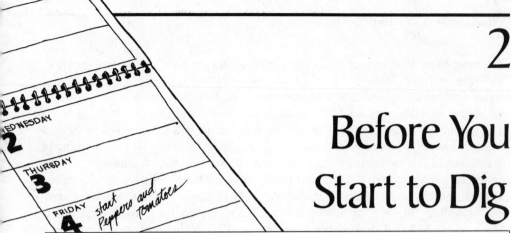

Before You Start to Dig

THE GAME PLAN

The Goal: It's time to get your backyard food production system underway. The first steps are planning the system and determining your food needs.

The Strategy:

1. Patience is the key to success—above all, take your time and proceed gradually and carefully.

2. Plan carefully and learn how to consider these factors in your planning process—time, space, aesthetics, skills and knowledge, costs, and tools and equipment.

3. Start to learn how you can save in each of these areas to get the most production for the least total investment from your backyard.

4. Start to develop sources of further information in each of these areas.

The most important suggestion in this entire book is to take your time—go slowly—have patience. Backyard food production, whether it be of vegetables or animals, requires considerable knowledge and skill. In other words, you can make disastrous mistakes very easily if you barge ahead without thinking through what it is you hope to accomplish. A little planning ahead will go a long way toward making your effort a productive success. The wonderful thing about gardening is that it allows you to legitimize daydreaming—it now becomes "planning." All experienced gardeners will tell you that planning is important. What they don't usually admit is that most of that planning was done ruminating while they were driving, or walking the dog, or just sitting in front of the fire on a cold winter night. Some people call that daydreaming; gardeners call it planning. It is very valuable time spent. Whether you call it daydreaming or planning, it will save you time, money, and even some sore muscles.

Issues to Consider in Planning Your System

If you're going to be a successful gardener, you've got to know what you're getting into and be sure that you don't already dislike it. Common sense tells us that if we don't like to do something, no matter how good it is for us or how much money it's going to save us, we won't stick with it. **There are a number of key issues to think about before you rush outside and start digging your garden. How much time and energy do you really intend to spend on this project, and what can you realistically expect to accomplish in that amount of time? How much space do you want to set aside for food production? How will you maintain the appearance of your property while producing all this food? Where can you get the skills and knowledge you will need? Do you know how to control your costs? How much equipment do you really need to get started? How much should you take on in the first year? What do you want to grow?** After you have thought a bit about each of these concerns, then maybe you will be ready to go out and turn the first shovelful. Judging from my experience, even taking as much as a whole year to think through all the considerations involved in backyard food production is not terribly unreasonable. I will admit, though, that we all want to get into a little gardening while we are doing all this thinking.

Saving Time

Your time is perhaps the most important variable in any effort to get into backyard food production. The challenge is to achieve a reasonable level of production without having to spend so much time that you sacrifice other activities you enjoy. This book is written on the assumption that at least one, and often two, members of the family are working full time to make a living, and that they don't wish to devote every minute of their spare time to food production.

How much time will it actually take? On the average, a beginning garden of approximately 200 to 400 square feet will take you between one and four hours a week to maintain, once you've done the initial digging and planting. That task can usually be accomplished by a couple in one or two weekends in the spring. That weekend's worth of hard work will give you a summer garden which will provide you with several hundred dollars' worth of fresh vegetables, and perhaps a bit extra for the freezer.

Logically, as you expand your food production system in terms of volume, season, and variety, you will be adding to the time it is going to take to maintain. But as you gain more knowledge and experience, you will be able to perform the necessary tasks more quickly and efficiently. Another important point here is that there are dozens of time-saving schemes that can ease the time pressure as you become experienced enough to take advantage of them. For example, as you learn how to use mulch throughout the whole garden, you will eliminate the time it takes to control the weeds. We'll be looking at ways to save time throughout the book, for each stage of a food production system.

Since most of us value our free time as a precious commodity, any tricks that help save time in our food production effort are very welcome. One caution, however, must be made about saving time. One of the appeals of chemical fertilizers, pesticides, and herbicides is that they will save you time. Those practices found in what is called organic gardening will tend to take more time than those using the chemical approach. This issue is discussed more fully in chapter 3, but in the end your decision about which course to follow comes down to a question of the short-term benefits of saved time vs. the long-term benefits of a more productive soil. Saving time now in fact could be harmful to your food production system later.

My view is that any productive activity, whether it be gardening, fixing cars, or building furniture, deserves the kind of care and time-consuming attention it takes to do it well in both the short run and the long run. For example, I recommend that all beginning gardeners start right off with permanent raised beds, rather than with the traditional flat rows. This method takes more time in the first two or three years of a garden, but then after that you can stop digging your garden altogether if you like. I have 800 square feet of garden in raised beds and don't expect to do much digging ever again. It has taken me four years to get it into that condition. While there is an initial time investment, this is one time saver that can make backyard food production a possibility even for the busiest people.

Space and Its Appearance

When you own less than a quarter of an acre of land, as most suburbanites and town dwellers do, the space available for a vegetable garden is going to be limited. There are a number of factors that need to be considered in establishing a site for the garden. This is an important decision. You can always change it back next year, but who needs that kind of wasted effort? A little planning now will save many headaches in the future.

Working with Shade
A major consideration in many backyards is finding where there will be enough sun. Vegetables do not grow in full shade, and many backyards have sufficient trees to create a major dilemma: Should you cut down a few of those big, old trees in the interest of a long-term investment in your food supply? I had to cut down a large ash tree to be able to begin my garden six years ago. I reasoned that, since it did not shade the house and thus did not help keep it cool, I could afford to lose one big tree for the garden, since I had several others to maintain the appearance of the property. It was not an easy decision. We feel great respect and affection for large trees, and besides that it can cost as much as $600 to have one removed. I still must plan my garden within the shading patterns of the other trees. It means that some of my garden gets just the minimum sunlight—five to six hours a day—but with excellent soil, average to good production is still possible. Also, a number of vegetables, such as lettuce, onions, and Swiss chard, can take partial shade during the day and do just fine. The need, then, is to plan your garden so that the shade-tolerant vegetables are in the shaded areas. The chart titled Interplanting Guide, in the Appendix, indicates which vegetables can tolerate some shade during the day.

The simple way to determine which parts of your garden are going to be partially shaded is to watch what happens on a sunny day. Remember that the pattern will be different in the summer than it was in the spring. Noting where the shade falls in the morning, at noon, and in the middle of the afternoon will give you some idea. For those of you who are interested in a more scientific approach to assessing your gardening space and its sun requirements, there is an excellent description of the procedures for measuring the amount of sun that is available for raising food in *The Integral Urban House* (see the Bibliography) on pages 53 to 56. This is a valuable book, and I will be referring to the work of the Farallones Institute, responsible for the Integral Urban House, in chapters to come.

Saving Space
As you think through the many possible ways to save space, remember to check out the books and magazines dealing with urban gardening problems. The folks in the city have an even greater space problem than those of us in the suburbs, and many good ideas can be gleaned from their approaches to space saving. **Here are some ideas to get you going on your own space-saving schemes: The compost pile can be hidden in a corner, behind a shed or hedge. Fruit trees can be trained flat up against a fence or a garage wall. Vine crops like pole beans can be trained to climb a trellis or some other vertical structure, taking up less ground space than**

When choosing the site for your garden, it's important to take into account the shifting patterns of shade cast by trees and tall shrubs in your yard. As shown here, a garden that is in shade during part of the morning *(top)* may enjoy full sun during the afternoon *(bottom)*.

bush varieties of the same crop. There are many other space-saving ideas, and I'll be discussing some of them, such as interplanting techniques, succession planting, and container growing, in later chapters.

Aesthetic Concerns

A vegetable garden can be a thing of beauty with a little planning ahead of time. Here are a few examples of ways to make your garden pretty as well as productive. A garden using raised beds that are curved into patterns produces a very attractive visual effect. Flowers such as nasturtiums and marigolds, planted among the vegetables, can add beauty to the scene while also repelling certain insects and pests at the same time. On the other side of the coin, a flower garden can include some vegetables artfully placed throughout, saving space in the vegetable garden while introducing more colors and textures into the flower garden. For example, a border of frilly lettuce or a background row of red-stemmed Ruby Swiss chard can have a visually stunning effect.

While I believe that there is sufficient evidence to show that leaving some weeds in and around a garden helps reduce insect damage to your vegetables, I tend to opt for the orderly appearance of a well-weeded and heavily mulched garden, especially in a suburban area. Our garden is our view from our back deck, so its appearance is important to us.

Gaining Knowledge

Recently I heard writer Vic Sussman speak about his suburban homesteading experiences, which were recounted in an informative and often hilarious manner in his book *Never Kiss a Goat on the Lips* (see the Bibliography). He said that his success was generally based on his acquiring knowledge first by reading and then by doing. He recommended reading books and magazines and then going out into the vegetable patch and applying a new piece of knowledge. I could not agree more. That can be a problem in a society such as ours, where people seem to believe that they don't have to read directions. Too many people buy insecticides and liberally spray them all over the place with no concern for the recommendations on the label. Or they buy cars and never check the operator's manual. I do not believe that you can approach food production in the same manner. Raising food is an activity in which it takes many years to achieve any degree of expertise. Reading and then doing are among the best ways I know to gain the knowledge needed to be successful and to avoid discouraging setbacks.

Learning from Research Centers

There is no dearth of written material these days about gardening and backyard food production. In the past ten years there has been something of a boom in the publishing business dealing with gardening. That has not occurred simply because people are more interested in growing their own food, but because there have been enormous developments in the knowledge of how to grow food in your backyard contributed by a number of very exciting research projects. The New Alchemy Institute in Falmouth, Massachusetts, has been working with food production, energy production, and the relationship between those two activities to produce some valuable new ideas for the backyard food producer. The Farallones Institute in Berkeley, California, mentioned earlier, has developed the Integral Urban House, which is a laboratory for testing an enormous number of ideas and techniques for food production, energy production and conservation, and resources recycling. The Rodale Research Center of Rodale Press is another prolific source of valuable information dealing with issues in backyard food production.

There are more than 20 research and demonstration projects in the United States and Canada that are expanding the base of knowledge we need for successful production in the backyard setting. A brief directory of these projects, titled Directory of Research Centers, can be found in the Appendix. Much of what my family has been doing on our suburban homestead reflects the ideas we have gained by following the work of these different groups. The problem for you, as for us, is how to keep up with all this helpful information without getting overwhelmed. The solution is magazines, books, and friends.

Magazines and Books

I am a big fan of magazines. I believe that they are even more helpful than books for the beginning gardener. You'll find some good ones that deal, at least in part, with backyard food production listed in the Bibliography. Most cover a wide range of subjects each month, some superficially, some extensively, so there is usually something in there for everyone. Over time you find most of the things you are concerned about covered in depth. Magazines are often ahead of books in getting out new ideas. They connect people who have like interests or questions. Every month they come in with their attractive covers and motivating articles that you can read at your leisure over the weeks until the next batch comes in. A magazine article takes 15 minutes to read while a book takes hours. There we have the time issue again.

Which magazines should you subscribe to? The list of magazines in the Bibliography includes my own editorial comments on each for you to take with a grain of salt. As you can see, I believe some magazines are better for beginners than others. Many of them are available on the newsstand. My advice is to pick up those you can buy at your magazine store, see in your local library, or borrow from some friends. After you look them over, you can decide how many you wish to subscribe to. I get four magazines and check out two others at my community library.

As far as I'm concerned, the most valuable aspect of magazines is being able to cut out the articles you have an interest in and throw the rest away (rather, recycle the rest). I have no interest in saving back copies of magazines. I estimate that the articles I save represent no more than 5 to 10 percent of the volume of the magazines from which they came. Five years of articles are stored in two file boxes, and if they are stacked in one pile, stand only 11 inches tall. That pile came from at least 240 magazines which have since been recycled, rather than stored in my attic where I couldn't get at them when I wanted to anyway. My filing system is very simple and I can usually find what I want in less than five minutes. On any one subject I won't have more than 10 or 15 articles to scan, so I don't worry about having any fancy detailed classification system. Simple as it is, I've found that my filing system for magazine articles provides me with much of the information I need.

My only other comment about magazines also applies to books. Just because something is in print, that doesn't mean it tells you all you need to know in order to make a sound decision or take immediate action. Articles may not cover all the information you need to apply the principles directly to your situation. Let me give you an example. A few years ago I read that a good way to store solar heat in a greenhouse was to stack beer cans painted black and filled with water along the back wall. This seemed like such a good idea that I immediately enlisted all my friends to this noble cause, collecting beer cans. It wasn't until after we had drunk a lot of beer, and I had painted over 1,000 beer cans, that I made an important discovery. We don't have enough sun during the winter in this particular part of the country for the mass of water in the beer cans to absorb sufficient heat to hold my greenhouse overnight. That issue had not been discussed in the article, and I hadn't, in my enthusiasm, pursued it. Consequently, we threw out 1,000 beer cans carefully painted black. What works for someone else may not work for you.

Next to magazines, there are a few books that I feel are also important resources for beginning gardeners. These, too, are listed in the Bibliography. The problem is that there are far more than a few books available. In fact, the selection available today is mind-boggling. I think everyone should have one or two basic references that cover the whole subject of vegetable gardening. The best ones are usually quite expensive, so you really don't want to make a mistake. I bought my first books on the advice of a good friend who was a real expert in gardening. If you don't have a friend with that particular skill, then the public library might have a range of books to skim before you go out and drop $20 on a basic gardening reference. However, my experience with libraries has been that their collections are pretty skimpy and tend to be a bit out of date. I am firmly convinced that the enormous volume of research completed in the past ten years makes most basic references older than that obsolete. If they only cost $5, then I wouldn't feel so strongly about it. But if you are going to put out over $20 then I'd think you would want books that take advantage of the latest research included.

One of the main concerns in selecting gardening books is whether the author is an organic gardener, a chemical gardener, or one who uses a bit of both techniques. Such biases have a major impact on the techniques and procedures that will be recommended in any particular book. Most of the books I've listed in the Bibliography reflect my own bias. That bias is fairly simple—I believe in using the organic method in raised beds, making use of intensive planting techniques.

In the end, most gardening books are reference books. Only a few are the kind that you would want to read from cover to cover on a cold winter's night. Consequently, unless you're a book collector, as a beginning gardener you don't need very many books. Here quality is more important than quantity. I own quite a few books related to food production, but I really only use three of them very often. They include a basic encyclopedia-type reference, a comprehensive book on insects and diseases, and a book about the intensive method of planting. The rest I dip into occasionally, but I have used my magazine articles far more often. What you will find is that books become more important as you get more experienced. I find that after five or six years of experience I'm more interested in buying a book dealing exclusively with some specific subject such as composting, container planting, or working with seedlings. In the beginning, I believe you should keep it simple.

Friends

Gardening friends are a major source of information, especially to the beginner. But they can also be a problem. Sometimes they can be intimidating with all their knowledge and advice. After all, there's nothing any of us would rather do than give advice to someone else. Of course, sometimes we overdo it. I myself have been guilty of this very sin! Nevertheless, if you are fortunate enough to have a friend or neighbor who is an accomplished gardener, take advantage of the opportunity for advice. He or she can help you avoid many mistakes.

Friends can also sell you on their biases, so balance what you hear with what you read. I remember being lectured one time by a very experienced gardener that compost would eat up all the nitrogen in my soil if I used it before it was two years old. I use compost that has gone from leaves to finished material in six weeks, so I was concerned that maybe he knew something I didn't know. I came back home and researched the 10 or 12 magazine articles I had on compost and checked my basic references. Unfortunately, they weren't very specific about the subject of nitrogen depletion if compost is used too soon on the garden. Finally I checked with my county agent, who's not too big on organic methods, but he was able to help me figure out that my six-week compost was just as finished as my friend's two-year compost. My friend is a very good gardener, but he had one piece of information which turned out to be incorrect. A beginner might have taken him at his word and not used the finished compost for two years.

Like most people who share the same interests, gardeners tend to form informal networks and rely on one another for information. I got into gardening because of a friend, and I still call him periodically when I have a problem I can't solve. People I have helped get into gardening do the same with me. Often the friend or neighbor won't know the exact answer to your question, but he or she may have the proper reference book or may know how to go about solving the problem for you.

That brings up the subject of friends and your own books. Some people refuse to lend books. They've been hurt frequently enough by losing valued books that they get tough and say no to everyone. A friend of mine quoted somebody who observed that books help no one when they're sitting on a shelf. I agree with that thought, and we lend books to friends. We lose a few, but we try to keep track of who has what so the losses are minimized. Borrowing books, if you are responsible about it, can be a simple and inexpensive way to get lots of good information. When you add up the collective libraries of four or five gardeners, then you have a respectable reference library just a phone call away.

Learning by Doing

Magazines, books, and friends have been my best sources of information and motivation. In the final analysis, though, I have learned far more by actually working in the garden myself than I have from the printed page. The variables that must be considered when raising your own food are far more numerous than one article or one conversation can cover. You must learn how to assess all these variables yourself and apply what you read or hear to the set of conditions that make up your particular garden environment. Learning about the effects of the climate and soil, about the productivity of different varieties, about feeding and watering requirements which vary from vegetable to vegetable can only take place in your own backyard as you do it yourself.

Other Ways to Learn

Let me make a quick observation about the fact that television, our omnipresent, overused communications addiction in this country, is not a major source of information about gardening. There are several excellent gardening shows on public television channels, a few of them in the early morning hours, often sponsored by the local extension service. Unfortunately, these shows have a major liability—they can't be referenced two weeks later when you actually need a particular piece of information. Television programs are a good motivator to get you interested in backyard food production, but I believe the printed word still serves as the best source of information.

However, when cable television comes into its own in the next five years, we may see a change in the role of television as an information source. Also, I'm confident that home computers will begin to replace many reference books and magazines in the next decade as sources of technical information about backyard food production (see the discussion in the Conclusion). National data banks on food production will be at our fingertips. For now, though, I recommend a couple of magazines, a few good reference books, and a good friend to help you get launched in your food production endeavor. Assume that some of your planning time will be taken up by investigating local references in the library, selecting your books and subscriptions, and finding a friend to be your gardening mentor.

Controlling Costs

There's an old economic cliche in this country that tells us that you have to spend money to make money, and it's true that setting up a garden does involve some initial capital expenditure. However, the cost of developing and maintaining a backyard food production system can certainly be controlled and kept to a minimum, allowing maximum savings from your efforts. Again, the admonition to begin slowly and plan carefully applies here. Purchase only the basics in tools and supplies, then expand your inventory gradually as you gain knowledge and develop commitment.

There are a number of cost-cutting tricks that help to increase overall savings from the vegetable garden. Unfortunately, most of them don't really come into play until after you have acquired a few years of experience. For example, I buy very little fertilizer and no insecticide. I use large amounts of compost and mulch and I use manual insect controls so that I can avoid those expenditures. But it took me a number of years to gain the confidence and ability to cut that cost. In the beginning I did use some chemical fertilizer and insecticide. As my soil improved and my skills developed, I cut those items out of my budget. Another way I save money is by growing my own seedlings. Some people sell or trade their extra seedlings, often covering their entire cost of seeds for the year. In chapter 7 I will talk about barter and cooperative buying of equipment and food. These can be major cost-saving activities. The big economic danger I have encountered in beginning a backyard garden is what my wife calls my nickel and dime problem. I can never get out of a garden supply store or a hardware store with just the item I went in to buy. It is amazing how something will rise in priority when a sale sticker has been added. If you want to realize the greatest cost savings you can from your food production system, then you must develop better discipline than I have in buying nonessential tools and supplies.

Sound Investments

Before I talk about tools and equipment, let me give you my investment philosophy, which will probably drive the accountants among you up the wall. **I believe that for capital investments that improve your own degree of self-reliance in the areas of food production and energy production, the total cost should be written off as soon as the item is paid for.** If I spend $3,000 for a solar greenhouse and pay cash, then I write off that cost in the first year. Normal accounting procedure would require me to project the value of the vegetables and the heat produced by the greenhouse and figure out how many years it would take to equal my initial capital investment. In my view, the issue is not the financial return on your investment for these items, but rather the increase in your own self-reliance and quality of life as you see it.

I believe that no one should purchase equipment, especially expensive equipment, that he or she can't afford. Therefore, if you can afford to build a greenhouse without hurting the rest of the family's economic condition, then write it off in the first year—sort of like a one-year investment. It makes sense to me. From this perspective, in the first year the lettuce I grew in my greenhouse cost about $700 a head. In the second year and all the years thereafter, that lettuce has cost me pennies a head. Again, in the first year my compost cost me $250, the cost of the shredder which I purchased cooperatively with a neighbor. But since then, I have produced many tons of compost every year, and it costs me annually the equivalent of about 5 gallons of gas and a quart of oil. My motto is: If you can afford it, and you need it, then buy it and write it off as soon as it's paid for.

Equipment and Buildings

Some of your planning time should be devoted to an inventory of the tools and equipment that you already own and a forecast of those supplies that will be necessary to launch your food production system.

How Many Tools Do You Need?

A very productive vegetable garden can be well managed for 20 years with only a shovel, a rake, a trowel, a watering can, and a 5-gallon pail. With a recycled paint can as a pail, that investment in tools would amount to about $30 (less if you go to yard sales). But even when buying these basic tools, you should go slowly. Quick decisions and impulse purchases can cost you a great deal of money, and much of it will be wasted. Everyone has his or her own style and work habits, so I will not suggest any list of tools, equipment, and buildings for the ideal backyard food production system. However, I do have some thoughts on the subject that might help you evaluate all the wonderful devices conjured up by American industry to separate gardeners from their money.

Hand tools vs. power tools is one basic issue to consider. I don't have a hard-and-fast policy, but I try to keep the power tools at a minimum and definitely try to confine my purchases to power tools that I can repair myself. Generally, power tools are more expensive to buy and to maintain. They are sold primarily to save time. I believe that hand tools are sufficient for the first-year garden. Even now my primary tools are a shovel, a rake, a manure fork for the compost, a trowel, several 5-gallon pails, and a watering can. In most cases, you can do just as good a job, and sometimes a better one, with hand tools. In the end it becomes an argument between cost and your time. When you get to a large piece of equipment, such as a tiller or a shredder, rental is often an attractive option, especially when you are just getting started in gardening.

Storage Space for Tools

After you've picked out all those handy tools you're going to buy, you need to think about where you're going to keep them. Limitations of storage space may affect your purchases. When you are working in the garden, you are not going to want to go all the way down to the cellar and rummage around behind the washing machine each time you need another tool. Naturally, the bigger the tool, the bigger the storage requirement, and storage sheds are not cheap. My three big storage problems are a lawn mower, a garden cart, and a shredder. All the rest of my equipment consists of hand tools that hang on the wall of our utility room. If your garden is going to be bigger than 600 square feet, then a rented or borrowed tiller might come in handy, but consider my recommendation that you start with hand-dug beds right from the beginning. That first winter after your first full summer of gardening is a good time to start thinking about whether you really want to invest in more equipment. That's the time you'll probably start thinking about paying your income tax, and a more sober review of your bank account is likely to prevent unnecessary purchases!

Buildings to Consider

Buildings are even more expensive than equipment. The storage shed is often the first step. A greenhouse or a root cellar are also attractive additions to a backyard food production system, but they represent a significant investment. They also represent an increase in the demand on your time as you grow your vegetables in the greenhouse or manage your storage in the root cellar. All these issues should be considered carefully before you make a decision.

Planning Does Pay Off

My final point in this discussion about planning is that I believe that there is a direct relationship between your ability to minimize your time investment in a food production effort and the amount of planning you put into each stage of its development. The value of planning never ends. It works like this: Mulching prevents weeds from growing. But I must plan ahead to figure out where and when I will get my mulching material. I like hay, but I want it to be free—that takes some planning. If I don't have to weed I save time. Here's another example: I want to get maximum production from my garden at all times, so I must do some planning to make sure I have some medium-size seedlings ready whenever another crop is

Careful planning is the key to having the kind of productive, good-looking garden that can serve as the focal point of the backyard landscape. At my house, the garden is our view from our back deck, and careful planning is essential so that I can keep the garden neat and attractive throughout the season.

being harvested. As the early cabbage gets picked, in goes a half-grown pepper plant. And here is one more example: If I plan ahead and make my own ice in advance for chilling vegetables after blanching them in the process of getting them ready for freezing, I will save some time when I want to freeze a batch between dinner and when the ball game comes on television. As our planning skills improve, our time investment in our food production system seems to decrease. Remember, other people call it daydreaming, but we call it planning!

The Beginning Garden

THE GAME PLAN

The Goal: In this first stage of the system, you'll start with a small garden to establish the garden site and to gain experience in garden planning and management skills.

The Strategy:

1. Think about your property as a system in which all parts interact, and choose the best site available for the garden.

2. Draw up a diagram of where you'll plant each crop.

3. Develop skills for making the best use of your time when doing garden chores.

4. Build one or two double-dug raised beds, and start a compost pile.

5. Do basic planting and maintenance chores, and practice the basic backyard integrated pest management system.

6. Start a recipe file of ideas for using the produce you grow.

27

Enough of the preliminaries. Let's get into developing your backyard food production system. The next five chapters represent a series of stages for the development of a complete system. You do not have to include in your own system all the components that are discussed, nor do you have to build your own system in the same order. The stages are offered in this order because they represent levels of increasing sophistication and complexity. Each takes some initial capital investment, some start-up time, and some more knowledge. If you take my advice and develop your system slowly, then you will develop it in stages over three to five years, rather than trying to do everything at once.

In this first stage of development, begin with a modest garden that will serve as a basic learning tool for gaining experience in seed selection, soil management, disease and pest control, and cooking your harvested produce. From the beginning you must deal with both planning and management issues, so that will be the focus of this chapter.

Planning Your Food System

The very first thing you must learn to do is to think about your entire property, all 10,000 square feet (one-quarter acre) of it, as a system. It is a system that is highly integrated, and it already has its set of checks and balances. You have sun, wind, rain, and air available in certain amounts according to your climate. Your property has trees, shrubs, grass, weeds, and maybe some flowers already in place. Your soil is of a certain quality, and you have a certain number of stones. Your house is located permanently on some sector of your property in some relation to the north-south axis. You already have a certain number of species of birds and animals, and you have your share of bugs and worms and other denizens of the air and the soil. This is your little ecological niche. In most cases, this ecological system is basically in balance, even with the introduction of people (your family). Now what you are about to do, in planning to develop a backyard food production system, is to alter that existing ecological system. Whether it stays in balance or goes out of balance depends a great deal on your careful planning of the changes you will make.

All Parts of the System Interact

Everything you do in one part of your little ecosystem has an impact on other parts. Cutting down some trees to get more sun for the garden may increase the heat in your house in the summer, and, if the trees are on the north side, their removal may make your house colder in the winter and less protected from the winter winds. Feeding the birds in the winter and building birdhouses around the property invites birds to help you fight insect pests in your garden, but they may also eat your garden seeds and young seedlings. I don't want to give you the impression that you might destroy the whole system if you are not supersensitive to the implications of each major step that you take. However, developing a sensitivity to all the inter-relationships among all the parts of your little ecosystem will help you make better decisions as you develop your backyard food production system.

Making Sound Decisions

One of your biggest problems, not shared by your friends in the country, is that you do not usually have a lot of options in selecting a site for a garden or a green-house. Your space is limited; your house is already located on the property; and your township probably has zoning laws that made sure that you have a big wasted front yard, thus limiting the potential backyard growing space. **Because of the limitations you face with an average suburban lot, it is essential that you have some sense of your future plans for your food production system (five or more years hence), so that you do not make a decision now that prevents you from doing something you want to do four years from now.** Planting an apple tree where you will eventually want to put a greenhouse is an example of this kind of mistake.

Sometimes it helps to have something to measure your plans against as you begin your daydreaming. I have three basic criteria against which I measure my various food production projects. Whether it is a decision to add another row onto the garden, to add blueberries along the back line, or to try growing herbs in containers on the back porch, **I check every decision against three goals:**

1. **Can I get maximum yield for the space?**
2. **Can I minimize my use of energy?**
3. **Can I minimize the time required by me or my family to do this task?**

The basic theme of this whole book is how to find the way to achieve maximum yield in food with the use of a minimum of energy (especially fossil fuels) in a lim-ited space with a minimum amount of time. Looking back over the five years of development of my own system, I find that it's possible to quantify the results I've tried to achieve in the two diagrams on page 30. Initially, I experienced a high investment in energy and time with a relatively low level of productivity. As I gained more experience and knowledge, I achieved a reduction in energy and time consumed with a major increase in productivity.

Actually I have what the information specialists call a closed loop process. I plan my activities for the year. I then carry out my plans. As I see what happens and learn by doing, I am reacting to that experience with new knowledge and in-sight which affects my plans for next year. Then the cycle begins all over again. There is nothing terribly new about that idea, but it does put the necessary empha-sis on the value of planning before you implement any major new projects. I don't think the goals listed above can be reached without it.

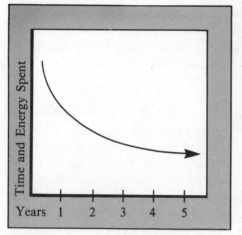 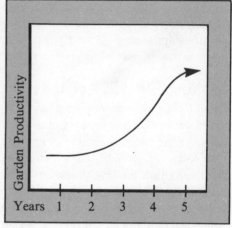

Over the years, the amount of time and energy you spend on the garden decreases.

Over the years, your garden's productivity rises!

Selecting the Garden Site

Most of us living in areas that have been settled for many years have to deal with the existence of large trees on and around our property. The ideal site for a vegetable garden is one that has full sun from sunrise to about 3:00 P.M. Morning sun is generally better than late afternoon sun, because it warms the plants faster. **If you have to cope with partial shade, as I do, then choose a site that gives you at least six hours of sun on your garden at some time of the day.** Plants like lettuce, onions, parsley, radishes, and spinach can take some shade and still produce well. A complete listing of vegetables that can tolerate some shade can be found in the chart titled Interplanting Guide, in the Appendix.

Even if shade is not a problem, it is best to have a garden that is not too close to trees and shrubs, simply because their roots compete for the nutrients and moisture your vegetables are going to need. **A garden does not need to be all in one place. Some of the most attractive and most productive gardens I've seen surround the backyard, using only the perimeter. Vertical space is also an attractive alternative that most of us overlook for growing vegetables.** The ground space next to trellises, walls of garages, and fences can support sizable amounts of cucumbers, squash, tomatoes, and even apples if you use the espalier technique of pruning, which I will discuss more fully in chapter 5.

Keep It Simple

No matter where you decide to start your garden, keep it very simple for the first year. A plot that is from 200 to 400 square feet is plenty if you have little or no

experience. Anything larger and you can be easily overwhelmed and give up the whole idea in one season. Also, a very common mistake made by beginning gardeners is to plant far too many different types of vegetables. It's very easy to lose complete control when drooling through a catalog in the middle of January. What's another 75 cents for just one more pack of seeds? You haven't had kohlrabi since you were a kid! But every extra vegetable variety you add brings with it a whole range of additional concerns that can complicate that first year's garden. Each vegetable you grow has its own watering and feeding requirements. Each has its own set of insects that attack it and its own group of diseases that can damage it. Consequently, I feel that the beginning gardener should resist all temptation to have more than ten different types of vegetables in that first year's garden. This will give you an excellent variety of fresh food for your table without overwhelming your gardening efforts.

Rows or Raised Beds?

You have a basic decision to make when you get down to actually designing your garden once you've picked your site. You can plant in rows or you can plant in raised beds. **My advice is that you start right off with raised beds, and I'll explain why. There are some major advantages to double-dug raised beds instead of the rows which have been traditional in this country since its settlement. Space is a luxury in most backyards, and rows waste space.** A garden laid out in traditional rows has paths between every row of plants. Therefore, only about 30 to 40 percent of the total space in the garden is devoted to growing plants. The rest is used for paths. On the other hand, if you set up your garden using permanent beds that are 3 to 4 feet wide, then you are increasing the percentage of space devoted to growing plants. There are now fewer rows, and so now you will have from 60 to 80 percent of the space in your garden devoted to growing plants, or almost double the space used for growing in the garden laid out in rows.

Beds take more work to dig, at least initially, as we'll discuss later in the chapter. If time is a critical problem, you might compromise and build one good bed and use rows in the rest of your first year's garden. This fall and next year you can build more beds as you get the time.

A growing bed is usually 3 to 5 feet wide, no wider than you can comfortably reach from the permanent path. Not only do you get an increased yield per square foot from beds, you also save on water and fertilizer. Since you have permanent beds, you have permanent paths. Consequently, you don't have to fertilize or water the paths—ever. In addition, using the permanent paths eliminates soil compaction problems that can greatly reduce your yield. In a row garden you don't know where the rows are going to be from year to year, so you end up using fertilizer and water in the paths where they are, of course, wasted.

There's no doubt in my mind that beds are far superior to rows. Just because of the more efficient use of growing space, beds allow you to double your production

This close-up shows how raised beds are constructed—the gentle mounded shape allows me to plant on the sides of the bed as well as the top and results in an even better use of the available space.

over rows. Furthermore, beds allow for the use of what are called intensive methods of gardening, which can increase your production up to tenfold over rows. We'll discuss those techniques in detail in chapters 4 and 5.

One way to make garden production computations a bit easier is to have beds that are either 4 by 25 feet or 5 by 20 feet, so that you have a bed that covers 100 square feet. That's a convenient round figure to use in computing plant spacings and seed orders.

Making the Garden Layout

I believe that all beginning gardeners should sketch a layout of the garden before beginning to plant in the spring. All you need for this first-stage garden is a rough plan showing where you will plant each vegetable. As you gain more experience, perhaps you can plan in your head or use some simple notes. For the first few years, though, a sketch can be very helpful. It doesn't need to have the precision of a blueprint or the detail of a photograph.

No matter what you plan on your sketch, you will make some changes as you actually get into the laying down of seed. The sketch, along with several of the charts you'll find in the Appendix, will help you to decide how much seed you're

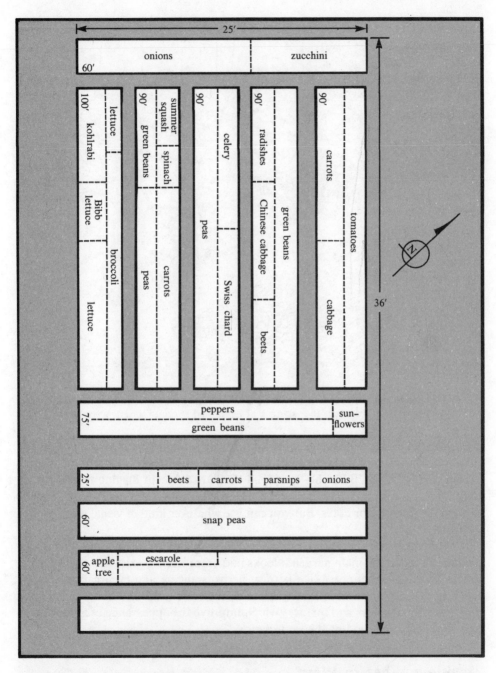

A garden plan in progress; this plan shows the first plantings. The outside dimensions of the garden area are 25 by 36 feet, but there is a total of 800 square feet of actual bed space (the number inside each bed indicates the square feet of growing space in that bed).

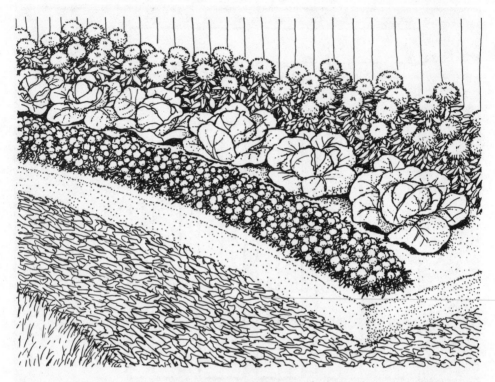

You don't have to confine your food-growing activities to the main garden plot. Vegetables can be tucked into flower beds, too, to make use of additional space in an attractive way.

going to need to buy. The sketch will also help you visualize what part of the garden has to be dug first. **All plants don't go in at the same time, so if you plan your layout carefully, you'll be able to spread the hard labor of digging the first beds over almost a month.** I like to use graph paper for my sketch, with lots of room around the borders for notes. But you can use whatever kind of visual guide works best for you.

Remember when working out your garden plan that there's planting space available outside the main garden. Nooks and crannies also exist throughout your flower beds. Compact crops like lettuce, herbs, spinach, and even carrots can be stuck in and around other planting areas in the front yard and at the side. They add a variety of colors and textures which improve the appearance of a flower bed and produce some food at the same time.

Deciding What to Plant

Let me say again that when it comes to choosing what to grow in the garden, one of the most common mistakes of the beginning gardener is planting too many types of vegetables and planting too much of each vegetable in the first year. If you have more than ten types of vegetables in your first garden, then you may have too many.

It is relatively easy to determine what to plant—you should plant those vegetables that you and your family most like to eat. There is a simple exercise to help you choose crops according to your eating habits. Consult the chart titled Planting Guide, in the Appendix, which lists the 50 most common vegetables that you might grow. Then divide that list into three categories:

1. Those vegetables your family enjoys the most and eats frequently, at least once every two weeks.
2. Those vegetables that the family likes okay, but eats infrequently.
3. Those vegetables you haven't eaten before, but that you would like to try.

The leftovers are those vegetables that you and your family don't like at all. These you can forget about.

For the first-stage garden, you should pick no more than ten vegetables from your number 1 list and then pick one from your number 3 list just for fun. If you still have trouble making a final selection, you might consider those listed on the chart titled Some Criteria for Selecting Vegetables to Grow in Your Garden.

Some Criteria for Selecting Vegetables to Grow in Your Garden

Most Productive per Square Foot	Highest Market Value	Highest Nutritional Value
Tomatoes (supported)	Tomatoes	Broccoli
Peppers	Bunching onions	Spinach
Squash	Leaf lettuce	Brussels sprouts
Green beans (pole)	Turnips	Lima beans
Beets	Summer squash	Peas
Lettuce	Peas	Asparagus
Peas	Onions (bulb)	Artichoke
Carrots	Green beans	Cauliflower
Cauliflower	Beets	Sweet potatoes
Broccoli		Carrots

You might want to focus especially on those vegetables that give you the highest yield per square foot of garden space, or you may want to get the most nutritional or economic value from your first gardening efforts.

In any case, the chart titled How Much to Plant, in the Appendix, shows how much you can expect to get from a 25-foot row of most of the vegetables you will be planting. This will help you decide how much to plant. My advice is to underplant rather than overplant in the first year. There's no rule that says you have to use all the seeds in a packet. Most of them will store very well for at least another year. A modest garden with ten kinds of vegetables will give you plenty of food for the table and a little left over to give away or put up. What you don't want in this first year is to feel overwhelmed. It's a real emotional setback to plant something, tend it and nurture it, and then have so much that you see the harvest rotting on the vine. Next year will be plenty of time for getting a better handle on volume and increasing it to meet your needs.

Organic or Not Organic?

The next consideration to deal with after you have thought about your garden layout and what kind of vegetables you will be planting is whether or not you will maintain your garden using organic principles. Organic gardening treats the soil as a living and breathing organism. The organic gardener fertilizes and cultivates with methods that are as close to nature's ways as is possible and practical. This means using natural minerals and organic fertilizers. Synthetic chemical fertilizers, insecticides, and herbicides are avoided.

Organic gardening has finally come into its own in recent years. While we are still many years away from seeing the majority of our commercial farmers return to the organic methods their grandfathers used, the backyard gardener can now use organic techniques and not be considered a nut. Organic gardeners are still in the minority, but their numbers are growing every year. Why? Because the facts are on their side. Organic methods have been shown time and time again to produce higher-quality crops in greater quantity once those methods have been firmly established.

I am not a purist, but I can hold my own in a conversation with most other organic growers. Perhaps the purest organic philosophy is held by Masanobu Fukuoka, a Japanese farmer whose book *The One-Straw Revolution* (see the Bibliography) should be on everyone's "must read" list. He uses what are sometimes called natural farming techniques that incorporate organic methods. Fukuoka does not believe in cultivation of any kind. He spreads his seeds over the surface of the soil. He utilizes neither chemical fertilizers nor compost, but lets the decomposing residues from his former crops restore the nutrients to the soil. He rejects weeding by tillage as well as the use of any herbicides. (Some weeds do get pulled by hand.) This somewhat primitive-sounding approach to agriculture consistently gives him per-acre production levels that equal or exceed those of any other farmer in Japan.

While I don't go quite as far as Fukuoka, **I believe that organic techniques are logical and necessary for the backyard food system. I have four reasons for my position. The organic method avoids waste, it saves energy, it increases produc-**

tion, and it prevents harmful chemicals from being ingested into the body. I use compost and I dig my garden, but I buy into the rest of Fukuoka's approach to food production.

Every spring, I am reminded of the wastefulness of our suburban life-style in this country. On the first nice weekend in the spring, as I do my jogging around town, I see people doing their spring cleanup and putting the trash out by the curb for pickup by the township trash trucks. Invariably, in many of those trash piles will be several large bags which formerly held 50 pounds of chemical fertilizer. In those same bags will now be the material that had been carefully raked up from the yard to be taken away and burned. That means that residents take commercial fertilizer, which took considerable energy to make and to transport, and use it to replace natural composting material that is free and would do the same job. On top of that, they take that compostable material and put it out so that more energy must be used to truck it to an incinerator so that more energy can be used to burn it up! That is a classic exercise in waste of both organic resources and energy.

The organic method improves production because it works in harmony with Mother Nature—who is far more complex than any of us will every truly understand. When I first started out, I supplemented the meager compost I had with some commercial fertilizer. My plants grew okay, but I did notice that my soil had no earthworms. They had been there in the spring when I first prepared the garden, but they were not there in September. I learned later that earthworms don't like soil that has had synthetic fertilizers added. They either die or move on. I also learned that earthworms produce their weight in castings every day, and that their castings supply nutrients in a form that is readily usable by plants' roots. The worms also aerate the soil to a depth of 6 feet, and dead earthworms are rich in nitrogen, which is sometimes difficult to get in natural form. I realized that I had traded a short-term convenient feeding with the chemical fertilizer for the more impressive long-term benefits of healthy soil full of earthworms.

It is the micro- and macro-life in the first few inches of topsoil that break down organic material into nutrients in the form that is needed by plants to grow and thrive. This living population includes billions of bacteria, fungi, mites, protozoa, millipedes, sowbugs, earthworms, and many other denizens of the soil. The application of large amounts of chemical fertilizers, pesticides, and herbicides to your garden will kill off most of these beneficial soil-dwelling creatures. You will then be entirely dependent upon commercial preparations to produce the food in your garden. I don't like the trade-off. **In the beginning, the organic method takes more time and you lose a small percentage of your produce to the bugs. However, after a few years, that organic method gives you a superior crop from soil that is continually increasing in its productive capacity each year.** It's like a good investment program. After the initial capital investment, the profits just keep growing year by year.

Garden Management

When you think of your backyard as a food production system rather than as a garden, then you find yourself thinking about managing that system rather than simply about keeping up with your garden. In order to get maximum production for the least energy spent and time consumed, you must become a good manager. **For effective management of your vegetable garden there are five general areas of concern, and they are all interrelated:**

1. Soil maintenance—including preparation, feeding, and watering
2. General upkeep—tying up the tomatoes, thinning the seedlings, and other plant-related chores
3. Disease and pest control
4. Weed control
5. Harvesting.

The Two Types of Management Activities

All of these management concerns break down into two very distinct, but equally important, classes of activities, both of which are needed for the most productive results. These are the planning activities and the day-to-day chores that I will call the reactive activies.

Planning activities don't end with finishing your garden sketch and ordering your seeds in January. They go on throughout the year. These are the kinds of activities that help you take care of those day-to-day responsibilities more easily. Two important planning activities are the continuation of learning about plant growth and gardening techniques and development of your information sources. Both of these were discussed in chapter 2.

Another planning activity that you'll need to start practicing here in the first-stage garden is collecting supplies before you need them. Every year you know you will need certain materials for mulch and for compost. Planning ahead for their collection is a way to reduce the frustration level during the busiest part of the growing season. I collect leaves in the fall to be combined with grass clippings in the spring and summer to make compost. Without the leaves, my grass is of little use for compost. Also, I have three rain barrels to collect water in case a drought hits in August, another example of planning ahead.

All these planning activities are important, but too little attention is given to the reactive skills one needs for the day-to-day management of a productive garden. These are skills that you can develop and improve as you go along. I mention them so you will be conscious of what seem like little concerns, but are the difference between superior production and average production. **Let me mention four reactive skills that I believe to be important:**

1. Use of Short Time Periods. On any given day there are 25 things that you could be doing in your garden. Your ability to use five or ten minutes almost every day will keep the garden under control and reduce the burden on the weekend considerably. Pull a few weeds. You don't have to pull the whole row today. Snip the suckers from half your tomatoes, and do the others tomorrow or the next day. Feed the broccoli tomorrow; take care of the cabbages next weekend. Your ability to use small snatches of time each day will go a long way toward preventing the garden from becoming a burden.

2. Development of Good Observational Skills. This was a hard one for me. Your ability to spot those few little insects before they take over can mean the difference between minor damage and disaster. Noticing that leaves are a bit wilted on a cloudy day instead of waiting till they have fallen over from thirst can have major impact on your final production levels. It took me some time really to focus down on the details of my plants. In the beginning I didn't even know what to look for. Having gardening friends come through my garden was always a big help. They saw things I didn't even know to look for. Every problem has a cause. The plant may be wilted, not because it is thirsty, but because its roots are being eaten by maggots. The green beans have spots on the leaves because you handled them when they were wet. I remember the first time I spotted ants on my apple tree and knew that they were there to tend their aphids. I felt like I was really getting along in my observation skills. Every year you learn a bit more, and see a bit more, and marvel at the wonder of it all.

3. Acquisition of Good, Quick Data Sources. You can't know everything and you don't have time to reread a 200-page book to find out what to do about squash borers in an organic garden. The charts in the Appendix are the product of seven years of trying to keep track of the basic information I gathered in my reading and learning over that time. They give me quick and simple answers. If I want more details I can go to my library, but often the charts are sufficient for a quick reference. My other quick references are my gardening friends. They call me and I call them. The informal exchange can be helpful. You should develop your own sources that are comfortable for you.

4. Establishment of Priorities among Tasks. This is another tough one. There is *always* something to do in the garden. While it's amazing how many of those tasks can go undone with little consequence to the harvest, others are critical to a satisfactory harvest and cannot be deferred. The trick is learning what to do and what to let go until you have a few extra minutes. Weeding can always be delayed, but proper feeding and watering are critical to the plants' effective growth. Turning your compost pile or mulching the cabbages can always wait for a few days, but the transplanting of the seedlings when they are ready and not yet root-bound in their pots is not good to delay for very long. This skill of priority-setting comes only from experience and, unfortunately, from your failures. We plan, we do, we learn from our mistakes, and we plan a bit differently next year. Learning to sort out the priorities of your gardening tasks can make this process more successful.

This brings me to my final point on garden management. It doesn't help to make a mistake one year and then do the same thing wrong again the next year. **Remember your mistakes and learn from them. You can keep records or you can trust your memory.** I use a combination. I have found that a garden calendar, sold in most book stores in the early spring, is handy for making little notes for the next year. I've tried more elaborate record-keeping projects, but they get lost in the hustle and bustle of the summer season. In the Conclusion I will talk about how the home computer will be helping us in this task in the near future. In any case, if you are good at keeping notes, you will have an advantage over the rest of us who depend too much on our memories to avoid mistakes in the garden from year to year.

Soil Management

I look at soil management as having three major areas of concern: preparation, feeding, and watering. Each of these activities takes some knowledge and experience. Here I will deal primarily with preparation and discuss feeding and watering more fully in the next chapters.

Once your garden is under way and you have some experience, you will find that soil preparation for the spring planting really begins in the previous fall when you get your garden ready for the winter. Activities such as sheet composting, planting cover crops, and heavy mulching all contribute to the vitality of your soil in the spring. However, I will assume that you are just beginning and talk about your initial double digging of one or more beds for the first spring planting.

Double Digging

Double digging is a special method for preparing your soil and it is just plain hard work. It requires that you dig down to double the normal depth when breaking up soil for planting. There are no shortcuts, and by the time you are only half finished you really have to believe that it is all worthwhile, because your muscles will be telling you that there's got to be an easier way. But double digging is definitely worth the effort.

In this first year, when you're just getting started, you might find it easier to rent a tiller to do the initial breaking up of the sod and topsoil. But to develop the most productive raised beds, the hard work of double digging by hand cannot really be avoided. Of course, you can pay someone else to do it for you. And remember that, once the bed is constructed, its maintenance each year becomes easier and easier.

Few people think much about the root systems of their plants. Yet many plants have as much or even more growth below the ground as they have above. The root systems of many plants, such as tomatoes, will go down 6 feet deep if the soil conditions will let them. When you double dig a bed you are making a major contribution to improving the ability of the root systems of vegetables to provide maximum nutrients to their plants. Because the soil is loose, the roots can penetrate it more freely, making for heavier, stronger root systems. This allows more moisture, air, and nutrients to be absorbed by the plant. These conditions are ideal for roots to work at their peak efficiency: More nutrients equal better production.

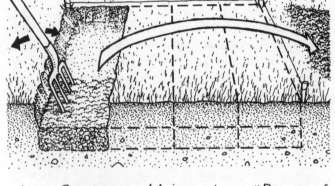

Double digging is the best way to prepare the soil for raised beds. Begin by digging a trench at one end of the garden, and transport that soil to the other end of the plot. With a spading fork, loosen the subsoil in the bottom of the trench.

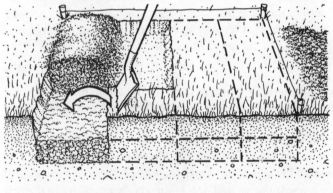

Dig another trench next to the first one, shoveling the topsoil into the first trench. Loosen the subsoil in the second trench.

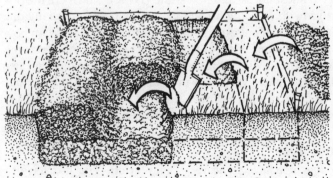

Repeat the procedure to work your way across the garden. The topsoil hauled from your first trench is used to fill your last trench.

While some folks, like John Jeavons (the author of a popular book, *How to Grow More Vegetables;* see the Bibliography), believe you should double dig every time you plant, the generally accepted standard today is that you should double dig a new bed for the first two or three years, then again two or three years later, and then very seldom thereafter if sufficient compost and mulch are applied each year. You could get by nicely never digging that bed again if you work in lots of those organic materials each year and let the earthworms and their little friends do their digestive magic. I don't double dig my garden anymore, having done it three times in five years. I loosen up the soil with a rake before planting and that's about all the preparation I have to do in the spring.

Double digging is not all that complicated, as you can see in the illustrations. The reason the technique is so specific with each step is that you must be concerned about keeping the top 2 inches of soil still on the top when you finish. Don't forget all the micro- and macro-life that is critical for producing plant nutrients in a form that plants can readily use. You don't want unintentionally to wipe out the entire micro- and macro-population in one digging. A 100-square-foot bed will take you anywhere from 5 to 15 hours for the initial digging. The time required depends on the type of soil, how many rocks you encounter, and the speed at which you work. After the initial digging, the same bed takes about two hours to double dig. Usually you should dig a bed several days before you plan to plant so that the ground has a chance to settle and your bed won't sink later on. Ideally, you dig on one weekend and plant on the next. I haven't always followed that rule, because of time, but I haven't found myself in any serious trouble so far.

Soil Improvement
There are two tasks that you need to perform early on in order to do any kind of a good job in soil management. You need to get a soil test and you need to start your compost pile.

You can get a soil test packet from your county agricultural agent. It costs about $3 or $4 and will be mailed to you if you call his office. The test will reveal the basic condition of your soil in terms of its pH (degree of alkalinity or acidity) and the balance of nitrogen, phosphorus, and potassium (NPK), which are the primary nutrients for plant growth. Reading a good gardening book, especially one specializing in organic methods, will help you to interpret the test and explain how to rectify any problems that show up. Without this soil test you are really starting in the dark with your new garden. My first test showed me that I should not use manure on my garden because it was very high in potassium, which my soil has in abundance. I was all prepared to put a liberal layer of manure on my garden until that test result came in and prevented what would have been a serious mistake.

Your First Compost Pile
Your first compost pile does not have to be very fancy at all. You just have to start it. Unless you have a shredder, you should avoid collecting too many sticks

and fibrous materials, at least in the beginning. But from day one, you should never again automatically throw all your kitchen scraps in the trash. Except for meat products and grease, all food wastes from your kitchen, including coffee grounds and tea bags, should go into the compost heap. It's not all that difficult to find an inconspicuous place to locate it. We'll talk later, in the next chapter, about getting a high-production composting operation going. I'll say this again, but it is worth saying—it is impossible, absolutely impossible, to add too much organic material to your soil. You will be a very unusual gardener if you can ever say that you have more compost than you can use.

I find making compost one of the most satisfying activities in my garden. It seems, though, to be one of the most misunderstood activities among beginning gardeners. They fear bad smells and believe the process to be very complicated. My satisfaction comes from taking things that have been thrown away by other people, such as leaves and grass clippings, and making them into a product that creates rich soil and promotes plant health. The transformation of a pile of leaves, grass, and garbage into crumbly black humus that smells fresh and earthy is little less than miraculous and not very difficult.

People's misunderstanding about compost may have come from some of the early magazine literature on the subject, which tended to prescribe somewhat precise and exact formulas for compost production. It must have seemed to some gardeners that composting was more trouble than it was worth. When a novice tried to do it on his own, the pile often smelled and attracted flies and rats. Consequently, compost has gained an unfortunate reputation among suburbanites and their township governments as well. Some suburban boards of health actually discourage compost piles because they are considered a public nuisance. **But compost, when properly made, does *not* attract rodents, does *not* smell, and is *not* in any way a public nuisance. The pile can be located unobtrusively in a corner of the yard and can be attractively sheltered.**

The fact is that composting is very easy, as soon as you understand how it works. The simple explanation is that compost is produced by billions of microorganisms breaking down the raw organic material into humus, which looks and feels like soil. These microorganisms require a certain sort of environment in which to multiply and to continue the breakdown process. If you create that environment, you get beautiful compost. If you don't create and maintain that environment, you don't get compost. Now that's pretty simple. The environment is not all that precise, and you have a great deal of leeway in how you go about building your pile. **Essentially a good compost pile needs four elements: some carbon-containing materials, some nitrogen-containing materials, oxygen, and some moisture.**

The carbon materials are the dry things like leaves, straw, sawdust, and twigs. The nitrogen materials are usually the green things like grass clippings, garden wastes, household garbage (no meat products!), and weeds. Manure is a nitrogen material but it is not available to many of us in the suburbs, and is not really needed anyway. The ideal ratio between the amount of carbon materials and the nitrogen materials is somewhere between 25:1 and 30:1. That's 25 parts of dry stuff to 1 part of green stuff. My experience has shown that I can get down to as low as a 10:1 ratio, as long as I keep the oxygen level very high. This is accomplished by turning the pile frequently. In any case, this ratio allows the microorganisms to eat and reproduce. If you have too much carbon (i.e., too many leaves and not enough green things), then the decomposition process will slow down and may take as long as two years if you just let the pile sit. If you have too high a proportion of nitrogen materials, then the pile will get putrid and begin to smell and attract flies. In the beginning it's best to err on the side of too much dry material.

Oxygen availability is really a function of whether you use an active method or a passive method to make your compost. The passive method means you simply build your pile and let it sit undisturbed. This method takes a year to two years to produce finished compost. The active method means that you turn the pile and mix the ingredients one or more times. The mixing adds more oxygen and speeds up the decomposition process. If you turn the pile every two or three days, you can get finished compost in just three weeks.

The moisture level is important and is easily maintained. Some water is needed by the microbiotic life as the decomposition process is proceeding. Some books say how much you should sprinkle the pile as you build it, but I have found a way to avoid that issue. I let my raw materials—leaves, sawdust, straw—sit out in the weather to get rained on. When I build a pile, they are already damp. Then I cover my pile with a sheet of plastic (a roof would do the same thing) to keep the rain from soaking the pile. My pile is just slightly damp, not too wet or too dry. It's as damp as a carefully wrung-out sponge. This procedure has worked very well for me.

Planting and Caring for the First-Stage Garden

There is no need for me to get into planting instructions in this book. There are many excellent books available that go into great detail about the culture of almost every vegetable you can imagine, and some you've never heard of. In the Appendix you will find a number of charts which give the basic data for planting most vegetables. I strongly recommend that you get at least one good general book on vegetable gardening and review the planting discussion, at least for the ten vegetables in your first garden. (I've listed a few of these books in the Bibliography.)

Caring for the garden as it grows is something that you'll learn with time. I'll be discussing feeding and watering at length in the next chapter. But even in the first-stage garden, your plants will need care. If you've been able to make compost, put it on the garden whenever you have a finished batch. Spread it in an even layer around and between your plants. If you have compost available at planting time, dig it into the garden beds before planting your crops.

There are no hard and fast rules about watering, especially at this stage of the game. If you experience a dry spell, or if you notice that your plants look droopy in the evening or early morning (*don't* check them in midafternoon—the hot sun makes even nonthirsty plants look limp then), you should water them. Use a sprinkling can, bucket, or hose, and just try to give them a good, thorough soaking once or twice a week while the dry weather lasts. If you can, direct the water to the base of the plants, where it will soak down to the roots more quickly. In the second-stage garden, watering will become more crucial.

Disease and Pest Control

It is in the area of disease and pest control that the new gardener has the toughest test of his or her organic philosophy and management skills. It is particularly tough in a new garden. **A brand-new garden is more vulnerable to disease and insect damage than is an established one.** Diseases and bugs will tend to hit the weakest plants. Because of the condition of the soil and the inexperience of the gardener, the plants in a new garden are usually not as strong and healthy as those found in a garden that has been worked for three or four years. Consequently, the beginning gardener is more likely to experience that traumatic combination of anger and sorrow when he comes out to check on his precious plants and finds that the entire broccoli crop has been lost to cutworms, or the tomatoes are coming in with blossom end rot, or some other atrocity is being perpetrated upon his good works by a tough and ruthless Mother Nature! In disease and pest control, first-hand experience backed up by your acquired knowledge is the best approach to controlling these problems.

In recent years, a new approach to insect control has been developed for commercial agriculture; it's called integrated pest management, or IPM. This method involves using a number of different techniques simultaneously to control insect pests. These techniques include rotating crops, companion planting, biological insect controls, and chemical insecticides as a last resort when necessary. This IPM system is still in its infant stages and has yet to be proven cost-effective for large-scale agricultural applications. Nevertheless, I like the concept, since with some minor adjustments it is the same as the organic method for insect and disease control. I use what I will call my backyard IPM approach for organic gardeners.

I must make an important point here. The organic gardener does not expect ever to completely eliminate all the insect pests in the garden. A balanced ecological system will always have a good mix of the good guys and the bad guys. As a result, most organic gardens have a little bit of insect damage, but it's inconsequential to the total harvest. It's natural for the beginning gardener to become upset when he or she sees one leaf on one plant with a few holes in it from insects. The first reaction is often to do something quickly that will prevent one more leaf from being damaged. Thus the chemical gardener moves into action with his sprayer or duster and gives that row of beans, or whatever, a good spraying. This will, in fact, eliminate any more damage to the leaves. But unfortunately, that same spraying will also eliminate the beneficial insects such as ladybugs, lacewings, and even honeybees. So, as soon as the spray washes off in the next rain, the beans are even more vulnerable to insect attack than they were before. The natural predators have been eliminated with the first round of pests.

Fighting off the next wave of pests requires even more chemicals than the first time did, because the predators are no longer helping out. Over time, insects develop a resistance to certain insecticides, and even stronger poisons must be used to have the same effectiveness as before. This becomes an endless cycle that is not only very expensive, but terribly hazardous as well. **Once you start using chemicals, you are dependent upon them from then on, because you have weakened or even eliminated the natural checks and balances that operate in a garden's environment.** So try to learn to tolerate the few pests and their damage for the greater good of the entire garden.

The organic gardener is comfortable with what we might call "relative damage." The concern is to "manage" the insect pests in the garden, not to eliminate them. The trade-off for the loss of a small percentage of the crop in an organic garden is a growing environment that outproduces the chemical garden if it is well managed.

My simple backyard IPM system involves a number of steps that are taken in priority order. The philosophy is that it is better to prevent insect damage than to have to fight it after the pests have arrived. The last two steps then are taken only when the other steps have failed. My experience has shown that after a few years of this approach, the last two steps of using sprays and botanical poisons are seldom necessary.

The Backyard Integrated Pest Management Process
Here are the steps in my backyard IPM system, in order of their priority:

1. **Maintain garden hygiene.**
2. **Rotate crops.**
3. **Build soil health.**
4. **Use pest- and disease-resistant varieties.**
5. **Learn pest emergence times and habits.**
6. **Use interplanting and companion planting.**
7. **Use biological controls.**
8. **Use physical controls.**
9. **Use natural sprays.**
10. **Use botanical poisons.**

Don't be alarmed at the length of this list. It is not as complicated as it may sound. Becoming comfortable and skillful in using all these steps effectively will take a number of years and that is okay. Most beginning gardeners start with step 11 (that I do not even include in my list), which is to use chemical insecticides.

In my opinion, steps 1 through 6 yield far better results in the long run, but they take a number of years to begin to have their full impact.

1. Garden Hygiene. This means simply to keep your garden in a condition that minimizes the opportunities for insects to breed and multiply. No piles of rotting weeds or vegetable refuse should be allowed in the garden; no stagnant water or piles of wood or things that can harbor insects underneath. Some insects will dwell under mulch, but if the mulch is dried, this will not be much of a problem.

2. Crop Rotation. Even in a small garden this helps. Don't plant your cabbages in the same place next year; try to follow heavy-feeding crops with light feeders or soil-builders like legumes. Moving the crops around confuses the insects and keeps concentrations of bug populations from building up.

3. Good Soil Health. I have dealt with this subject in some detail. I believe that compost is a key ingredient for good soil health. Healthy soil yields healthy plants. Since insects tend to attack plants weakened by poor growing conditions and unbalanced nutrients, good soil is one of the more effective prevention techniques.

4. Resistant Varieties. If your area has a particular problem with a certain insect, then sometimes you can find in a seed catalog a variety of the vulnerable vegetable that is resistant to that insect. A good example is the cucumber beetle. It can leave a virus which will wipe out your cucumbers in short order. There are now a number of cucumber varieties that are resistant to that virus. Here again your agricultural agent can be helpful to you.

5. Pest Emergence Times. This is a most helpful, but quite difficult and complicated strategy. If you know when a particular insect will turn up in your garden you have a real advantage. You can plant varieties of affected vegetables that mature earlier or later than the expected emergence times of the attacking pest. At least you will know when to start looking for the pests so that you can catch them early before they multiply.

6. Interplanting and Companion Planting. These techniques involve planting certain plants close to each other, because one tends to repel certain insect pests that attack the other. We will discuss this concept in much more detail in chapter 5.

7. Biological Controls. By biological controls I mean all the natural predators of harmful insects. This includes beneficial insects, birds, toads, and bats. The more you can do to attract these insect eaters the better. I will deal with this in more detail in chapter 5.

8. Physical Controls. There are all kinds of physical controls that have been developed over the years to keep down the population of harmful insects. Some are more effective than others, but they are all worth considering. This category includes such things as traps, black light, dormant oil, diatomaceous earth, paper collars, wood ashes, flour, and all manner of other repellents, lures, and traps that are used by organic gardeners around the world. Traps using a sex lure or pheromones for Japanese beetles and gypsy moths are becoming very popular. None of these physical controls will eliminate a particular pest, but they will limit the numbers of a pest so that damage to the garden is minimized.

9. Natural Sprays. These include the hundreds of home remedies that have been developed by organic gardeners over the years. Some are designed to repel the insect, and others are designed actually to kill it. These sprays include such deterrents as soapy water, garlic, red pepper, and "bug juice," which is made by blending the bugs themselves in water. A more detailed discussion of these methods can be found in chapter 6.

10. Botanical Poisons. These are insecticides that are derived from plants; they are poisonous to insects but generally harmless to humans and animals after a few days. They include pyrethrum, rotenone, and nicotine preparations. These sprays are definitely effective, but like chemical sprays, they do not discriminate between harmful pests and beneficial insects. While these materials can be very toxic when applied, even to humans, they break down very quickly and lose their toxicity for people and animals after a few days, unlike the chemical insecticides. These are discussed in more detail in chapter 6.

Since it takes a number of years to master the backyard integrated pest management approach, what should you do for this first year or so when you get hit with your first bean beetle attack? As I said before, I think that it is terribly important to learn how to be observant. If you spot them early, many bug infestations can be stopped cold by some simple handpicking. This is one area where I relax my principles regarding oppressive child labor. Children seem to have much sharper vision for spotting small insects than do adults. I have been known to offer very minimum wages, such as five bugs for a penny, and turn a couple of little kids loose in the bean patch. I rationalize this crass behavior with the assumption that the kids are learning about nature and can always use the money.

In any case, I suggest you try to deal with harmful insects in your garden in the same order as my little IPM list does. If everything else fails, then by all means use a botanical poison such as rotenone. But use it with great care and then try to find ways to avoid using it next year. Believe me, as the years go by, organic control of insect pests gets easier.

Eating Your Produce

As I've said before, our national diet does not focus very much on vegetables—we are a meat-loving country. Consequently, many of us were raised in families where the vegetables played a very minor role in meals. They were often overcooked, and were usually just boiled and served with a little butter and salt and pepper. While various ethnic groups have brought their own vegetable specialties (such as stuffed cabbage, borscht, and eggplant parmigiana) into our diet, most of us have not learned to prepare and enjoy the full range of fresh vegetables that we have the potential to grow in our own backyard gardens.

The key point here is obvious—if you don't eat what you grow, and if your garden production doesn't represent a significant percentage of your diet, at least in the summer, then you won't save very much money for all of your time and energy.

Part of developing a food production system, therefore, is learning how to make maximum use of your produce on the dinner table. In subsequent chapters I will discuss how to go about saving your produce for later use. You can store, freeze, can, process, and dry your vegetables and enjoy them all year long.

What may be a new experience is learning how to use vegetables fresh from the garden every day. The most obvious problem is that when a certain vegetable is ripe, you usually have enough to eat it every day for two weeks—not an exciting prospect for everyone. Here is where a few years of experience will make a world of difference in your garden planning in the spring. **The trick to having a varied harvest is to stagger your plantings so that you will have a variety of fresh vegetables available continuously from June through October.** Once you have a quantity of vegetables available at any one time, then you need to learn how to vary their preparation. Experimenting with new recipes can be fun, and there are numerous cookbooks on the market that are devoted exclusively to vegetables. The combination of produce guarantees that you won't get bored and that you will be able to make better use of your produce from an economic standpoint.

About half the vegetables you will grow can be eaten raw, in salads, or with tasty dips. Some people like some of them better after they have been blanched for a minute or two (green beans, broccoli, and peas are often blanched this way). All vegetables can be cooked (even lettuce!) either by themselves or in dishes such as soups, stews, and casseroles. Vegetables can be sautéed, steamed, boiled, baked, and stir-fried. They can be combined in endless ways, and they can be served with many different sauces. In other words, the vegetable garden offers an almost infinite variety of tastes and textures that is interesting and even very nutritious. However, keep in mind that the less you cook them, the more nutritious they remain.

The key to making the best use of your garden is to develop your own vegetable recipe file. While cookbooks do organize a section on vegetables, they seldom have more than two or three recipes for each one. Most recipe books spend much more time on the meat dishes. Newspapers and magazines are often great sources of a wide range of interestingly varied recipes for vegetables. When various vegetables are in season, food editors usually feature preparation hints. I clip the interesting recipes and set them aside in a pile. Once a year or so I spend an afternoon in front of the TV pasting recipes on 5 by 7-inch cards. My recipe file has a divider for each individual vegetable. Recipe books will give me about 5 recipes for eggplant, for example, but I have almost 20 in my file and it grows each year. Believe me, when the eggplants come in they keep coming in. By the fourth week of eggplant season, you are really motivated to try a recipe that you haven't tried before!

While most general recipe books have a section on vegetables, if you are like me, you have many books and can't remember which one had that wonderful recipe for red cabbage. I've solved that problem by simply noting the book and the recipe title on a 5 by 7-inch card and slipping it in my file. Then, when I am looking for something to do with green beans for the umpteenth time, my card file is my primary reference, because it includes all the recipes from my books that I once spotted and decided were worth trying.

Another practice for the cook to consider is the use of fresh herbs in vegetable dishes. Having a half-dozen different fresh herbs available can add significant zest to all your meals. The problem is learning how to use them and then remembering that you have them handy out in the garden. If you start off simply, with some basil, dill, oregano, parsley, and chives, you will find that they are easy to grow and that they really do add a new dimension to your salads and your cooking. You'll soon learn, too, that herbs are used in larger amounts when they are fresh than when they are dried. Drying intensifies their flavor.

The Economics of the First Stage

When you draw up your balance sheet of costs and savings at the end of this first stage in your food production system, you will probably find that you just about break even. It's hard to calculate precisely how much you will have saved in this first year. I don't take the time to keep the kind of detailed records that I'd need to get a good, hard estimate of the dollars-and-cents value of my produce. Some of what I grow you can't even buy in most grocery stores—Swiss chard, kohlrabi, and leaf lettuce, for instance. The Gallup poll I've referred to earlier in the book produced a statement that a 600-square-foot plot (20 by 30) produced in 1980 dollars roughly $360 worth of vegetables at a cost of about $20. That results in a profit figure of about 60 cents per square foot of garden. It also assumes an experienced gardener with a garden that has already passed the initial capital investment stage.

I estimate that a beginning gardener, with an average first-year level of experience, can figure on about 50 cents per square foot in value of the produce, using 1981 prices. A good gardener using a well-prepared, intensively planted garden with raised beds can expect to get from $1.00 to $1.50 per square foot after three or four years of experience. Then that 600 square feet mentioned above produces up to $900 in savings, a figure that begins to make a real difference in the family budget.

In this first stage, the capital investment in tools and other things that won't be repurchased later tends to bring the savings down to a break-even point. That is the price for the training and the experience you're gaining during this first year. One of the most knowledgeable writers in the field of gardening and food production is Nancy Bubel, who has a number of excellent books and many fine

Economics of the First Stage

Item and Use in Food Production System	Initial Capital Investment	Operating Costs and Savings
Garden maintenance Seeds, plants, and natural fertilizers for garden of 200–400 sq. ft.	. . .	$15–$25 covers the basic annual costs, and you can expect $100–$200 in savings beyond that (assuming you save about 50¢ per sq. ft. of garden).
Garden tools and equipment All-purpose hoe	$7–$10	Properly cared for, it lasts indefinitely.
Scuffle hoe (for weeding— optional)	$14	Lasts indefinitely.
Spade	$8–$33	Lasts indefinitely.
Garden rake	$10–$20	Lasts indefinitely.
Trowel	$2–$5	Lasts indefinitely.
Garden cart or wheelbarrow	$39–$150	Lasts 5–10 yrs. with care.
Watering can	$6–$45	Lasts 10 yrs. with proper care.
Hose	$15–$20	Lasts 5 yrs. or more.
Gloves	$2–$10	Usually replaced every 2 yrs.

Comments: As with everything else, the higher the quality of the garden tool you purchase, the longer it will last. So for $100–$150 you can have a summer garden that will save you just about the same amount of money—$100–$200. Remember that if you had exactly the same garden again next year, you would invest only about $25 and still have the $100–$200 in savings.

articles to her credit. **This gardening expert identifies three ways to increase your garden savings: Produce more valuable crops, cut your costs, and increase your productivity.** It is that last point, increasing your productivity, where I see the most potential for increasing your savings, and you can do it without having to increase the amount of space taken up by the garden. The chart above gives you a rough idea of the costs that you might expect to incur in this first-stage garden. You may already have some of the equipment. You also may choose to spend more money than is indicated here. These figures are just a guide to help you with your planning. This same chart will be expanded at the end of each chapter as we move our discussion through the five stages for developing a backyard food production system.

The Summer Garden

THE GAME PLAN

The Goal: Your aim in the second stage of your backyard food
production system is to have a summer garden that supplies
most of your fresh vegetable needs during the growing season,
plus a little extra to store or put up.

The Strategy:

1. Think ahead to long-term crops like fruit trees and berries and
   where you'll put them.

2. Plan a year's supply of food for your household; then pick two or
   three vegetables of which you'll grow a year's supply.

3. Expand the garden by adding a bed or two, and plant crops
   closer together at equidistant spacings.

4. Try some different varieties.

5. Make and use more compost.

6. Water to maintain consistent soil moisture levels. Test the soil
   and add organic fertilizers as needed.

7. Learn new ways to cook and serve varying amounts of vegetables
   to keep pace with garden production. Can or freeze for winter the
   two or three vegetables of which you're growing a year's supply.

The second stage of your backyard food production system involves moving from your beginning garden to what is called a summer garden—one that is primarily designed to produce all your fresh vegetables for the table during the growing season, and that will also produce some excess for storage. **For the second stage, you must start to learn about how to store and preserve some of your food for later use. You will have to learn some new planning techniques, because you will be expanding the size of your garden, and you'll begin to use some new growing techniques designed to increase the production per square foot of your vegetable patch.**

Planning Skills Needed for the Summer Garden

One of the interesting developments that occurs at about this time in the creation of a backyard food production system is the rather sobering realization of how much you have to know to develop and manage such a system. At this point you've had some experience with your modest garden. You've subscribed to some magazines which have given you all kinds of good ideas to adopt in this second year. You've read a couple of books (or parts of a couple of books) and have two or three more on hand for winter reading. Gathering the information you need isn't that difficult. Even understanding each issue as it comes along doesn't really strain the brain cells. What does get very complicated, very quickly, is the integration of all this information in your head so that you can manage the production system and still lead a somewhat normal life in the suburbs.

Thinking about getting the soil improved, collecting some material for the compost ahead of time, planting some more seedlings for a later crop of cabbage, and trying to decide where to put the dwarf apple tree can clog a person's consciousness from time to time. On top of that, you might start to panic when you find that you really don't understand how squash borers get into the zucchini, so how can you prevent them from destroying your next crop? There is so much to learn and so little time to get everything done! However, if you talk to someone who has been growing food for five years or more, he will tell you to relax. Learn what you can when you can, and put in as much time as you feel you want to on your food production efforts. You'll find that you will strike a comfortable balance between what you know and what you need to know as you gain more experience.

I am a firm believer in the idea of "readiness to learn." We use it in educational theory to understand the development of children, and I think it works for adults as well. We pass an enormous amount of information through our brain each day, with relatively short-term retention. But when we are ready for a particular piece of information, we grab it and remember it for the rest of our days. That happens to me all the time when I read something in a magazine that really clicks and solves a problem I've been having, such as how much lime I should put on my soil to improve its pH level. I didn't really know when I had to put lime on the garden, assuming I needed it, because I didn't know how long its effects lasted. When I read that ideally lime should go on six months before a lime-loving plant is planted, I learned that it is a much longer-lasting additive to the garden than I had suspected. I can apply the lime in the fall and it will be available to my plants the following spring. I had been afraid that it would leach away. I had probably read that same information three years earlier, but I wasn't far enough along in my experience to be ready for it. While you must know a great deal to manage a backyard food production system properly, you will learn as you go, so don't get discouraged about how much you don't know. When you are ready, you will master all the techniques you need. Now let's look at a few more planning skills that may be helpful.

Thinking Ahead

While most of your food production efforts can be developed slowly over the years, there are a few crops that require you to think a bit ahead, because they take a number of years even to begin producing. **If you intend to have fruit trees, nut trees, berries of any kind, or asparagus, then you may want to make some decisions about the location of these crops soon, since they require a permanent location and need 2 to 6 years of lead time to produce any food.** Asparagus takes 3 years to be ready to harvest, and that bed can stay in place for 20 years. Depending on their variety, fruit trees can take 4 to 6 years before fruit is ready to pick. In any case, the location of these long-term crops is important in your long-range plan for developing your backyard system. Let me give you a few examples.

For instance, the folks who developed the Integral Urban House in Berkeley, California, decided to replace their front lawn with strawberries as a ground cover. You may not wish to go quite that far, but their work suggests that the front lawn, or at least part of it, is a possible site for some of this long-range planning. The people at the Integral Urban House also make extensive use of a traditional pruning technique called espalier on their fruit trees to save space while still offering an attractive component to the appearance of the yard. The fruit tree itself must be placed in a good sunny site, but if you also intend to use the espalier pruning method, it must be located so that the supporting structure can be enlarged as the tree grows bigger.

A very long-range view is recommended by Bill Mollison, who wrote *Permaculture One* and *Permaculture Two* (see the Bibliography). He believes that the decision about placement of trees, nut trees for example, should include consideration of their impact on the climate control of your property. Trees can serve as a windbreak that cuts the north winds in the winter, and they can produce shade which can help cool the house in the summer. Some nut trees take up to ten years to begin to produce a decent crop, and that calls for very long-range planning indeed.

You won't have to deal with all of these issues at the same time. Your primary concern will still be the garden that you plant each year. Nevertheless, some of the daydreaming you do during the winter months, or as you are turning the compost, can center on some of these long-range considerations.

There is another issue that gets raised when you begin to expand the size of your garden and increase your level of production: You will be ready to get into storing some of that excess food for later use. We will talk about canning, freezing, and storage later in this chapter. However, this excess food should not be produced haphazardly. You should be able to plan which vegetables you want to have in extra amounts and how much extra you really can use. The first step is to determine how much of each vegetable you really need.

Planning a Year's Supply

Figuring out how much of any vegetable to grow to produce a year's supply for your family is not all that easy. It is likely that different people in the family enjoy different vegetables. Your consumption can fluctuate with the seasons or simply with the whim of the cook. A 100-square-foot bed will produce varying amounts, according to the productivity of the soil, the weather, and your ability as a gardener. Your storage space is another limiting factor. You may be able to grow potatoes, but your climate may prevent you from being able to store them without refrigeration.

You are not going to be producing your year's supply of many of your vegetables in the second-stage garden, but I believe that it is helpful for you to know what that target would be if you did decide to try to grow it all yourself. The chart titled 67 Common Foods lists all the foods that you might conceivably be able to produce in your own backyard. Obviously, this varies with climate and the size of your backyard, but it gives you a starting place. Run down the list and identify all those foods that your family enjoys. Then take that list and identify all the preferred foods that you might be able to grow in your backyard food system, given the limiting factors mentioned in the previous paragraph. Now you are ready to compute your year's supply for each one.

The easiest way to determine your year's supply of each type of food is to sit down with the person in the family who does the food shopping. Most families these days shop on a weekly basis. A rough estimate of how often something has been purchased is fine for this exercise. **Figure out the frequency with which you eat a particular vegetable by times-per-week or times-per-month, and multiply by**

52 or 12 to get an estimate of your weekly or monthly consumption. We have pota-toes at least twice a week almost every week of the year. On the other hand, we have parsnips three or four times in the entire year. I am the only one in the family who likes green peppers, so I compute my needs accordingly.

Once you have estimated the frequency of use of each food, then multiply that figure by the amount your family consumes at each meal. Most frozen foods in the grocery store are packed in 10-ounce containers. If you eat green beans twice a month all year, using one package at a meal, then you'll need about 15 pounds of green beans for your year's supply (24 meals at 10 ounces per meal = 240 ounces = 15 pounds). If you check the chart in the Appendix titled How Much to Plant, you will find that a 25-foot row of green beans in a peak year will produce about 15 pounds. A 15-foot bed that is 4 feet wide will produce more than 15 pounds. One bed planted in green beans, then, will meet your needs for the year.

This brings us to a very important observation. **If you are going to try to grow as much of your fresh food as you can, and you live in the United States where over half the country has a winter season, obviously you will not have every fresh vegetable available to you in every month.** We've become very spoiled in this coun-try with Florida, Arizona, and California providing all of us with fresh produce 12 months a year. We gardeners can pickle our fresh cucumbers, but we can't store our fresh cucumbers so that we can have them in a salad in January. It is possible, but difficult, to grow cucumbers in a greenhouse, so if you are going to try to achieve some degree of self-sufficiency with your vegetable production, then you will find yourself changing a few eating habits—not many, but a few. You'll be eating some foods on a more seasonal basis, rather than during every month of the year.

A person who has a backyard food production system producing food 12 months a year in some ways can have food of more variety and far better quality than the person who depends on the local grocery store. There are, of course, some foods found in the grocery store that can't be grown at home, such as bananas and artichokes. Also, we find certain vegetables and fruits fresh in the stores in winter that we can't have fresh from our gardens, even though the quality and flavor of those foods leave much to be desired. On the other hand, the home producer will have many things fresh in January, assuming he has a greenhouse or solar grow frame, that are not available in any grocery store, including leaf lettuce, Swiss chard, and many kinds of oriental vegetables. I'll be discussing grow frames and greenhouses in later chapters.

After thinking through your vegetable preferences and yearly consumption, pick two or three vegetables that you like and that you can grow in quantity in your summer garden. Plan to store or preserve the excess in some way for use later on in the year. Green beans, tomatoes, and carrots are three excellent candidates for producing much of your year's supply out of a summer garden.

67 Common Foods

Foods	Family Enjoys	Frequency per Month	Amount per Serving	Year's Supply
Vegetables				
Asparagus				
Beets				
Broccoli				
Brussels sprouts				
Cabbage				
Carrots				
Cauliflower				
Celery				
Collards				
Cucumbers				
Eggplant				
Garlic				
Kale				
Kohlrabi				
Lettuce				
Onions				
Parsnips				
Peppers, chili				
Peppers, green				
Potatoes				
Pumpkins				
Radishes				
Spinach				
Squash, summer				
Squash, winter				
Sweet potatoes				
Swiss chard				
Tomatoes				
Turnips				
Yams				
Seeds, Nuts, and Legumes				
Beans, kidney				
Beans, lima				
Beans, mung				
Beans, navy				
Beans, pinto				

67 Common Foods—*Continued*

Foods	Family Enjoys	Frequency per Month	Amount per Serving	Year's Supply
Seeds, Nuts, and Legumes– *continued*				
Beans, string				
Chick-peas				
Lentils				
Peanuts				
Peas				
Peas, black-eyed				
Peas, split				
Soybeans				
Sunflower seeds				
Walnuts				
Fruit				
Apples				
Apricots				
Blackberries				
Blueberries				
Cantaloupe				
Grapes				
Grapefruit				
Lemons				
Limes				
Oranges				
Peaches				
Pears				
Plums (prune)				
Strawberries				
Watermelon				
Meat and Meat Products				
Chicken				
Rabbit				
Eggs				
Fish				
Carp				
Trout				
Other				
Honey				
Maple syrup				

Management Skills for the Second Stage

In this stage, you'll be focusing your efforts on increasing the productivity and efficiency of your food production system. It's time to consider expanding your garden's size and to undertake some intensive methods to increase production and save money.

Expanding Your Garden Plot

This second stage of your food production system requires a bit more space, but in no way requires a full-size operation of 1,000 square feet or more. **A summer garden with six to eight beds, or 600 to 800 square feet of growing area, will offer you all the challenges you need plus enough extra produce to put up for winter.** As you will see in the next section, intensive methods are very productive, but they are always a bit more time-consuming than conventional single-row techniques.

A garden this size can produce a very significant quantity of food, even with only one year's gardening experience. If you just scan the chart titled How Much to Plant, in the Appendix, you'll see that a single bed will produce 30 pounds of green beans, or 50 pounds of cabbage, or even 70 pounds of cucumbers! If you can imagine having six or eight beds, each producing this quantity of food, you can begin to appreciate the potential of your growing efforts.

Increasing Production
Using Advanced Planting Techniques

Advanced planting techniques used in conjunction with raised beds can increase the production of a garden ten times over the production levels of a garden planted in conventional single rows. Permanent beds and advanced planting methods produce such significant increases in production per square foot of space, because you space plants more closely together and, for various reasons, they grow better. **The catch is that these production methods take considerable skill and cannot easily be mastered in just one season. The best approach to learning and using them is an incremental one—give yourself two or three years to become really familiar with the use of all the advanced methods for increasing your garden production.**

Very briefly, these high-production methods include a number of concepts that are put into practice simultaneously. Intensive planting means spacing plants much closer together than the traditional distances recommended on seed packages. Interplanting involves planting different types of vegetables in among each other in order to take advantage of differences between the plants in terms of maturation dates, root structures, and foliar structures. This means that you get maximum production in a limited space. Companion planting involves bringing together groups of vegetables and herbs in an effort either to improve the production of each

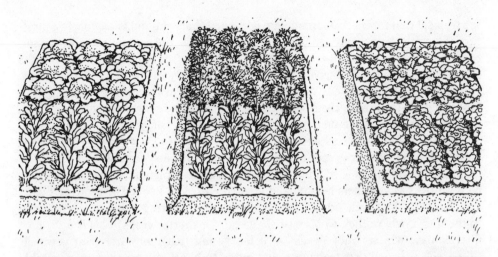

If gardening in raised beds is new to you, keep planting and maintenance chores simple by planting just one or two crops in each bed until you gain more experience.

variety, or to repel certain pests. Succession planting means that you provide an immediate replacement plant for every plant that is harvested, so that no garden space goes unused. Crops like peas, broccoli, and lettuce can follow each other in the same space over the course of a single season, to give you three crops from one space. Finally, rotation means moving your crops around the garden each year, never planting the same thing twice in a row in the same spot, in order to have the least impact on soil nutrient levels and to prevent the buildup of disease-causing organisms in the soil. While the combination of these five concepts greatly increases productivity, their implementation is obviously a challenge even to the experienced gardener.

So that you're not overwhelmed by trying to learn and practice intensive techniques that may be unfamiliar to you, I recommend that in this second phase you just focus on learning to plant your vegetables closer together in the beds—this will still improve your production, but won't confuse or overwork you with too many new tasks at the same time. As I mentioned above, this technique is called intensive planting. I'll discuss intensive planting now and cover the other advanced production techniques more thoroughly in the next chapter.

Intensive Planting

It's a fact that plants grow better when they are closely spaced and properly cared for. **Your aim in intensive planting is to locate your plants in the bed so that all the plants are equidistant from each other in all directions, and so that the outermost leaves of each plant just touch the surrounding plants at maturity.** This creates a canopy of foliage over the bed that has the same effect as the canopy over the tropical rain forest. A microclimate is created that is humid and cool. The moisture is kept in the ground and below the leaves, while the canopy acts like an umbrella to keep the soil cool and moist and protected from the burning rays of the direct sun. These conditions are ideal for rapid, steady plant growth. If you have enriched your growing beds with sufficient nutrients in the form of compost and other organic fertilizers, then putting the plants so close together will give you a much higher rate of production per square foot than you got using rows.

Until you gain more experience with beds, it's best to restrict each bed to one vegetable, or at least keep sections of the bed for only one vegetable at a time. The literature on intensive gardening shows that different plants can be combined in beds on the basis of their heights and growth patterns. The lower-growing plants are placed to the south side of the bed, and taller-growing plants are positioned to the north, where they won't cast shade on the shorter crops. This is a form of interplanting which is not as easy as it looks, and that's why I suggest you wait till next year to try that technique. It's easier to have only one kind of vegetable in a given area, so that when the crop is harvested you can conveniently rework that section of the bed in preparation for putting in your second crop. The chart titled Planting Guide in the Appendix gives intensive spacings for most commonly grown crops.

To get the maximum production per square foot from your raised beds, space plants equidistant from one another in all directions. The plants should be close enough together that, when fully mature, their outermost leaves just touch.

Laying out the plants in an equidistant fashion definitely allows you to have more plants per square foot, but it can be a little confusing until you get used to it. My father devised a tool for me that's proved to be really handy for planting in equidistant spacings. As you can see in the photo, it is nothing more than an oversized compass that can be adjusted with a wing nut to whatever planting distance you're working with.

In the first year of my food system, I simply used the between-plant spacings given on the seed packets as my equidistant spacings. The next year, after I had

This homemade giant compass makes it easy to measure plant spacings in the garden. All you do is adjust the arms to the spacing distance you need for a particular crop, then tighten the wing nut to hold them in that position.

gained a little confidence in the idea, I cut those distances down to about three-quarters of what the seed packets prescribed. In most cases it worked very well. You can use this rule of thumb yourself, and the Planting Guide in the Appendix should also be a help.

Varieties—Do They Make Any Difference?

One of your most important decisions as a gardener is choosing what to plant. Some varieties of vegetables take some special attention, so let's talk about varieties.

One of the most unsettling experiences for the beginning gardener is paging through the first seed catalogs and discovering that there seem to be at least 20 different varieties of every kind of vegetable imaginable! Not only do you have to choose from over 50 vegetables, but you have to choose from all those varieties as well. Every single one is described as the most perfect example of its kind, so how do you choose which will be best for you? There are a number of ways to deal with the problem—you can ask another gardener, you can ask the county extension agent, or you can guess. I guessed.

All those multitudes of vegetable varieties are created for very specific reasons. Some are resistant to a particular disease. Some are designed to withstand extremes in climate. Others are created for higher production, better flavor, better color, or a different taste. Still others are bred to prefer a longer or shorter day-length, so that they are better suited to the North or the South. Additional confusion is created by the existence of both hybrid and nonhybrid varieties. Without getting too deeply into the technical differences, nonhybrid varieties have been bred to themselves for many generations so that they possess a very uniform set of genetic traits. Nonhybrids tend to be the older vegetable varieties that have been grown for years. A hybrid, on the other hand, is a variety that has been artificially cross-pollinated by combining two or more uniform strains to produce a new variety that contains certain characteristics of each of the parent strains. Hybrids tend to be more expensive, but they also have characteristics and benefits, such as resistance to disease or larger fruit, that are not always found in the traditional nonhybrid strains.

The only time you have to be concerned about whether your seed is hybrid or not is when you decide you want to save your own seed at the end of the season to plant next year. The nonhybrid variety will produce uniform seed from which you can grow plants like the parent year in and year out. But the hybrid is not so stable. The seed from a hybrid plant will not produce a plant that's genetically identical to the parent if planted the next year—in other words, it won't come true from seed. What this means is that you can save your own seeds of nonhybrid varieties, but you can't with hybrids. The seed package will almost always tell you if a variety is hybrid or not.

A final decision as to which is the best variety for you can only be reached after a number of years of experimenting. Some varieties work better in the early plantings and others do better as fall crops—cabbages are a good example. Early cabbage is good to eat fresh, and the late-maturing varieties are intended for long-term storage over the winter. Vegetable varieties also differ in appearance and flavor. Some varieties store more readily or freeze with a higher quality. Other varieties are attractive to northern gardeners because they mature faster. I plant multiple varieties of many of my vegetables. I have an early-ripening tomato, a main-crop tomato, and a storage tomato. They get planted at different times in the season, so my planning has to take that into consideration.

No doubt you will find a friend who swears by a certain variety as being the most productive, and you might try it only to find that it is a dud for you. This can happen because you have different soil or different amounts of light available, and you may feed and water the plant differently. Consequently, while your friend uses variety A, you might find that B works better for you. The fact of the matter is that you have to find the best varieties of each vegetable one by one and all by yourself. You can get all the advice you want, but in the end you have to try over the years to find which ones you prefer.

The best way to experiment with different varieties is to plant a couple of different ones of many of your vegetables each year. Keep the one that works the best and try another new one alongside it next year. Then keep the best of that match and try another one. After a while you will settle on your favorite. This process does require at least a minimum effort in record keeping, because you have to know which variety is where in your garden so you can buy the right one next year. Some people keep very detailed records of comparative data, but I've never been able to muster the discipline to do that. I simply label the plants in the garden with the proper variety, then observe the differences and try to remember which to buy the next year. I miss a few now and then, but I figure that I have 50 more years of gardening ahead of me, so I'll correct some of my mistakes next year. The point of this discussion is that varieties do make a difference, and over time you will choose the best varieties to suit your situation.

The Composting System
In the first stage I recommended that you begin a basic compost pile. There is an increasing need for compost as you expand the scope of your food production activities. For stage two, I suggest you get a bit more serious about your composting program. As I mentioned in chapter 3, there are many systems for making com-

My three-stage composting system supplies me with compost throughout the growing season. The pile on the right is nearly ready to use. The center pile is in the process of being built, and the plastic cover will keep it damp until it's complete. At left are leaves and other materials that will be shredded and stored until there's enough to start a third pile.

post, all of which work very well. I've referred to a couple of books on composting in the Bibliography, and you'll find it helpful to look them over. My system works for me, and I offer it to you to consider along with the others that you read about. Eventually you will settle on an approach that fits the amount of time, storage space, and interest you have to offer. **I generally use only five things in my compost pile—leaves, grass, weeds, garden waste, and household garbage.** I use no manure, lime, or rock powders that are found in other systems. With those five materials I produce about 3 tons of gorgeous compost each season.

In the fall I collect about 100 bags of leaves that have been set out for the trashmen by neighbors. I shred those leaves, reducing their volume considerably, and then store them together as a mulch on the garden over the winter. In the spring I put them in a pile in my compost area. As I accumulate grass clippings, garbage, and other green material (nitrogen materials), I build a pile about 4 by 4 feet, which is a bit bigger than what is considered the minimum size for an effective compost pile. I run that pile through my shredder every week or two, and build up to three piles at a time, depending on the availability of green materials and my time. A pile is usually ready for the garden in about a month to six weeks. Most gardeners aren't interested in such a large system, and do just fine with one pile which they may turn two or three times during the season. You may find that one pile is enough for you in stage two, but you'll undoubtedly want to expand your composting operation in the next year or so.

I have had my compost tested by the county extension service and found it to be almost neutral in pH and high to very high in phosphorus, potassium, calcium, and magnesium. While leaves are acidic when they are whole, they become neutral when properly composted. I generally supplement my compost with some blood meal to provide the necessary nitrogen to balance the phosphorus and potassium.

Using Compost
I use all this compost in three ways. In the process of transplanting seedlings in the spring and throughout the season, I always put some compost in the hole I make before planting the seedling. This is done for the littlest lettuce plant as well as a shrub with a 2-foot ball of roots. I also use compost in the spring as a soil conditioner by simply laying an inch of compost over the entire garden as I prepare it for spring planting. That is worked in a few inches as I prepare the beds. Finally, I use compost extensively as mulch, which also acts as a fertilizer. I put 4 to 6 inches of compost around almost all my plants in the garden to keep weeds down, to hold in moisture, and to feed the roots slowly as the rain trickles down and leaches the nutrients contained in the compost. After a few years of putting about 5 inches of compost into your raised beds, you will have a growing medium for vegetables that cannot be surpassed.

Rich, crumbly compost makes an excellent mulch for growing plants. Just spread it several inches deep around the plants. It adds nutrients to the soil and helps to retain moisture and to moderate soil temperatures.

Watering—A Critical Function

The quantity and quality of the production of your garden is directly related to the proper watering of your plants. Unfortunately, it is not all that clear to most of us when to water and when not to water. Here again, as with compost, three different books will say three somewhat different things about the principles of watering. I suggest you read at least a couple of the sections on watering in the general references listed in the Bibliography to see where you fit in among all the approaches. In the end, it is not all that difficult after you've experimented with the problem for a year or so. **There are some critical variables which really affect how much you will have to water. Do you use mulch? If so, water less. What type of soil do you have? If it's sandy, water more. Leaf and root crops generally take more water, while fruit and seed crops take less. What is your weather? Dry and windy means more water.**

I think the most important issue to resolve is how to maintain a *consistent* level of moisture in your garden. It is the wet/dry fluctuations that can really hurt your production levels. My approach, in southeastern Pennsylvania, is to try to buffer the extremes in moisture as much as possible. By planting intensively and by using lots of mulch, I hold the moisture longer. By loading my soil with compost

A simple wood cover will keep mosquitoes and other unwelcome insects from taking up residence in your rain barrel.

over the years, I enable it to hold more water per cubic foot for longer periods of time. By planting my plants in slight depressions or in furrows in the beds, they get a higher percentage of the rain water than if the beds had a flat surface around the plants allowing more runoff.

Since we generally get fairly uniform rainfall in our area, I don't have to water too often. At the same time, I have learned to observe the signals. I feel the soil under the mulch, maybe down an inch or so. If it's even slightly dry, I will water. I keep track of the rains and generally ensure that the garden gets some water at least once every week from me or the rain. Root crops, leaf crops, and the squash generally get extra during the week. I have three rain barrels that store 150 gallons of nitrogen-rich rain water. This water is used mostly for seedlings, since I have seedlings in various locations almost all season long. Seedlings need water almost daily, depending on the weather.

Most of the experts say you should not water your garden with an automatic sprinkler. It wastes water and it gets water on the leaves of some plants that don't like water on their leaves. However, since rain obviously puts water on the leaves, and because the sprinkler saves time, I have broken that rule for many years. I am usually careful to water in the late afternoon to enable the plants to dry off a bit before dark, so I have for the most part avoided any disease problems because of my bad practice. With 1,000 square feet of garden, watering by hand or with the hose takes a chunk of time I am just not able to give.

The ideal setup, and one that is in my plans, is a permanently installed drip irrigation system. This requires special hoses, nozzles, and controls that are spread throughout the garden in a systematic fashion. The water is applied slowly drop by drop, providing moisture to the roots, the place where you want it, and only in quantities that are needed. Once the system is installed, it cuts your watering time down to almost zero, and it can save you from 20 to 40 percent of the amount of water you used previously.

A drip irrigation system is another example of a capital expense that doesn't get amortized. In an average garden you can spend from $50 to $150 on a drip system, depending on how automatic you want to have it. **What you must do is compare the cost of the system to the 20 or 30 hours you would save in a season as well as the difficult-to-measure increase in the production levels of your garden that are due to more effective watering.** If you are concerned about maximum production with least demand on your time, and you can afford it, then such a system is definitely worth considering. There are numerous systems on the market, and a trip to your local garden center should give you a chance to compare some of them. Write to the manufacturers for further information.

Feeding the Garden

As it is regarding watering, the gardening literature can be a bit confusing about the different approaches to fertilizing your vegetables. I won't go into all the technical issues here, since most basic gardening books cover the subject better than I could. Let me simply emphasize the key areas of concern. I'll let you learn about the details as you do some more reading and get some experience.

I believe that the most important factor in having well-fed plants is the quality of the soil, and that is directly related to how much compost you are able to add to your garden each year. I'm assuming that I have convinced you to work toward an organic method of gardening. Your guiding principle should be to add compost, then add more compost, and then add a bit more compost just to be sure. With that somewhat simplistic formula you'll be guaranteed a good supply of the essential nutrients in your soil, which in turn makes it quite difficult to have a nonproductive garden. As I mentioned in the previous section, I make lots of compost—about five or six good-size piles each year. While it takes at least two or three hours a month to produce that much compost, it eases considerably the complexity of watering and feeding problems in the garden.

One of your first concerns related to feeding should be to get a pH reading on your garden's soil. An imbalance in either direction will make it difficult for the plants to absorb nutrients efficiently from the soil. As I said earlier, a soil test from your agricultural extension service is the best way to get this information accurately. Lots of books will tell you how to get your pH balanced if you have a problem—add lime to acid soil or acid peat moss to alkaline soil, for example. But they seldom point out that properly made compost has an almost perfect pH reading, and adding large quantities of compost will help keep your pH level at a good point for growing most vegetables.

The three basic foodstuffs for growing plants are nitrogen, phosphorus, and potassium (the NPK you always hear about). Again your soil test is going to tell you where you stand in terms of these nutrients. The most important thing to remember as you try to figure out how to give your plants the proper amounts of nitrogen, phosophorus, and potassium is that these elements are only truly effective if they are themselves balanced in quantity in the soil. **You will have healthier plants if you have relatively low NPK readings that are balanced than if you have an unbalanced situation with high nitrogen, medium phosphorus, and a low potassium reading.** The balancing of the three nutrients is almost more important than the actual quantity of each in the soil.

The process for getting the elements into balance takes some skill and experience. The problem is complicated if you have one element, as I did, that is very high. My potassium readings were off the scale. The only way I could get my soil balanced was to increase the nitrogen and phosphorus content by adding materials high in those two elements but low in potassium. When I got a balanced reading of all three elements, I let the growing of the plants bring all three readings down to a more normal level. Utilization of these nutrients by the plants as they grow and the leaching action of the rain takes the NPK readings down. In my case, I've had to avoid using any manure or wood ashes for a number of years until some of that naturally high potassium was used up by my vegetables. This may be an unusual case, as many gardeners struggle with soil that is far too low in all or most of the necessary nutrients. In any case, the point is that you can't just haphazardly dump fertilizer materials onto your garden and assume it'll help. It might hurt.

To get a handle on this feeding issue, you will have to rely on the advice of your favorite organic gardening book, after you have applied the variables of your own local conditions. You may be limited by the availability in your area of some of the organic fertilizers that are recommended in the books. The charts titled Approximate Nutrient Composition (%) of Organic Materials and Feeding and Watering Guidelines, in the Appendix, give you some guidelines.

Using Your Summer Produce

It might seem unnecessary to talk about how to use the vegetables you have grown in your summer garden, but the efficient use of the harvest can be a problem. Most people who haven't had a garden before have a little trouble remembering, day in and day out, that all that fresh food is out there. As I mentioned earlier, on the other side of the coin, some folks get very tired, very quickly, of green beans, green beans, and more green beans! **Very often, the person who planned the garden is not the same person who does the cooking. Consequently, the gardener and the** cook need to work together if maximum benefits in food value and cost savings are to be realized.

Gardener and Cook Work Together

Here is where that recipe file that has been organized for each different vegetable comes in handy. The cook's ability to use the vegetables in the volume and variety that become available each week or so is directly related to the gardener's ability to plan the planting of the garden so that everything doesn't ripen at the same time, and so that not too much of one kind of vegetable is grown. Another good technique is to stagger the plantings of a particular vegetable. One-third of the crop goes in at the first planting date, one-third is planted in three weeks, and one-third is planted three weeks after that. It doesn't make much sense to put in the time and money to grow fresh vegetables if no one wants to eat them, or the family gets tired of eating the same vegetable constantly.

A properly planned vegetable garden can produce a quantity and variety of foods that does not overwhelm, but rather stimulates and excites. My father, who was raised in Vermont, tells of his family's special tradition when each of the fruits and vegetables in their garden first became ripe each season. When the first peas came in, supper that evening was a huge bowl of fresh green peas and bread and butter—nothing else. When the strawberries became ripe—a big bowl of fresh strawberries and bread and butter was the supper for that evening. It was a celebration supper, a time to savor each fresh fruit and vegetable all by itself as it became ripe for harvest.

The Versatility of Salads

Our family members have become worshippers of the salad. **The summer garden offers infinite possibilities for wonderful salads. The salad can be a side dish or the main dish; it can utilize leftovers, fresh-picked vegetables, or both.** For example, small amounts of carrots, spinach, lettuce, radishes, scallions, broccoli, and parsley mixed with some leftover macaroni make a marvelous light supper and take advantage of the great variety available in the summer garden.

We Americans don't appreciate raw vegetables as much as people in many other cultures do. We want to cook everything, often eliminating most of the food value as well as most of the flavor from our food. Several cooking techniques that are becoming more popular here are stir-frying and steaming. Both of these methods are especially good for lightly cooking vegetables, if they must be cooked. We use our wok a great deal to stir-fry lightly an assortment of fresh produce from the garden. It's quick and easy, and the process saves many of the nutrients that are lost when vegetables are boiled.

Most of us also like to peel many of our fruits and vegetables, which generally takes away that part of the product that contains the highest concentration of nutrients and flavor. We're used to the tough skins of vegetables that we get in the super-market—vegetables that were bred to endure the rigors of transcontinental travel to get to our dinner table. **Fresh vegetables and fruits from your summer garden, when picked at their peak, before they get too large and tough, are tender and only need to be washed, not peeled.** The peels of fruits and vegetables are an especially good source of fiber as well. Ideally, fresh carrots, cucumbers, tomatoes, summer squash, parsnips, and eggplant should not be peeled whether they are eaten raw or cooked. Even potato skins seem to be enjoying a resurgence as a stylish hors d'oeuvre.

As you get more involved in backyard food production, you will find a need to evaluate and probably make some changes in the family's eating and cooking habits as you become more productive. One way to make the best use of your produce is to learn to store it for later consumption. I'll discuss canning and freezing below and cover some other storage techniques in subsequent chapters.

Canning and Freezing

No matter how imaginative you become as a cook, you are inevitably going to produce more vegetables than you can eat fresh from your summer garden. You now have two choices—give the excess away to friends and neighbors or find a way to preserve it for later use. While it's nice to be generous to your friends, I believe that it's important to learn how to preserve and store as much of your own food as you can in order to create the greatest cost savings for your gardening efforts.

The two most common methods for preserving food these days are freezing and canning. **Almost all fruits and vegetables can be frozen and retain most of their flavor and nutrient quality. Most fruits and a few vegetables can also be canned with good results.** When you compare the two methods, each has some strengths and some weaknesses. I believe that both methods are of value and should be used. Canning saves you a bit more money. Several studies have shown that you can save 40 to 60 percent of the cost of the same product in the stores if you use home canning. Freezing saves you 30 to 40 percent over the cost of the same product in the store. Once you learn the techniques and have the proper equipment, both processes take about the same amount of your time. Canning takes a little longer in total time spent, but you don't have to be involved for every minute. The equipment for freezing is quite a bit more expensive than for canning, but then many people already have a chest-type freezer, so they are all ready to go.

My advice would be to learn how to freeze first and then get into canning. Most of the early vegetables—peas, green beans, broccoli—freeze very well. Later in the season you get into tomatoes, peaches, and applesauce, which are often canned. I have listed in the Bibliography three excellent references dealing with processing fresh produce (*The Blue Book, Putting Food By,* and *Stocking Up*). Any one of them will serve your needs in the beginning.

Some people are concerned about the possibility of food spoilage during home freezing, and especially, during canning. Loss of food from spoilage does happen occasionally, but it is very rare for someone to get seriously ill. In fact, there have been relatively few cases of illness from home-canned food recorded in the entire United States. Whenever I read about someone who has had a problem, he or she has usually done something stupid. **There is one rule in freezing and canning that virtually guarantees safety and success. That rule is "always follow the rules"!** Both canning and freezing processes have been streamlined into such a simple and routine set of steps that failure can only occur if you don't follow the steps. But follow the steps you must. Each step has been developed to avoid a potential problem. Read the instructions, follow the steps with no variation, and you will have made the most of your harvest by storing the excess for later use.

One further note about canning: There are two methods of canning, the water bath method and the pressure cooker method. My advice is not to bother with the water bath method, and begin immediately using the pressure canner, or pressure cooker. This saves having to buy some equipment that isn't necessarily very expensive but which does take up storage space. You can handle all canning tasks in a pressure canner, but you can handle only acidic products like fruit and tomatoes in a water bath canner.

I have a slightly different perspective about canning than is usually found in the literature. **I generally use freezing as the method to preserve fresh foods from my backyard system, and I use canning to preserve processed foods.** Most of the fresh vegetables, such as peas, green beans, and broccoli, are frozen directly from the garden. Foods like tomatoes and peaches take some processing, such as cooking down or adding syrup. They could be frozen, but they are just as good canned and then they don't take up valuable space in the freezer.

Finally, most of my canning efforts are directed toward home-processed foods such as baked beans, sauerkraut, applesauce, and soups. The pressure canner is a wonderful way to take advantage of some of the food you just can't buy in the stores. It takes almost the same amount of time to make a stew for 15 as it does to make one for 6. Make a big batch, serve your stew, and process the excess in the pressure canner while the dishes are being washed. Home-canned stew is far superior to store bought, and it takes little extra time and energy to put up. Make a big pot of soup stock and can a few pint or quart jars on the side. Then you have the makings of almost instant homemade soup by adding some fresh or home-frozen vegetables from garden with some meat leftovers.

Some people may be wary of getting into freezing and canning because they view them as terribly time-consuming procedures—taking time that few of us can afford. This is not really true. **The secret to saving time in canning and freezing is to handle small quantities of produce at a time.** Once you learn how to handle the very simple steps of freezing, you can put up six to ten packages of green beans in less than a half an hour, during the same time that you are cleaning up after supper or watching the evening news on TV. The assumption here is that you had fresh green beans for supper so you had to pick and clean some green beans anyway. Especially if you have any help at all from other members of the family in the cleaning and cutting of the vegetable prior to freezing, the freezing process itself is quick and easy. At our house, only once or twice in a season does the whole extended family rally to put up a couple of bushels of peaches or tomatoes. All the rest of our canning and freezing is done in small batches and consequently imposes very little on our daily routine.

There is little question that your ability to store foods for later use will be a primary determining factor in how much money you can save as you develop and expand your backyard food production system. Fresh vegetables in season in the summer are usually pretty inexpensive. It is in the winter when we begin to pay for transporting our vegetables from California that our own food production efforts really begin to pay off.

The Economics of the Second Stage

At this point in the development of a backyard food production system many of your investments are only indirectly related to your savings from the garden. Composting equipment and watering equipment serve to improve the overall production of your garden but are very difficult to evaluate in terms of the specific savings that such items create. Freezing and canning can make a great contribution to your food savings, but your own preferences and the degree to which you get involved in these activities will determine how much you will actually save each year.

The chart below gives you some idea of what each of these components of your food production system will cost. **The expanded summer garden can mean a savings of $250 to $400. If you buy a shredder, a chest freezer, and a few other odds and ends, you have not saved much money in the final accounting for the year. On the other hand, you have made an investment in long-lasting items which will make contributions to your cost savings in future years.** My theory again is "If you can afford it, buy it, and write it off in that same year." The increase in your garden's productivity with some decrease in the time it takes you to manage your garden increases your return on your investment over the years.

Economics of the Second Stage

Item and Use in Food Production System	Initial Capital Investment	Operating Costs and Savings
Garden maintenance Seeds, plants, and natural fertilizers for garden of 400–600 sq. ft.	. . .	$25–$40 covers the basic costs, and you should end up with from $250–$400 in savings to the family food budget. This assumes you produce 65¢ worth of food per sq. ft.

Economics of the Second Stage—*Continued*

Item and Use in Food Production System	Initial Capital Investment	Operating Costs and Savings
Garden tools and equipment		
Shredder (for compost)	$400–$800 (buy) $30/day (rent)	This machine costs from $10–$40 to operate each yr. It is difficult to compute actual savings.
Manure fork	$14–$38	. . .
Galvanized watering can	$6–$45	. . .
Sprinkler (hose attachment)	$10–$25	. . .
Drip irrigation system	$50–$250	These can take some maintenance after a few yrs. of use.
Food processing equipment		
Chest freezer (9–15 cu. ft.)	$250–$500	You can figure it costs you from 10–20¢ per lb. of food that is in the freezer for an average of 6 mos. Home-frozen foods save you from 30–50% off the cost of the grocery store's frozen food.
Pressure canner	$40–$80	Canning costs you about 3–10¢ per qt. and saves you 40–70% off the cost of canned goods at the grocery store.
Water bath canner (used only for high-acid foods)	$15–$25	
Jars and lids	$10–$30	The experts say you should buy new lids every yr., so you'll spend $3–$5.
Canning tools (tongs, etc.)	$10–$25	. . .
Vegetable steamer	$6	. . .
Wok set	$15–$40	. . .

Comments: Without including the shredder and chest freezer, which many folks won't include in their second year, you are saving up to $400 just from your garden's production. If you decide to get into freezing and canning, you could add up to $200 more to that savings figure without too much effort, for a total saving of $600. Being conservative and using lower figures, your $40 for the garden and let's say $75 for some modest canning and freezing will still save you $300, which is a net gain of almost $200. That is a very conservative figure.

Multi-Cropping and Extended Season

THE GAME PLAN

The Goal: In this third stage, your backyard will supply most of your vegetable needs for the whole year, your garden will reach its final size, and you'll extend the growing season.

The Strategy:

1. Review and amend your garden plan throughout the season.

2. Pay close attention to varieties—choose those that meet your particular needs and continue to experiment with others.

3. Expand the main garden to 600 to 800 square feet; tuck additional plants into flower beds and small patches elsewhere.

4. Build a simple cold frame and use it to harden off seedlings early in spring and extend the harvest later into fall.

5. Increase productivity by practicing intensive planting, interplanting, companion planting, succession planting, and crop rotation.

6. Plant and maintain a few fruit trees, nut trees, and berry bushes.

7. Save space by growing vine crops vertically and gardening in containers.

8. Learn new processing and storage methods: Make juices and pickles; dry herbs, fruits, and vegetables.

In the third year, your goal will be to see how much more you can produce in the same amount of space. **There are at least four ways to increase the productivity of your food system:**

1. **You can add more beds, maybe getting to the final size that is possible in your suburban or city backyard.**
2. **You can plant your garden earlier in the season and grow things later in the season than you have in the past.**
3. **You can develop what I call the master gardening techniques such as intensive planting and succession planting to increase the yield of your garden.**
4. **Finally, you can make better use of space by using a vertical trellis, fence, or frame and growing things in containers in odd spots around your property.**

Which of the four approaches you take (and you may want to try them all) will depend upon your situation. You may decide, for example, that adding an extra bed to the main garden will increase your productivity to the point where your yearly vegetable needs are supplied. Or you may prefer to keep the same size garden and use the space next to a fence for vertical culture of vining crops. After reviewing the planning considerations for the third stage, this chapter will deal with these four approaches to increasing the productivity of your food production system. Afterward, some ideas about cooking and processing will be discussed.

Planning the Third-Stage Garden

Now that you are getting into a more complex garden system that depends for its success on the integration of an assortment of cultural techniques, you will find that the planning you do each year will change as well. For the stage-two, or summer garden, most gardeners order their seeds for the whole growing year sometime in January or February. Then they sketch out their garden layout for the year and set down their expected planting schedule. For a basic summer garden this approach works fine. But for the stage-three extended season garden that employs multi-cropping techniques, this approach to planning will not work. **At this stage in your gardening career, you should be doing a little planning all the way through the season.** While you might buy most of your seeds in January (when the best quality seed is available), the planning of your garden layout and the planting schedule is likely to be changing throughout the growing season. A spell of exceptionally cool weather, for example, will set back your summer crops, probably in turn delaying your fall plantings. Consequently, you will always be fiddling with the layout and the planting schedule to adjust for the many variables that affect your production throughout the growing season.

Selecting Varieties

Your plans now will reflect much closer attention to the many different varieties you can get of each of the vegetables you select for your garden. **The experimentation with varieties that you began last year will continue in this third stage. You will be looking now for the best varieties for early planting and then later for the best varieties for late-season planting—they will be different. You will be more concerned about specialized traits like disease resistance, and will even be starting to appreciate and distinguish the subtle but very real differences in flavor among the different varieties.** This ongoing process of determining the varieties that best suit your taste buds, your soil, and your climate takes many years and for most people turns out to be one of the most interesting facets of the gardening experience.

The Final Garden Plot

Two years of experience in food production is sufficient to allow you to make some final decisions about the permanent layout of your backyard food production system. As I said in chapter 1, you must continue to look at your whole property as your garden. Your garden consists of the fruit trees, the berry patch, the various containers, and small patches slipped inconspicuously into the front and side yards, as well as the main garden in the back. **In stage three you'll be ready to start planting the permanent crops. In addition, you should now be able to pretty much figure out how much food you want to produce and how much space you will need to produce that amount of food.** The big question is whether or not you have enough space on your property to reach that goal.

Most people don't realize how much they can really produce in a relatively small space in the backyard. In fact, as your gardening skills increase each year, you'll find that you actually need less space each year to grow the same amount of food. **At stage three, a garden of 600 to 800 square feet that incorporates the techniques discussed in this chapter, will supply most of the total vegetable needs of a family of four.** The space needed beyond 800 square feet is often dedicated to permanent plantings such as an asparagus bed and berry patch.

Soil Preparation and Digging

Let me here make a brief comment about rotary tillers. If your garden were planted in the traditional system of widely spaced single rows and were as large as 800 square feet, you might feel a need to own your own rotary tiller. However, when your garden is set up in permanent raised beds, as this book recommends, I don't think the tiller is as essential. To put it simply, the beds don't need to be dug each year, and the nongrowing areas are only pathways, which don't have to be dug at all. By the time you reach the third stage, the only heavy digging you'll need to do is if you're adding new beds to the main plot.

As I explained earlier, I don't dig my beds every year any more. I just pile on more compost and work it into the top few inches of the bed. At deeper levels, I let the earthworms and the roots of the growing plants keep the soil well worked. For me, a tiller is of no value. Some people with permanent raised beds still use their tillers each year to work the top part of the beds, and that's fine. But since a decent tiller costs over $500, I think it's well worth your while to think over carefully whether your need of a tiller is critical before you rush out and make such an expensive purchase. If I had to choose between a tiller and a shredder, I'd take the shredder every time.

Extending the Season with a Cold Frame

One of the easiest ways to extend your growing season is to use a cold frame. It is a minigreenhouse that is constructed of simple materials and can add many weeks to the beginning and the end of the traditional growing season in your area. Let me distinguish first between a cold frame and what is currently being called a grow frame. The latter is a more sophisticated cold frame with heavy insulation and special design features that allow you to grow vegetables in it throughout even the coldest winter weather. We will discuss these grow frames in the next chapter. A cold frame is simply a bottomless box with a glass or plastic cover that allows the sun to shine in. Its primary job is to protect nonhardy cool-weather vegetables from frost damage, either in the early spring or in the late fall. If you can protect these plants from frost, you can extend their production time by several weeks. It's as simple as that.

Making the Best Use of a Cold Frame

There are at least four ways in which a cold frame can help to increase your total production: It allows you to plant spring crops early, harden off seedlings safely, shade spring crops in hot weather to prolong their harvest, and extend the harvest season for fall crops.

In spring, you can plant cold-loving plants like lettuce, radishes, and spinach from seed in a cold frame several weeks ahead of your usual outdoor planting time, and harvest the crops two to three weeks earlier than normal. You can also use the cold frame to harden off seedlings that you have started indoors under lights or in a greenhouse. The hardening-off process gets the plants acclimated to the chilly nights and lessens the chance of damage from the cold after they are planted in the garden. I combine these two ideas and start lettuce, Chinese cabbage, and spinach in my greenhouse and then transplant them when almost grown into a cold frame. This technique gives me fresh garden lettuce four weeks before my neighbors.

In the summertime, you can replace the glass of the cold frame with an old window screen, and continue to grow lettuce even in the hot weather. The screening

This simple cold frame is made of bricks that are stacked but not mortared—it's easy to disassemble when not in use. In spring and fall, the glass cover provides a warm environment for early or late crops.

In early summer, the cold frame can be covered with a screen to provide ventilation and shade that prolong the harvest of cool-weather crops like lettuce.

protects the lettuce from the hot rays of the direct sun, while allowing plenty of air circulation. The shading also helps keep the soil cooler and moister.

In late fall you can transplant into the cold frame cold-tolerant plants like lettuce, parsley, Chinese cabbage, endive, and escarole, and keep them growing a month or even six weeks after the first serious frost, which signals the end of production for many gardeners. Here in the Philadelphia area, we are eating fresh leaf lettuce from our simple cold frames into the first two weeks of December. Sometimes we actually have to brush away the snow to get at the lettuce. I'm convinced that lettuce grown under these conditions has a far better flavor than does lettuce grown in the spring.

By using a cold frame and other protective devices such as cloches and hot-caps, you can keep your garden really productive right into the winter months. Growing cold-tolerant plants also helps to increase your production levels, at a time when your neighbors are cleaning up their gardens for the year. In addition to those mentioned above, the list of fall crops includes collard greens, kale, parsnips, Brussels sprouts, a number of oriental vegetables, and Swiss chard. You'll find that when you add them to your garden, the months of October and November can be just as productive as are July and August, if you're willing to expend a little effort and build a cold frame.

Building a Very Simple Cold Frame

A cold frame can be made of almost anything, especially discarded materials. An old storm window is a very good starting point. People are always throwing these into the trash, and they make ideal cold frame covers. All you need then are four low walls for the window to sit atop. You can find good designs in books at your local library for cold frames made from one piece of old plywood. I have taken to using old bricks for the walls of my cold frame. While you can make a wooden cold frame that will break down for storage, I found that one made from loose bricks stores away just as well, and I happened to have the bricks. I simply make a little box of the bricks (with no mortar) just a bit smaller than the old storm window that I have liberated from someone's trash. This structure sits on one of my growing beds, and I plant directly into the garden. On sunny days I prop up the window to allow air circulation, and at night I let the window sit flat on the bricks, to hold in the heat collected during the day. I can build a cold frame of any size this way, depending on where in my garden I wish to set it. And when the weather warms up and the plants are big enough, the entire cold frame can be dismantled and the plants left to grow to maturity right where they are. No transplanting is necessary—a real work-saver for you.

Some gardeners are fortunate enough to have a permanent space available for a cold frame. If this is your situation, you may opt to put in a cement-block foundation and build a more substantial structure that will last for many years.

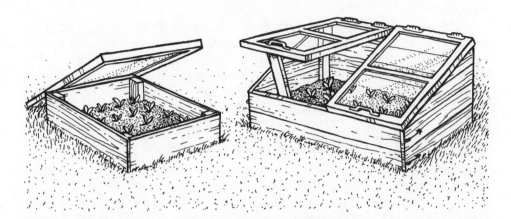

One of the simplest cold frames you can make is a bottomless wooden box that's covered by simply laying an old storm window on top *(left)*. If you're more ambitious, you can angle the sides of the box and attach storm-window covers with hinges. This kind of cold frame *(right)* should face south, in order to collect the maximum amount of sunlight.

My advice is to start off with as simple a rig as you can manage. You want to locate your frame where it gets plenty of sun and is protected somewhat from the north winds. I bank leaves or sometimes compost up around the sides of my brick cold frame to help insulate it a bit from the winds. No doubt, you will think of a couple of design changes you will want to make next year; you can get a bit fancier then.

Growing Plants in the Cold Frame

A cold frame does take a bit of tending, but the techniques are not difficult and really are based on just plain common sense. If it is allowed to stay closed during a bright, sunny day, it can build up enough heat to cook your plants. The temperature should not get much above 80 degrees if you want to keep your cold-loving plants happy. Consequently, you have to keep track of the weather and on sunny days open up your frame for ventilation. Another reason to ventilate your cold frame, especially in the spring, is to avoid damping-off, a fungus disease that is fatal to young seedlings. At night you must close the cover to keep in the heat that has been stored in the soil during the day and to protect the plants from the frost. If the temperature is going to go much below freezing, the plants can often be saved by simply covering the entire frame at night with an old quilt.

Watering in the cold frame is a bit different from watering in the regular garden. Generally you'll need to water less, since the closed frame tends to keep in moisture. In the springtime I often use flats to hold the seedlings I am hardening off. Then if a severe cold snap comes roaring in I can easily carry them back into the house.

When you consider that you can extend your growing season by eight to ten weeks with the skillful use of one or more cold frames, the effort required to construct and manage them seems well worth it. By using materials recycled from the trash, the cost is minimal. And to be able to pick fresh lettuce in early March even before the peas are in is a special treat for anyone.

Advanced Production Techniques

Over the years I've been generally confused by a number of terms that are being used more and more in magazines dealing with gardening. It wasn't until I finally sat down a year or so ago and put them all together that I finally felt I could say that I understand what intensive planting, interplanting, companion planting, succession planting, and rotation mean. I found that part of my confusion was due to the fact that many writers had improperly used some of these terms interchangeably in the articles I'd read. The terms, of course, are not interchangeable. Each one represents a different gardening technique that will in some way increase your production per square foot. Each of these methods will increase your production without requiring additional space. When two or more techniques are combined, they will increase your production many times over.

These terms were defined in chapter 4, but I think that the easiest way to understand these concepts and then to be able to use them is to view them in a linear way, as progressive steps. This is a somewhat artificial approach, but I think it will help those of you who may have been confused, as I was, by some of the sloppy

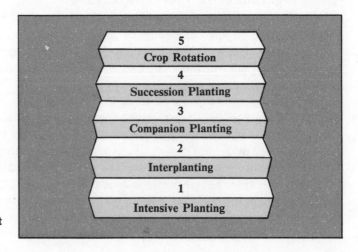

The steps to the highest levels of productivity.

uses of these terms in magazine articles. Each concept is related to one or more of the others. For the purpose of this explanation, however, let me introduce them as a series of progressive steps, each of which builds upon the gains of the previous step. The diagram on page 84 shows what I mean.

If you follow this diagram, you first learn to use intensive planting techniques. Then you can learn about interplanting techniques. That prepares you for tackling the concept of companion planting. From there you move on to succession planting methods. And finally, you can handle the concept of rotation. Let me explain in turn each of these five steps toward advanced production capability in your backyard food production system. You might find it helpful to set aside one of your garden beds this year and experiment with these techniques to learn how to use them.

Intensive Planting

I've already discussed intensive planting techniques in some detail in chapter 4. However, let's review the key points again for emphasis, especially since it's essential that you fully understand intensive planting techniques before you can really understand the other four concepts. Research by John Jeavons and others has demonstrated that vegetables can often be planted closer together than the distances recommended on seed packets. The ideal intensive spacing allows the leaves of adjoining plants just to touch each other when the plants are fully grown. When you plant in a bed instead of in rows, this method will allow the foliage to form a canopy over the soil, which helps keep the soil from drying out and overheating on sunny days. This is good for the roots.

It's important to remember that when you pack plants into a bed in such an intensive fashion you must be very conscientious about giving them sufficient food and water. Liberal applications of compost and other organic fertilizers are essential for the intensive planting techniques to work effectively. But the result will be increased production in the same amount of space.

Interplanting

Once you understand how to use intensive planting, you can then move on to the next step and try some interplanting in your intensive bed. **Interplanting means growing two or more types of vegetables, usually only two, in very close proximity to each other (that is, intensively planted) so that they combine certain characteristics to each plant's mutual benefit.** Taking into consideration such characteristics as height, growing period, and root structure, you can design combinations that allow all the plants to thrive and often increase their production and quality over normal growing techniques. There are lots of effective interplanting combinations. As you will see, it takes a bit of time and considerable patience to figure out how to use all these combinations in your garden.

Here are the five basic approaches to interplanting:

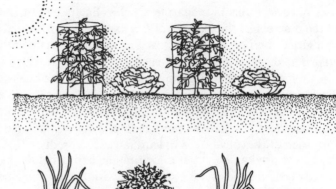

Plant vegetables needing lots of sun, like tomatoes, next to those that can stand a bit of shade, such as lettuce.

Combine plants according to their aboveground growth patterns, putting taller-growing plants, such as onions and carrots, next to shorter growing plants, like lettuce.

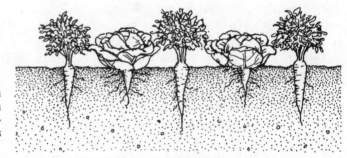

Plant vegetables with deep root systems, such as carrots, next to shallow-rooted crops, such as cabbage.

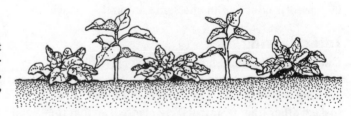

Combine vegetables that have a long growing season, such as eggplant, with short-season crops, such as spinach.

Plant vegetables that are heavy feeders, such as kale, with crops that are soil builders, like soybeans.

While the obvious value of interplanting is to make your use of space more efficient (in a sense making intensive planting even more intensive), there is another significant value to interplanting that is just now being explored by scientists. An exciting discovery is that insects often locate the plant they prefer to eat by its smell. That means when you plant five rows of green beans next to each other, you make the Mexican bean beetle's search much easier than if you had interplanted those same beans with two or three other kinds of vegetables and herbs in an intensive bed. Interplanting creates a kind of aromatic confusion for the insects, which apparently reduces insect damage as compared to typical damage expected in gardens planted in rows or even intensive beds of individual plants.

As you will see shortly, interplanting is critical to the concepts of companion planting, succession planting, and rotation. The chart on page 88 gives a partial list of some of the variables you may wish to consider when undertaking your first interplanted, intensive bed. A more complete chart covering more vegetables, titled Companion Planting Guide, can be found in the Appendix.

Companion Planting

Companion planting is simply a more sophisticated form of interplanting. All companion planting combinations are really examples of interplanting, but all interplantings are not necessarily companion plantings, because the only goal of interplanting in itself is to save space. **In companion planting, plants are grown together in order to take advantage of some complementary physical or chemical relationship that is beneficial to one or both of them. The purpose of a companion plant is to improve plant growth, to improve the soil, or to help control insects and weeds.**

Companion planting works in a number of different ways, depending on the type of plant in question. Some companions are helpful to each other because of substances excreted by the roots of one of the plants. Marigolds repel nematodes from such vegetables as beans and eggplant by virtue of the root excretions they put out. Sometimes plant aroma will repel insects. Sage, for example, has a strong scent which repels the cabbage butterfly, an insect that bothers cole crops (broccoli, Brussels sprouts, cabbage, and cauliflower). So sage and cole crops are also good companions. The pollen from the flowers of some plants will attract certain insects. These plants can serve as trap crops that lure pests away from the vegetable crop. Some crops make good companions because of their complementary nutrient needs. Corn and beans, for example, can be planted together, because corn is a heavy feeder that demands lots of nitrogen, and beans fix nitrogen in the soil. What the corn takes the beans help give. Companion plants always have some chemical or physical benefit for each other.

The characteristics I've described above mean that companion plants can play a number of different roles in the garden. They serve as nursery plants which help attract and support growth of beneficial predator insects that will help keep invad-

One example of a classic pair of garden companions is corn and beans. In this case, the benefit is nutritional: The bean plants fix nitrogen in the soil—nitrogen which the corn needs in abundance for good growth.

ing pest populations under control. Strips of weeds such as dandelion, lamb's-quarters, wild carrot, and goldenrod, strategically planted throughout the garden, will support many species of beneficial insects. Other companions serve as repellent plants, discouraging damaging insects by spines, toxins, or odors. Some common repellent plants include mint, marigold, nasturtium, petunia, members of the onion family, and sage. Finally, some companions act as decoy or trap plants,

Some Classic Garden Companions

Vegetable	Companion	Enemy
Beans	Corn, potatoes, catnip	Onion family
Cabbage family	Onions, celery	Tomatoes
Carrots	Onion family	Dill
Corn	Beans, peas, potatoes	Tomatoes
Cucumbers	Radishes	Potatoes
Peas	Carrots, turnips	Onions
Peppers	Carrots	Fennel
Squash	Corn	Potatoes

serving as alternative feeding sites for harmful insects. Nasturtiums, for instance, attract aphids and lure them away from members of the cabbage family. As I mentioned in the section on interplanting, companion planting almost always has the additional benefit of mixing up the plants in your garden, which confuses the ability of insect pests to find the plants they most like to eat.

Identifying successful companion planting combinations is as much a mythology as a science. Many people have had a wonderful crop one year and attributed it to the fact that two particular plants were next to each other. But the wonderful crop could just as easily have occurred because of perfect weather, better soil conditions, or a plant variety that was particularly well-suited to that climate. The proximity of the two plants might have been entirely irrelevant. Nevertheless, enough people have been practicing companion planting for enough generations that much of what you read can be taken as generally accurate. The chart titled Some Classic Garden Companions lists some of the most common companion combinations, which are accepted by many gardeners as being beneficial to production. The chart titled Companion Planting Guide, in the Appendix, will give you more ideas. There is no question that other companion combinations exist, but these I will leave to you to discover over the years.

Succession Planting

Succession planting simply means planting a new plant immediately upon harvesting a mature plant, so that you get at least two, and sometimes even three, crops from the same space over the course of a growing season. For example, when the peas are finished you might immediately plant eggplant in their place. Succession planting, however, does require a fairly good knowledge of growing characteristics and the maturation times of the vegetables in your garden. Peas are a cold-weather crop, so you can't start them in June after the spring lettuce is done. Green beans need warm soil to germinate, so they can't go in with the peas and spinach.

The trickiest part of succession planting, the aspect that's hardest to learn, is timing the start of the second crop if you are going to use transplants. If you are going to plant eggplant in the place where the spring peas were, you'd be wasting valuable growing time if you waited until the peas were harvested and then put the eggplant seeds straight into the ground. What you need to do is put in transplants. Eggplant can be started from seed in a greenhouse or cold frame six to eight weeks before you're ready to transplant it. So in order to make your succession work, you must first try to figure out when your peas will be harvested and then count back six weeks, to determine the date when you should start your eggplant seedlings. This process gets very complicated when you're planning succession crops for as many as 15 different vegetables having varying gestation periods! A good record book and the chart titled Succession Planting Guide, in the Appendix, will be a big help.

Succession Planting Ideas

Here are some of the favorite succession crop combinations from a few of the staff at Rodale Press. As you experiment with succession planting in your garden, you'll develop your own favorite combinations.

	Early Season	Midseason	Late Season
Lee Goldman, Executive Editor, *Organic Gardening* magazine	Leaf lettuce Snap peas Broccoli	Tomatoes Eggplant Peppers	Oriental vegetables Broccoli Lettuce
Ray Wolf, book editor	Lettuce (different varieties, of course!)	Lettuce	Lettuce
Marjorie Hunt, author of gardening books	Early peas	Celery root	Spinach
Rudy Keller, horticulturist	Peas Broccoli Early lettuce. . .harvest continues	Broccoli. . .harvest continues New Zealand spinach. . .harvest continues	Late carrots or beets
Eileen Weinsteiger, horticulturist, Rodale Research Center	Broccoli Lettuce Oriental greens Lettuce Spinach Lettuce	Carrots Lettuce Lettuce Tomatoes Peppers Beets	Lettuce Carrots Oriental greens Oriental vegetables Lettuce Cabbage

Rotation

Like the other advanced techniques, crop rotation is not that difficult to define. **Rotation simply means planting a given crop in a different spot in the garden each year. Rotation is practiced to balance the depletion of nutrients from the soil, to reduce insect concentrations, and to control disease.** Even different vegetables in the same family, such as broccoli and cabbage, which are subject to the same diseases, should not be allowed to follow each other in the same bed.

A general rule of thumb for proper rotation of your crops is to plant heavy feeders, followed by soil-builders, then by light feeders. With some help from a dose of compost, and maybe some other organic fertilizers, you'll be ready to start the cycle all over again. Succession planting may allow you to go through the entire

Blueberry bushes can be planted as a hedge to serve as a property divider or to screen off the compost pile from view of the house.

rotation cycle in a single year. The rapid successions make rotation absolutely essential, for repeated plantings of heavy-feeding crops in the same spot could seriously deplete your soil of nutrients in just a year or two. Never plant heavy feeders in the same spot twice in a row if you can possibly avoid it. If you can't avoid it, then you must at least add a lot of compost and give the soil a few days' rest before putting the second heavy feeder in the same spot.

Rotation gets a bit tricky when you try to keep track of which particular nutrients each vegetable takes from the soil, in order to compensate the losses later with other balancing rotations. For example, leaf crops consume lots of nitrogen and root crops consume lots of potassium. So it is better to follow beets with lettuce, than with carrots, another root crop. The chart titled Feeding and Watering Guidelines, found in the Appendix, should help you in planning your rotation system. Even if you rotate your crops over one bed, it will help to keep insects from taking over an area.

In summary, each of the advanced planting techniques by itself is not too difficult to understand and use in your garden. It's when you begin to combine their use, and eventually get to using all five techniques simultaneously, that the gardener's life becomes very interesting. But believe it or not, it's not all that complicated once you get used to it. Because each technique is so closely related to the others, after a few years of practice you'll wonder why you didn't use them years ago. On top of all that, you will be getting three to five times the production levels from your garden that you got before you used these techniques—not a bad return on your investment of time and energy.

Growing Fruits, Nuts, and Berries

When you consider your entire property as the base for your food production system, then there will be a number of opportunities to have fruit trees, berries, and

[Continued on page 94]

Some Reliable Fruit Trees for Beginners

Variety	Fruit and Tree Characteristics
Apples	
Golden Delicious (includes the many strains and sports)	Yellow apple that is good for eating and cooking. Moderately hardy tree that does well in all the apple-growing regions except the extreme northern and southern areas. Most are somewhat self-fruitful but make excellent pollinators for other varieties.
Granny Smith	Green to yellow apple that can be used for cooking or eating. Excellent variety for warmer climates found in the southern states.
Haralson	Red apple for cooking or eating. Excellent keeper. Very hardy tree, making it an excellent variety for the northern states.
McIntosh (includes the many strains and sports such as Cortland, Macoun, and Empire)	Red apple that is good for eating and cooking, although it does not keep well. A very hardy tree that is an excellent variety for the northern regions but will not do well in the South.
Priscilla	Red apple of good quality. Good for all apple-growing regions except the extreme northern and southern areas. Very disease resistant.
Red Delicious (includes the many strains and sports)	Red eating apple that stores fairly well. One of the most popular eating apples. Moderately hardy and fairly resistant to most diseases. Self-sterile.
Winesap (includes the many strains and sports)	Red apple that is excellent for eating and cooking; also a very good keeper. A hardy tree that will do well in all apple-growing regions except the extreme northern and southern areas. Susceptible to scab.

Some Reliable Fruit Trees for Beginners—*Continued*

Variety	*Fruit and Tree Characteristics*
Pears	
Bartlett	Yellow pear with an excellent dessert quality. A medium-hardy tree that will do well in all the pear-growing regions except the coldest spots. Although this is one of the most popular pears for homegrowers, it is very susceptible to fireblight. Needs a pollinator other than Seckel.
Clapp's Favorite	Yellow pear of good quality but a poor keeper. Grows well in all the pear-growing regions. Very hardy and self-fertile.
Duchess	Produces large, yellow pears. Very hardy and self-fertile. A reliable variety that is good for the northern regions.
Kieffer	A winter pear that is excellent for cooking. Will do well on a wide range of soils in all the pear-growing regions. A hardy, productive, and reliable variety. Somewhat resistant to fireblight.
Maxine	Large, coarse-fleshed pear with good quality. Hardy tree that is easy to care for and reliable. Resistant to fireblight.
Moonglow	Early yellow pear. Very hardy tree that will do well in all the pear-growing regions. Easy to care for and reliable. Resistant to fireblight.
Seckel	Small, sweet pear with excellent quality. Will do well in all pear-growing regions except the Deep South. Very hardy, vigorous, and healthy tree. Resistant to fireblight. One of the best for the homegrower. May be self-fruitful. Will not cross-pollinate with Bartlett.
Tyson	Pear with excellent flavor although grainy at the core. Very productive and vigorous. Somewhat resistant to fireblight.

maybe even a nut tree or two. **The key to success is to approach your fruit produc-tion like a landscaping exercise.** Fruit trees and berries prefer full sun, but they can stand a little bit of shade. Blueberries and gooseberries are shrubs in their own right, so they can be laid out as a hedge or they can stand alone as individual deco-rative bushes. I mentioned earlier that the Integral Urban House in Berkeley uses strawberries to replace grass as their ground cover. Dwarf fruit trees can be tucked into all kinds of little corners. Grapes can be grown over an arbor or up alongside a garage or a fence. All these fruit-producing plants can be integrated into the land-scape in a way that brings beauty to your homestead, as well as delicious food. Rosalind Creasy's *The Complete Book of Edible Landscaping* (see the Bibliogra-phy) gives many excellent ideas for using food-producing trees and bushes as aes-thetic additions to your property.

Planning Considerations

Care of fruit trees and berries does not take much time over the year, but it does require some important knowledge to make sure they produce to their maximum. You cannot just let them grow uncared for. They will respond to inattention with little or no fruit. Once or twice a year you'll need to prune your trees and bushes, you will have to properly feed these plants, and you'll need to protect them from pests and disease.

Just as in your vegetable garden, try to avoid the temptation to start off with six different kinds of tree fruits and eight different kinds of berries.

A Guide to Fruit-Growing

Fruit	Space	Years to Bearing	Average Production per Plant
Apples			
Dwarf	8-ft. circle	3–5	½–1 bu.
Standard	25-ft. circle	6	6–10 bu.
Blackberries	3-ft. row	2	1½ qt.
Blueberries, highbush	4-ft. circle	2	8–12 qt.
Grapes	8-ft. row	3	12–15 lb.
Peaches, dwarf	8-ft. circle	3–5	½–1 bu.
Pears, dwarf	8-ft. circle	3–5	½–1 bu.
Raspberries	3-ft. row	2	1½ qt.
Strawberries	1 sq. ft. per plant	1	1–1½ qt.

In the northern part of the country especially, the selection of tree fruits and berries for your yard must be made with care. As a general rule of thumb, the hardiest and easiest tree fruits to start off with are apples and pears. The best berries include strawberries, raspberries, blueberries, and certain grape varieties.

Another important thing to remember is that fruit trees usually take at least three to four years to begin bearing fruit, and can take up to ten years to reach their maximum yields. Nevertheless, their bounty is definitely worth your patience. My advice is to select just one or two types of fruit and grow two or three different varieties of each. The ideal is to plant an early-bearing variety, a mid-season variety, and a late variety so you'll have fresh fruit over a longer period of time.

The nursery catalogs can give you some details about this aspect of fruit growing, although they're hardly unbiased sources of information. Novice growers would also be well advised to seek advice from gardening neighbors and the local county extension agent. They will know better which varieties grow best in your particular area. The chart titled A Guide to Fruit Growing will give you a sense of the kind of space you'd need for some popular kinds of tree and bush fruits.

Nut trees require an even more careful review of what will grow in your particular climate. Nuts seem to be more sensitive to climate variations than some of the fruits and berries. Nut trees also take much longer to produce: ten years in some cases. Your agricultural extension office should be an especially helpful source of information if you want to add some nut trees to your system.

Space-Saving Options for Fruits

I think the most interesting challenge in growing fruit in your backyard is the espalier. This is a tree or shrub which has been specially pruned to grow flat against a wall or on a trellis. Dwarf apple trees and dwarf pear trees are excellent candidates for the espalier method of pruning.

While a mature espaliered apple tree looks like it would be complicated to train, the technique is not terribly difficult. It is somewhat more time-consuming than the pruning normally required for trees, though. There are three or four pruning sessions and some extra snipping of suckers needed each year. Still, this isn't much different from what most of us do to take care of our tomatoes or rose bushes.

Besides saving space, the espalier technique produces a superior crop of fruit. This occurs because more food is available to each individual fruit, more fruiting spurs are created on the tree, and the uniformity of the tree's structure allows for a more even flow of sap. All these factors, along with the improved ventilation and increased amount of sun reaching the fruit, result in larger and better-quality fruit.

Because espaliered trees take up so little space, you can have six to ten trees in a backyard which you might otherwise expect to accommodate only a few. And

THIRD STAGE—MULTI-CROPPING AND EXTENDED SEASON

because espaliered trees are so attractive, this technique can open up your whole front yard for fruit production while improving the appearance of your property. There are several excellent references listed in the Bibliography that will help demystify the espalier process for you. (See *All about Growing Fruits and Berries, The Complete Book of Edible Landscaping,* or *The Organic Gardener's Complete Guide to Vegetables and Fruits.*)

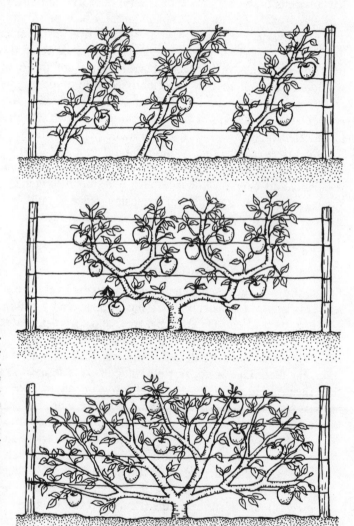

Three of the simplest espalier styles are the single cordon *(top),* the double-U *(center),* and the fan *(bottom).* If traditional forms like these look too intimidating or formal to you, you might want to create a sort of "natural fan" by retaining the main lateral branches in the angles at which they grow from the trunk instead of training them to more uniform shapes as shown here.

Dwarf varieties of some fruits and nuts can be grown in containers. A special type of dwarf variety, the genetic dwarf, is being bred particularly for culture in containers and other confined spaces. Although the trees remain quite small, they produce full-size fruit.

There is one other way to produce fruit, especially apples, even if you have no room in your own backyard for a tree. When you travel through a suburban neighborhood or a small town that was developed over 15 years ago, you often see numbers of full-grown apple and pear trees, completely uncared for, in front yards and backyards. They need pruning badly, and their fruit is small and deformed. These properties are usually occupied by the second- or third-generation homeowner who either doesn't know how to care for such a tree or doesn't want to care for it. Consequently, 4 to 8 bushels of potentially good fruit go to waste for each tree in that condition. My idea is to approach that person and offer to care for his tree in return for half the crop. Many people would be delighted to get good fruit and not have to worry about any of the work. Some people can get 20 or 30 bushels of apples each year just by offering to be foster parents for a few old apple trees whose owners don't care for them.

If you can find a friend with an apple cider press, you are then set for the year with sauce and cider, as well as delicious fruit all year. This is possible with no trees in your own backyard. Look around next time you are out driving or jogging. There are hundreds of trees just waiting for someone to spruce them up a bit. Their bounty is a fair return for a modest amount of work each year.

Vertical Gardening

Perhaps one of the most overlooked spaces for growing vegetables in the backyard is the space above the ground. Almost any vining vegetable can be trained to grow vertically up a wall or a trellis. Most of us tend to let our tomatoes, cucumbers, and squash ramble all over the garden. But when you train those sprawling branches up off the ground, the actual ground space needed to support four tomato plants, or eight cucumbers, or two squash plants is only 1 foot wide by 4 feet long. I have seen an entire garden growing in a 2-foot-wide bed around the perimeter of a backyard that was enclosed by a wooden fence. The entire fence served as a support for vertically trained vining crops, and the rest of the vegetables grew in the space just in front of the fence. This was a very productive garden that used only minimal ground space, because the gardener took full advantage of vertical growing techniques.

There are other good reasons besides space saving for adding vertical growing to your gardening skills. You can use your vertically grown crops to form a living

Vining crops like cucumbers, melons, and squash can all be trained to grow up a trellis or fence—using only a fraction of the garden space they'd need if left to sprawl on the ground. Heavy fruits, like the muskmelon shown here, should be supported with a sling tied to the trellis so they don't snap off their stems.

screen to hide a storage shed or a compost pile. The vertical garden can serve as a landscaping device that divides a section of your yard or garden for aesthetic reasons.

Vegetables suitable for vertical growing include pole, snap, and lima beans, cucumbers, muskmelons, peas of all kinds, winter squash, and tomatoes.

Supporting and Caring for Vertical Crops

The key to success with vertical growing is having the proper support system. At one time or another, we've all trained our tomato plants on wooden stakes that rotted out halfway through the season or broke under the weight of a full-size plant that was heavy with fruit. When the support collapses, part of the harvest is inevitably lost. Most gardening books seem to overlook these kinds of problems in backyard vegetable production. The best reference I've seen on the subject is Mel Bartholomew's *Square Foot Gardening* (see the Bibliography). He has made an extensive study of the subject and gives some excellent advice on making the best use of your vertical space and devising sturdy supports for the plants. **Supports can be wire mesh fences, wooden trellises, string nets, a wall, or a cage. You can**

also purchase plastic netting that's made expressly for this purpose. The most important concern in devising a supporting device is strength. The support must be substantial enough to bear the weight of the grown plant when it is filled with fruit. Large fruited crops like winter squash may even need to have the individual fruits supported by slings as they mature so that they don't fall off prematurely.

Bartholomew reports that growing crops vertically allows for more efficient use of sunlight and better air circulation, resulting in better growth. He has also found that pest damage is reduced, because pests are easier to see. Handpicking insects from a waist-high vine is much easier than crawling around on your hands and knees on the ground to poke under leaves.

Container Growing

Most of us think about container growing, especially where edibles are concerned, as being of interest only to urban apartment dwellers who grow some lettuce and tomatoes on their balconies on the fifteenth floor. Those of us with a backyard large enough to accommodate even a modest garden don't usually include container growing in our production system. That's a mistake. **If we are looking for maximum production in a limited space, container growing must be utilized right along with vertical gardening, espalier, and intensive methods.**

What to Grow in Containers

Containers are ideal for many of the kitchen herbs that the family uses regularly. Pots of herbs and salad greens can sit on the patio or deck right near the kitchen door, within easy reach of the cook. Parsley, basil, dill, chives, and oregano are all easy to grow in containers. Salad greens like lettuce, Chinese cabbage, and spinach are also good candidates for containers, because they are picked by the leaf, without cutting the whole plant. They grow well in containers, because their root systems are not that extensive, and consequently they don't suffer from the confinement as some other plants might. Cherry tomatoes make another good container crop. They are usually used in salads and often all you need are three or four for color or flavor. They grow extremely well in a container, and add a splash of color to the scene. Finally, the convenience of having salad crops close to the kitchen is a real blessing for the busy cook. The cook can pick the fixings for a salad in seconds. See the chart titled Vegetables and Fruits to Grow in Containers, in the Appendix, for some suggestions for container plants and varieties.

Managing Container Gardens

There are at least three things you have to keep in mind as you expand your production system into containers: the size of your container, the weight of the filled con-

tainer, and good drainage. The chart titled Container Planting Guide, in the Appendix, shows the minimum size of container that can be used for some common plants. I must emphasize that the dimension given for each is a *minimum*. If you want to ensure best growth and health in your plants, you should double the size given in the chart. There is always going to be some restriction to the root system of a plant growing in a container, but your goal is to give the plant as much room as is practically possible.

Of course, as the container gets bigger, it gets heavier. You control the weight of the containers primarily by adjusting the mixture of the growing medium you use. Never use plain garden soil in a container; it is too heavy and will compact, restricting root growth and hindering drainage. There are almost as many mixtures recommended for growing in containers as there are gardeners. Some people use a medium that is one-half compost and one-half soil. I use a mix of one-third compost, one-third vermiculite, and one-third soil. The idea is to have a medium that is relatively light, and that holds moisture but still drains well. If you are placing large containers up on a flat roof or on a raised deck, then you must be particularly

As you can see by the hot peppers, cherry tomatoes, and frying peppers growing in these pots, containers can add to your garden space and provide handsome decorative accents to your property as well.

A wide assortment of containers is available for growing vegetables, fruits, and herbs. For example, clay pots in varying sizes will accommodate herbs or compact vegetables like leaf lettuce;
a half-barrel or clay tub will hold a dwarf fruit tree or a berry bush; a rectangular wooden planter
can be used for several shallow-rooted vegetable plants or even interplanted vegetables and herbs.

sensitive to locating the container in such a way as not to endanger the structure
of the building. A container garden gains weight as the plants grow, and especially
right after it has been watered or rained on.

Good drainage is not only a function of the soil mixture. The material from
which the container is made has an effect as well. Plant pathologists have been noting that there has been a noticeable increase in plant disease since plastic pots have
become popular for the home and nursery. Ideally you want containers that can
breathe—porous clay or wood. However, if you have a good, light soil mixture,
and your container has drainage holes on the bottom that don't get clogged, then
plastic, wood, and metal are almost as good as clay and a great deal cheaper. Containers can be built from scraps found in the basement or in someone else's trash.
Garage sales are also a wonderful source of good-sized containers that cost near
to nothing. See the chart titled Container Planting Guide, in the Appendix, for
more details on container gardening.

Cooking and Processing Your Harvest

With an extended growing season, you will find that you will harvest a considerable
amount of excess vegetables and fruits that you must put up for later use. Canning
and freezing are the most popular methods for preserving foods, but you might
find that juicing, pickling, and drying are also attractive for certain kinds of foods.

Juices and Cider

Turning some of your excess vegetables and fruits into juice is an easy and very tasty way to store produce for later use. The most common kind of homemade juice is tomato juice. It can be made without any special equipment: The tomatoes are simply cooked down a bit and put through a sieve to remove seeds and skins. The juice is then canned in jars just as whole tomatoes would be. A mixed vegetable juice can be made by simply adding carrots, peppers, and other garden vegetables to the mixture as it cooks.

Some gardeners go a step further and buy an electric juicer that can produce fresh vegetable juice or fruit juice in minutes. Electric juicers are convenient—they eliminate the need to cook the food first. These machines cost anywhere from $40 to $110. As you'd expect, the higher the quality, the higher the price. The juice that they make can also be set aside and frozen for use in soups, stews, and casseroles. The beauty of electric juicing machines is that they let you utilize some of the vegetables that are too bruised or a bit overmature for conventional canning or freezing.

One of my all-time favorite juices is apple cider. If you have apple trees or have friends with apple trees, then making your own apple cider is not extremely difficult. If you can't find a friend with a cider press, you can take your apples to a commercial press, and they will make your cider for less than half of what fresh cider costs in grocery stores or farmers' markets. When cooked for a bit, fresh cider changes flavor and becomes what we know as apple juice. This juice can be canned or frozen, and may be stored for up to a year without losing its quality. Fresh cider left to sit in a crock for from four to six months becomes a wonderful cider vinegar that has lots more personality than the unexciting, uniform vinegar you buy in the store. Adding herbs to separate jars of your own cider vinegar gives you the basis for delicious, zesty salad dressings all year long.

Pickles

Almost any vegetable, and just about every fruit, can be pickled. There are basically four kinds of pickles: brined pickles, which include sauerkraut, dill pickles, and those big delicatessen cukes that used to come in a barrel; fruit pickles, which include things like your grandmother's pickled watermelon rind; relishes, which are all sorts of mixed fruits and vegetables including mixed mustard pickles and the chowchow of the Pennsylvania Dutch; and the fresh pack pickle, the most common kind of pickle made at home. Most of the pickle recipes that you see in newspapers and magazines make use of this fresh pack method. The product to be pickled is usually put in a light brine of some sort for from a few hours to overnight. Then the product is put into canning jars and processed. There are literally hundreds of wonderful recipes for this easy method of pickling. However, there are two pitfalls to beware of if you decide to try it on your excess produce.

One all-too-common pitfall for novice picklers is the temptation to make too much of one kind of pickle before you know if the family likes it. Many, if not most, recipes call for the ingredients to make at least 6 or 7 quarts of a particular pickle. You could end up with 12 pints of a garlic dill pickle that tastes just fine to you but makes the rest of the family turn up their noses. Unless you have a huge appetite for pickles, most of those jars will end up sitting on the shelf for years. The solution is always to make small batches, at least the first time. This way you might make six different batches of pickles in the season, giving you the kind of variety that should satisfy everybody's tastes. I seldom use quart jars for my pickles. Half pints are good for relishes, and pints seem to be the right size for me for most pickles.

Another problem that first-time picklers may encounter is the "it-doesn't-taste-like-Heinz" syndrome. It might sound strange, but it appears that in more and more families in this country where no homemade products have ever been processed and eaten, the flavors of commercial products set the standards for food preferences. Homemade products are inevitably compared to those commercial standards. This can especially be a problem where children are concerned. Every family must deal with this issue in its own way. But it can help always to have a variety of homemade foods available, so that everyone in the household can find those things they enjoy.

Drying Fruits, Herbs, and Vegetables

Drying food has some advantages, but unfortunately, there are a number of serious disadvantages as well. On the plus side, dried foods are easy to store, they take up little space, and they last almost indefinitely. All fruits and herbs and most vegetables can be dried. On the minus side, most vegetables are not terribly tasty in their dried form. The flavor of a reconstituted dried vegetable is nowhere near as good as that of a frozen or canned vegetable, and the texture is lost, as well. As far as I am concerned, however, fruits and herbs are definitely worth drying.

Food can be dried in a number of ways. Sun-drying is the cheapest way, and in most climates it is a satisfactory method. Here in humid Pennsylvania, though, it can be problematic. There are more foolproof methods, like putting the food in the oven, set at very low heat, or using a commercial dehydrator. Unfortunately, these methods are also energy-dependent and considerably more expensive than the solar drying process. We dry herbs over our wood stove, a method that goes back to earliest times.

The primary consideration if you're thinking about drying food is whether you will use the product after you've gone to the trouble to dry it. If you haven't had any experience with eating dried foods, then I'd suggest that you experiment first with drying herbs, and try making some fruit leather. Fruit leather is a chewy confection made from the puree of such fruits as peaches, apricots, or apples. The pulp is prepared and spread out in a thin layer on a tray to dry. It takes about a week or two to finish drying. Fruit leather has the consistency of taffy and a very good flavor; most kids love it on first introduction. Another plus is that it will store for a year. There couldn't be a better snack to replace the sugar-laden junk that we and our kids seem to crave so much these days.

You can buy dried fruits and vegetables in many health food stores and in some of the bigger food co-ops. You might want to try some of these products before you go to the trouble of building your own dryer, drying some of your produce, and maybe finding out that you and your family are not too fond of the results. At the same time, most gardeners have a number of herbs growing in their gardens each season. It is a shame not to dry some of them for use during the winter months. In some recipes, dried herbs are preferred to fresh, even if fresh are available. Herbs are easy to dry. Some dry better than others. Chives, for example, are better frozen than dried. Tarragon, thyme, parsley, oregano, and basil have excellent flavor when dried. With the cost of herbs in the stores today it is worth learning a little bit about the process of drying food.

The Economics of the Third Stage

When you learn to extend your growing season on both ends and use the advanced planting and growing techniques that have been introduced in this chapter, you can generally anticipate at least a doubling of the savings earned by your vegetable production. The chart titled Economics of the Third Stage doesn't quite double the value per square foot of production (it goes from 65 cents to $1 a square foot). I've deliberately made a conservative estimate, since many people will take a few years to become accomplished in the use of all these techniques.

The berries and fruit trees you planted will not produce any return on your investment for a few years. Strawberries will be harvested in the following year, but apples take at least four or five years. However, when they do start to bear, they'll keep producing for decades. Fruit trees, if you have the space for them, are a great long-term investment.

Saving on Equipment Costs

Purchasing the equipment for the various food processing methods discussed in this chapter can be less expensive if you take the time to tour garage sales and flea markets in your area. Many of these items, such as a kraut cutter, a cider press, and pickling equipment, might even be found in the attics and basements of senior citizens in your family, especially if they've ever lived on a farm. Often these items are just gathering dust, and your elderly relatives will be delighted to see them used again.

Economics of the Third Stage

Item and Use in Food Production System	Initial Capital Investment	Operating Costs and Savings
Garden maintenance		
Seeds, plants, and natural fertilizers for garden of 600–800 sq. ft.	. . .	$30–$75 should cover your basic costs, which will produce a savings of $600–$800 (assuming your increased skills give you a production level worth $1 per sq. ft.).
Berry bushes	$4–$10 each	Annual maintenance costs are minor. While it is difficult to estimate savings from berries and fruit trees, an average backyard orchard can ultimately produce from
Fruit trees	$7–$20 each	$10–$50 worth of food per yr.
Garden tools and equipment		
Tiller	$300–$900 (buy) $30/day (rent)	A tiller costs about $20–$40 a year to maintain. It will save time, but dollar savings are hard to compute.
Containers, tubs, and pots	$10–$150	Depending on how involved you get in planting food in containers, your savings can reach $50 in a year.
Cold frame	$15–$100	This contributes to your increased savings by extending your growing season and increasing your productivity.

[Continued on next page]

Economics of the Third Stage—*Continued*

Item and Use in Food Production System	Initial Capital Investment	Operating Costs and Savings
Garden tools and equipment–*continued*		
Small spray can for insect control	$10	. . .
Food processing equipment		
Dehydrator	$80–$180	Drying food costs about 2–3¢ per lb. You can save from $10–$50 a yr. in food and herbs.
Juicer	$40–$110	You can save well over $20 a yr. depending on how much your family uses it.
Cider press	$100–$700	You can save $15–$50 on your own and can barter home-pressed cider for almost anything else of value.
Pickling equipment	$10–$75	This will save you at least $10–$20 a yr.
Kraut cutter	$25	Here the quality is more important than savings.

Comments: Without considering the capital investments you may decide to make at this point in developing your system, this level of production and effort can give you $600–$800 in value from your garden, $100–$200 in savings from your canning, freezing, and drying efforts, and maybe another $100 from juices, container production, and fruit and berry production. Your food production system is now giving you over $1,000 a year in savings in your family's food budget!

6
FOURTH STAGE
Year-Round Gardening

THE GAME PLAN

The Goal: In the fourth stage you'll be producing food all year round, using a solar grow frame or greenhouse and/or parts of your home. You'll learn new techniques for increasing productivity and storing produce over the winter.

The Strategy:

1. Learn about the construction, costs, and maintenance of solar grow frames and greenhouses, and decide which structure will be best for you.

2. Begin to design the structure (whether or not you'll build it yourself); choose the site and plan the layout; select heat storage medium, construction materials, insulation, and glazing materials. Consider durability, aesthetic qualities, and costs of each.

3. Learn management techniques to make the best use of space and environment, to maintain plants, and to control pests in the structure.

4. Use sunny areas of your home for growing herbs and salad crops.

5. Start your own seedlings to increase productivity and get a jump on the season.

6. Save and store seeds for next season to cut costs.

7. Store root crops and winter vegetables in attic, basement, root cellar, and/or garden beds.

8. Grow sprouts indoors throughout the winter.

109

Many gardeners are satisfied to finish harvesting their produce and clean up their gardens in midfall. They pick the last tomatoes and peppers before the first frost finishes off most of what remains on the plants. In the last chapter I discussed how you can extend your growing season by as much as six to eight weeks. However, your gardening activities become particularly satisfying when you develop the ability to grow fresh vegetables all year long, even during the coldest of the winter months, by using a greenhouse or grow frame. By growing fresh vegetables in the middle of the winter, along with using your stored produce such as carrots, turnips, and cabbage from the root cellar or other dry storage spaces, you can have your own homegrown fresh vegetables on the dinner table every day of the year. In the coldest weeks of January, fresh salads and steamed greens from the greenhouse combine with baked potatoes and buttered carrots from the root cellar to make a meal that is second to none. It tastes especially good because you grew it all yourself. In this chapter we will discuss the skills needed for producing food all year round.

Having a continuing harvest all year long doesn't just happen. Growing vegetables throughout the winter takes equipment and growing skills that are considerably different from those required in your summer garden. You'll need a special structure—a solar grow frame or a greenhouse of some sort. You will need to learn about how to establish various dry storage areas in different parts of your home. And you'll find that you will need to change your cooking and eating habits a bit when you have an abundance of fresh Chinese cabbage, Swiss chard, and root vegetables available to you every day. As a bonus in addition to giving you fresh vegetables, the greenhouse will offer you a fascinating and relaxing activity that virtually eliminates the midwinter doldrums that all of us gardeners seem to suffer. Puttering around with lettuce seedlings in a warm greenhouse, while outside it is 10 degrees and the snow is piling up, is as satisfying a feeling as I've ever experienced.

Starting with a Solar Grow Frame

The solar grow frame is a relatively new device on the gardening scene. It's an excellent example of how an old way of doing things can be updated with modern technology to make a considerable contribution to our ability to become more food self-sufficient. **A grow frame is simply a cold frame (described in the last chapter) that has been redesigned to include insulation, night shutters, and very tight construction (including caulking) so that it can be used to grow certain vegetables throughout the winter. The most common size for a grow frame is about 4 by 8 feet.** In most parts of the country, the traditional cold frame has usually finished its service by the early part of December and doesn't get used again until sometime

A solar grow frame can provide you with a continuing harvest of fresh greens and other vegetables all through the winter.

in March. But the solar grow frame can do everything a cold frame does and, in addition, can be used to grow greens in the coldest January weather.

For most people, it's probably wiser to begin the experience of winter growing with a grow frame, rather than to plunge right in with the much more expensive greenhouse. A greenhouse usually represents a major capital investment, so it should be investigated very carefully. A grow frame can be built for from $450 to $800 and can serve as the first step toward a full-size greenhouse. Even if you add a greenhouse to your food production system later, you will continue to use the grow frame, so it's by no means a waste of money.

Building a Grow Frame

As noted earlier, the most common size for a solar grow frame is about 4 by 8 feet. It can sit on a concrete foundation or on a bed of gravel. You can locate it almost anyplace in your yard as long as it gets good sun. It's a bit more comfortable to work in when it is protected by a building on its north side. However, I think the most important siting issue is convenience to the kitchen door.

The grow frame is normally made of wood, but it's very tightly constructed and heavily caulked to eliminate virtually every crack and pinhole that could allow cold air to get in and warm air to escape. It looks very much like the traditional cold frame with its glass- or plastic-glazed doors. The grow frame, however, is always double-glazed to create an insulating layer of air between the two glazing surfaces. You can use glass, plastic, or film glazing, depending on your budget and your preference. The chart titled Glazing Materials for Grow Frames and Greenhouses sums up the characteristics of some popular glazing materials.

Glazing Materials for Grow Frames and Greenhouses

This chart rates common glazing materials for solar grow frames and greenhouses in terms of seven important characteristics. The last two columns on the right assign a numerical rating to each material's overall performance as an outer glazing (T_1) and an inner glazing (T_2).

Rating of Single-Layer Glazing Materials		A	B	C	D	E	F	G	T_1	T_2
Rigid	Glass	4	5	1	5	4	2	3	24	15
(125 mil)	Thick acrylic	4	5	1	4	4	2	3	23	15
	Polycarbonates	4	5	1	4	5	1	3	23	14
Semirigid	Reinforced fiberglass	4	5	1	4	5	3	5	27	18
(25–40 mil)	Thin acrylic	4	4	1	4	4	3	5	25	17
	Vinyl sheets	4	4	1	3	4	3	4	23	16
Flexible film	Polyethylene	3	1	1	1	2	5	5	18	15
(4 mil)	Vinyl	4	3	1	2	3	4	5	22	17
	Mylar	4	4	1	3	3	3	5	23	17
	Acetate	4	5	1	1	2	4	3	20	17
	Tedlar	5	3	1	3	3	2	3	20	14
	Teflon	5	3	1	3	3	1	3	19	13

KEY:
1	Bad	A	Solar transmittance.
2	Poor	B	Infrared absorption.
3	Good	C	Reduction of heat flow.
4	Very good	D	Weatherability (ultraviolet, ozone).
5	Excellent	E	Resistance to tear, fracture, and scratching.
		F	Low cost.
		G	Installation and maintenance.
		T_1	Total of A through G. Evaluates materials' potential as an outer glazing.
		T_2	Total of T_1 minus D and E. Evaluates material as an inner glazing.

NOTE: Reprinted from *The Solar Greenhouse Book,* edited by James C. McCullagh, Rodale Press, 1978.

The angle of the glazing is important. Horticulturists at the Rodale Research Center found that frames with the glazing angled high (more vertical than horizontal) performed better than frames in which the glazing was angled low. The more vertical glazing makes better use of the sun. Research has also shown that the choice of glazing materials is not critical to the performance of the crops grown inside. However, you should consider durability, ease of installation, and cost when making your selection.

At night, an insulating shutter is pulled down between the glazing and the plants to prevent the escape of heat collected from sunlight during the day.

Another important component of the grow frame is insulation. Grow frames are insulated along the three sides of the structure, the belowground area, and the north-facing back wall. It's important to make every effort to insulate every surface that could possibly allow heat to radiate out of the structure. Styrofoam panels have been used successfully in insulating the grow frames at the Rodale Research Center. These panels are easy to work with and install.

While insulation technology has made the biggest contribution to the grow frame's production capability, the addition of a movable night shutter has also been an important improvement. As you can see in the photo above, the grow frame incorporates a shutter device that is pulled across the glazing every evening to further prevent the loss of valuable heat that was captured inside the structure during the day. The combination of the tight construction, heavy insulation, double glazing, and the night shutter allows the grow frame to withstand below-freezing temperatures for many days on end, as long as a few of those cold days have some sun. The grow frame has worked successfully in all parts of the United States and southern Canada.

What to Grow in the Grow Frame

What can you grow in one of these devices when the temperatures are cold and the days are short? **My own experience and the experiments at the Rodale Research Center indicate that the most successful vegetables in grow frame conditions are the oriental greens—the Chinese cabbages and mustard greens.** Some of them grow even better in such cool temperatures than during the spring or fall season outdoors. The oriental vegetables can survive and even continue to grow, though at a slower pace, when temperatures are down in the 30s. I've also had good luck in the grow frame with many types of lettuce, endive, escarole, and even Swiss chard. A partial listing of these cold-loving plants for the grow frame appears below. A more complete list is included in the Appendix. You may not be familiar

Vegetables for Solar Grow Frames and Greenhouses

These vegetables are most adaptable to the cool conditions in a solar grow frame:

> Chinese cabbage, mustard
>   greens, and other leafy
>   oriental vegetables
> Endive
> Escarole
> Kale
> Leaf lettuce
> Swiss chard
> Turnips (oriental types especially)

These vegetables can be grown in a solar greenhouse:

> Basil (if temperatures don't go
>   too low)
> Beets
> Chinese cabbage, mustard
>   greens, and other leafy
>   oriental vegetables
> Chives
> Endive
> Escarole
> Kale
> Leaf lettuce
> Parsley
> Radishes
> Spinach
> Swiss chard
> Turnips

with some of these vegetables, but I suggest you give them a try. They are easy to grow, delicious, and very nutritious.

The grow frame does not take too much time to manage and maintain. However, it does take some attention each day in order to control ventilation and to open and close the shutter each morning and evening. **You must bear in mind that the vegetables in the grow frame will mature more slowly than they would outdoors in the spring. That's because of the cooler temperatures, the shorter days, and the weaker sunlight.** One nice aspect of winter growing in the grow frame is that you'll have fewer problems with bugs. Also, you don't need to feed and water your plants as often in the winter, because they are growing more slowly.

A typical 4 by 8-foot grow frame operating at peak capacity will produce about **5 pounds of salad and cooking greens every week, with a slight reduction during the coldest weeks.** This is a fine addition to any family's diet, especially when the lettuce and greens in the grocery store look so anemic and limp after their long trip from the fields of California or Florida. Five pounds of greens is a significant weekly volume, especially if you use them raw in salads.

The Solar Greenhouse

If you enjoy growing fresh vegetables in your grow frame, then maybe you're ready to take the plunge and build a solar greenhouse. Greenhouses have been with us for centuries, but the concept of the solar greenhouse is only a few decades old. The solar greenhouse has introduced an important new concept for raising plants: dependence on the sun for heat, with little or no supplemental heat from electric or gas heaters. The traditional greenhouse (and there are an estimated eight million home greenhouses in this country) has to be heated during the winter with a system run on electricity or gas. In the past, home greenhouses were used primarily to grow flowers and house plants. But with the introduction of solar greenhouses came a new interest in using home greenhouses to grow food. The skyrocketing costs of fuel may have done more than anything else to propel the idea of the solar greenhouse into the forefront of gardeners' attention. In response, the hobby greenhouse manufacturers have now introduced a variety of prefab kit models and plans for solar greenhouses in a range of sizes and shapes.

The solar greenhouse incorporates all the design features of the solar grow frame, with a number of important additions. Like the grow frame, the solar greenhouse is very tightly constructed, heavily insulated, and double glazed, and it often has movable insulation such as curtains or shutters for keeping heat in at night. But in addition, it contains some medium, usually water or stone, for storing heat from the sun to be radiated back into the greenhouse at night, and it has some form of ventilation system built in. Some greenhouses are completely passive, using no mechanical fans or blowers to move air around, while others do incorporate some sort of device for mechanically circulating air. Temperatures in a properly designed and constructed solar greenhouse should seldom drop below freezing in any part of the United States. In many locations, they will seldom go below 40 degrees. And if there is sufficient mass to store heat during the day, the daytime temperature will often stay below 80 degrees, allowing the vents to stay closed or at least opened only a crack.

Designing the Greenhouse

One of the first issues you have to consider in designing your solar greenhouse is whether you will use it to produce heat for your home as well as to produce food

FOURTH STAGE—YEAR-ROUND GARDENING

A solar greenhouse doesn't have to be obtrusive. My own greenhouse, as you see here, is located on the second floor and was carefully designed to blend in with the architecture of our house.

for your table. It is extremely difficult to design a greenhouse that performs both functions with equal effectiveness. A solar space designed to collect maximum heat for the home is seldom a satisfactory environment for growing vegetables. The temperatures there go too high during the day, and the extreme temperature fluctuations between day and night hinder effective plant growth. On the other hand, a solar greenhouse that produces food effectively will produce only a modest amount of excess heat for the home. This is primarily because the best solar greenhouse for plants is one that captures the most solar heat in the storage medium for use by the plants at night. In short, if you want solar heat for your home, use a design other than a solar greenhouse, such as a sun space.

The solar greenhouse can be free-standing or it can be attached to the home. Either way, you need a site that faces south. As you can see in the accompanying photo, I not only attached my greenhouse, but I also put it on the second floor. This is my second solar greenhouse. My first was built from scrap lumber and old wooden storm windows. My father and I designed and built it. We made a few mistakes, but it worked just fine. It cost about $500; my current one cost over $3,000. I did the basic design and hired an architect and a contractor to do the construction. Obviously, you do what you can afford. Both greenhouses have produced excellent food. If you plan to have a greenhouse built professionally, you can figure the costs to be about the same as for new residential construction ($35 a square foot in 1982 prices).

Whether you build it yourself or have it done by someone else, you would be wise to do most of the basic thinking and design work yourself. You can pick the site and you can figure out the internal layout that you want. You can decide whether your heat storage will involve rocks, water, or both. Those are all very important decisions that you'll be able to make for yourself after a bit of study on the subject.

I put my greenhouse on the second floor to take advantage of the fact that I was going to have a wood stove underneath it in my family room. The wood stove serves as a backup heating system. Putting an attached greenhouse on the second floor was the only way I could have a growing area that would not be shaded by big trees.

I'm not going to delve into the details of the design principles of the solar greenhouse. It's beyond the scope of this book, and there are a number of excellent books available on the subject. Some are listed in the Bibliography. (My favorite for beginners is *The Solar Greenhouse Book,* edited by James C. McCullagh. It is very helpful for figuring out the best design for your particular situation and pocketbook.) I will, however, point out a few of the mistakes I made with my own solar greenhouse, and share with you some of my biases as well.

Most books recommend that you insulate the north, east, and west walls of the structure, leaving only the south for glazing. I didn't follow that recommendation and glazed the east wall as well as the south. I'm sorry that I did, and I'll probably cover it up and insulate it one of these days. I lose much more heat through that east wall than I gain in the early morning on sunny days. Another important rule is never to skimp on insulation. In fact, it's difficult to have too much. The primary problem in managing a solar greenhouse is how to keep in the heat. Every inch of insulation helps to ease that problem.

I did not include in my design any movable insulation, such as shutters or curtains. Now I wish I had. I can still do it, but now that all the inside benches and storage areas are in place, it would be very complicated to install any movable insulation. I'd advise you to plan from the start to have movable insulation for your glazed areas at night. Design it right into the initial construction of the greenhouse, and don't forget that you'll need a place to store it during the day. It's the storage of the insulation devices that has me stumped at the moment. All the current research shows that movable insulation makes a significant difference in overnight heat retention, and is well worth the modest extra investment.

The decision about which material to use for glazing is a very individual one. There are many kinds of glazing on the market, and each manufacturer says his product is the best for one reason or another. The glazings also represent a rather broad range of prices. Study the books and articles and go with what you think will be best for your needs. Consider things like convenience, cost, ease of installation, and durability when picking the glazing for your greenhouse. I chose a double-walled STP acrylic material, because my greenhouse is so close to the street, in range of the prankster's brick. I would have preferred glass, but I couldn't afford the kind that would repel a brick. The STP acrylic isn't transparent, so consequently I have lost some of the light that I need in the short days of midwinter when the sun lies low on the horizon. Maximum light transmission should be very high on your list of important variables as you design your solar greenhouse. There's plenty of light in the summer, when your plants are growing outdoors. But in the winter, that's not the case. The plants really show the difference, too; they grow more slowly and are more spindly when they lack sufficient light.

The next thing you need to consider in designing your greenhouse is how to provide for storage of the heat that accumulates during the day, as the sunlight enters through the glazing and is transformed into heat. Like your choice of glazing, this is a very individual decision that will be affected by your site, the materials available, and your pocketbook. There are many options to consider. You can store water in containers that are usually dark in color or painted black. You can build your beds on top of a layer of crushed rock. You can line the walls and floor with masonry of some sort. The deep beds of soil are themselves a source of additional heat storage.

If you go with water as a storage medium, try to find a container that will be cheap and will last a long time. As I mentioned in an earlier chapter, my first greenhouse included plans for a somewhat unique water storage system. I read somewhere that beer cans made good free storage devices, minus the beer, of course. So a number of my friends who believed strongly in recycling set about to help me in my task of collecting over 1,000 empty beer cans. After a diligent effort for one whole summer, we achieved our goal. I carefully painted all the cans black and then tried to figure out how to stack them along the back wall of my solar greenhouse. The long and the short of it was that my ingenious system just didn't work. The cans didn't stack as well as I had hoped. I didn't appreciate that different brands of beer have different designs for the bottom of the can. As it turned out, the small cans really wouldn't have provided enough mass to store the necessary heat. I switched to using 5-gallon honey cans for water containers, and the trashmen spent a number of weeks wondering what we were doing with 1,000 beer cans painted black. Unfortunately, there were no recycling facilities in that town, so our recycling effort fell short of the complete cycle.

One of the trickiest problems in designing your heat storage system is figuring out how much storage mass you need. A useful rule of thumb is to provide 1 to 2 gallons of water or 1 cubic foot of masonry or stone for each square foot of glazing

The raised planting areas in my greenhouse make watering and other gardening tasks quite convenient. This photo shows the last of my spring transplants almost ready for planting out in the main garden.

FOURTH STAGE—YEAR-ROUND GARDENING

This view shows additional planting areas against the back wall of my greenhouse and the water-filled, black-painted honey cans that serve as the heat-storage medium.

in the greenhouse. A review of the rapidly growing body of literature on solar greenhouses will provide you with some other formulas for calculating heat storage, and also a vast range of creative ideas for recycling various materials and containers for heat storage. I like 5-gallon honey cans because they stack so well, and you can often buy them used from an apiary supply store at a very reasonable price. Properly painted with a rust-retardant dark paint, they should last six to eight years before they start to leak.

An important design component that I seriously underestimated when planning my solar greenhouse is the ventilation. I have two ceiling vents equipped with automatic vent openers that open and close them according to the temperature. They work just fine. My problem is that the vents are not big enough. When I am at home on a sunny day, I can rig some fans to blow the excess heat into the house. But when I'm not there, I depend on the vents to open when the temperature climbs toward 80 degrees. They open all right, but they're just not big enough to allow enough air movement to prevent the temperature from going above 80 degrees on very bright, clear days that aren't too cold. One rule of thumb for ventilation is that the total vent space should be almost one-sixth of the area of the glazing. I have 120 square feet of glazing and 2 square feet of vent area—a tenth of what I need. Air must move freely in a solar greenhouse, so fans are almost a must. Again, you will find many points of view on this subject in the literature. Study it carefully, and by all means, don't skimp on the venting area.

Managing the Solar Greenhouse

In the northern two-thirds of the United States and in all of Canada, a solar green-house will occupy a part of your food production activities during almost nine months of the year. The objective is to use every square inch of growing space in the greenhouse as efficiently as possible during these months. This means relying heavily on the use of succession planting techniques. In your garden, you try to keep every square foot producing something or other all the time. The same princi-ple applies to managing the greenhouse, only it is even more critical. You may only

When planning your greenhouse, be sure to provide enough ventilation. This illustration shows the vents I installed in my greenhouse, compared to the amount of vent space I really ought to have, as indicated by the dotted lines.

have 20 or 30 square feet of growing space in a small solar greenhouse. Consequently, you must learn every trick in the book to keep each square inch producing food as much as possible.

Unless you live in a southern location, the greenhouse season actually begins in August when you start a crop of vegetables and herbs out in your garden to be transplanted into the greenhouse when they are almost full-grown in late October. These plants might include Chinese cabbage, several varieties of lettuce, escarole, endive, parsley, dill, basil, and perhaps just a few flowers for color. I transplant these plants right from the garden into my greenhouse beds in order to preserve as much of their root systems as I can to reduce transplant shock. In September and October you'll be starting a second planting of vegetables out in the garden, to move into the greenhouse as seedlings in late October. They will continue to grow and replace the first crop sometime in late November or in December. This second planting could include several varieties of Chinese cabbage, some lettuce, and several oriental greens. These will go from the garden into pots or containers for a month or so before going into the greenhouse beds.

The normal growing period in a solar greenhouse is roughly November through March. The ideal is to have the first greenhouse crops ready to pick on November 1, while you still have late vegetables available outside in your cold frames.

During the cold months of December, January, and February, your crops should be at various stages of maturity. This will give you a steady flow of greens for cooking and for salads with relatively little time spent on your part each week to produce them. This is the time of year to relax a bit.

In February, the solar greenhouse takes on the additional task of serving as the nursery for the first plants to go out into the cold frame and then into the main garden in April and May. There's a chart in the Appendix titled Seed-Starting Tips listing all the vegetables that can be started in your greenhouse to get a jump on the season. I start two or three varieties of lettuce and some Chinese cabbage in early January to put out into the cold frame in early March. Those seedlings started in February get hardened off in the cold frame and then go directly into the garden in late April.

In the northern parts of the country, some people continue to use their greenhouses for starting seedlings for succession planting during the May-through-September outdoor growing season. Usually, though, the greenhouse is left empty over the summer, because it's very difficult to keep it from getting too hot. This is the best time to do some important maintenance tasks, such as repairing, caulking, and thoroughly cleaning every surface in the greenhouse.

Like the solar grow frame, the solar greenhouse, with its cool winter environment, is best suited for growing oriental greens and salad greens. In the chart titled Vegetables for Solar Grow Frames and Greenhouses, earlier in this chapter, you'll

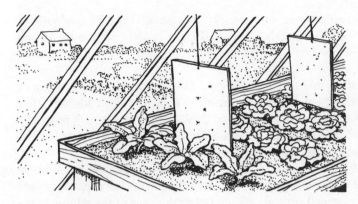

An effective control for whiteflies in the greenhouse is to suspend among the plant foliage some boards that have been painted yellow and then coated with motor oil or another sticky substance. The bugs are attracted to the yellow color and are trapped by the oil.

find a partial listing of the kinds of vegetables and herbs that thrive in the solar greenhouse. You'll find a more complete list in the Appendix.

Insect control in a greenhouse can be a challenging task, especially for the beginner. The environment in a greenhouse is ideal for a population explosion of certain insects. The most common pests are various sorts of aphids and whiteflies. Learning to control these little troublemakers takes more than one growing season for most of us. You can lose control of them in a very short period of time—a matter of days. It is extremely difficult to get rid of a serious insect infestation once it's gotten out of control, and at the same time avoid using some kind of chemical spray.

Horticulturists are generally in agreement that the best way to handle bugs in the greenhouse is to prevent them from getting there in the first place. And in my experience, the experts are correct! The first rule of pest and disease prevention is sanitation. Keeping the greenhouse clean and free of little piles of debris goes a long way to keep down insect infestation. What usually happens is that you inadvertently bring the bugs into the greenhouse on plants moved from the garden or brought from the store. **Those same observational skills I mentioned in an earlier chapter become very important here in the greenhouse. When you bring in new plants, always inspect them carefully—for aphids especially.**

While prevention is definitely the best and the easiest cure, there are a number of steps to take to control these little pests if they do appear. The cardinal rule when combating pests is that time is of the essence—the sooner you act when you spot a bug, the more likely it is that you'll succeed in controlling the invasion. There are a number of organic sprays you can try, such as soapy water and red pepper solutions. These nontoxic repellent sprays have proven successful for many gardeners. Another good control technique is the use of yellow panels to trap whiteflies. USDA scientists have found that whiteflies are attracted to the color yellow, for some reason. I've installed in my greenhouse three panels, each about a foot square, painted yellow and covered with a sticky substance. (I use Tanglefoot, but motor oil will also work.) The panels are placed right in the beds, down among the foliage of the plants. Just like flypaper, the whiteflies stick to the yellow panels and die.

As a last resort, if an infestation really gets out of control, then dusting or spraying the plants with rotenone or pyrethrum, which lose their toxicity after about three days, usually bring things under control. Using these strong botanical poisons should only be done when all else fails. Once you have had a few battles, though, you'll find that you get better at preventing the next attack.

A modest-size solar greenhouse (about 8 by 10 feet) really does not take an inordinate amount of time to manage. Getting established in the fall generally takes a few afternoons. After everything's set up, you can take care of the minimum requirements of watering and feeding, and do a little transplanting as well, in one or two hours a week.

In the fall you need to revitalize the planting beds with new compost and get in the winter's supply of potting soil. I use a growing medium of one-third compost, one-third vermiculite, and one-third garden soil. Some people pasteurize their soil in the oven before bringing it into the greenhouse, to eliminate any pathogens that may be in the soil. I haven't found that step necessary, at least not so far. In fall there is also usually some last-minute caulking to do in the greenhouse, along with some general housecleaning.

Because the greenhouse garden is small and controlled, plant maintenance and transplanting from then on take little time. On the other hand, you can go into the greenhouse with the intention of simply planting a few lettuce seeds for the next succession and find yourself coming out three hours later having had a wonderful time puttering around and feeling completely relaxed and at peace with the world. If goin' fishin' is the classic therapy for the summer, messing around in a greenhouse is surely the ultimate gardener's therapy for the winter.

Growing Vegetables in the House

After all this discussion about growing vegetables in a grow frame or a greenhouse, I must point out that salad greens and herbs can also be raised perfectly well in the house during the winter. Crops like lettuce, parsley, dill, endive, and escarole are relatively easy to grow in hanging pots in the sunny windows of your home. They are attractive plants in their own right and add a variety of color and texture to the appearance of any room.

Another trick is to bring things into the kitchen in hanging pots just as they're ready to pick. That way there is always a hanging pot or two of lettuce or Chinese cabbage to brighten up the kitchen. These greens are then easily accessible for

A sunny kitchen window is a good place to raise herbs, some seedlings, or even a pot of leaf lettuce for winter eating.

dressing up a salad, and growing space is freed up in the greenhouse or grow frame to get something else going sooner.

If you haven't got a greenhouse, you can still grow winter salad greens or get an early start on your spring crops of lettuce, greens, and herbs down in the cellar under fluorescent lights. For example, here's a simple way to grow leaf lettuce: You plant a dozen leaf lettuce seeds, later thinning to leave the six sturdiest little plants. The plants will grow just fine if you keep the lights suspended a few inches above their tops (adjustable chains make this simple). The lights must be on for 12 to 16 hours a day. I use a timer so I don't have to remember to turn the lights on and off each day. After three weeks, you can plant 12 more seeds to get six more little plants. When the first lettuce plants are about 3 inches tall, transplant them into hanging pots (three plants fit nicely into a 10-inch pot.) After a few weeks in a sunny window, you can start adding a few leaves of fresh lettuce to your winter salads. With two or three hanging pots in a window and replacement plants coming along under lights, you can grow almost all your salad greens throughout the winter without much trouble. Supplementing these greens with some sprouts (discussed later in this chapter) gives you fresher and tastier greens than you could ever expect to find in the stores.

The Importance of Starting Your Own Seedlings

The only way to use the limited space in a grow frame or a greenhouse to maximum productive advantage is to learn to grow your own seedlings in some place other than your main beds. If you plant seeds directly into a greenhouse bed, you are using that bed at less than its maximum production capacity for one to two months. Seeds should be started in flats or in other containers designed for that purpose. As the seedlings grow, they will need to be transplanted one or more times into individual pots or other containers where they can grow to a size that makes putting them into a bed practical. Growing your own seedlings is almost essential if you're going to take advantage of succession planting techniques either in your greenhouse or out in your main garden during the summer. Producing healthy seedlings is a challenging activity. It's one thing to sow seeds directly into the garden and then thin out the extra plants. It's quite another matter to transplant a delicate little seedling with just two leaves and a hairlike stem. But all it takes is some practice, and the rewards are certainly worth the effort. The Bibliography lists several good sources of further information on growing and handling seedlings. See also the chart titled Seed-Starting Tips, in the Appendix.

Seedlings under Lights

While you have to learn about feeding, watering, and transplanting techniques, the two primary concerns in growing healthy seedlings are sufficient light and enough space for the roots to grow. I've had the best luck starting my seeds under lights. I have two 48-inch fluorescent light fixtures rigged in the cellar so that they can be raised or lowered according to the height of the growing plants. I don't use the

A metal utility shelving unit to which you have attached fluorescent light fixtures can function as a basement nursery for starting dozens of vegetable, herb, and flower seedlings. The lights should be about 6 inches from the plant tops, so start with the flats elevated on bricks or boards, and gradually lower them as the plants grow.

more expensive grow-light bulbs. Normal cool white or warm white tubes seem to work just fine. I keep the lights about 6 inches above the plants and have them turned on for 12 to 16 hours a day. This procedure gives me healthy plants almost every time.

My attempts to start seedlings in the greenhouse have not been as successful, because in the winter months they can't get as much light as I can provide with the fluorescent fixtures. Plants that can grow outdoors in partial shade, like lettuce and Chinese cabbage, do pretty well, but light-loving plants like tomatoes, broccoli, and cauliflower get a bit spindly because they really need more light than I have available in the greenhouse in the winter.

While light, water, and food are important, I have found that the hardiest seedlings are those whose roots haven't been seriously harmed by the transplanting process. At this stage in its development, a plant's root system grows faster than its leaves and stem, and the plant can quickly become root-bound. Also, the transplanting process, no matter how carefully undertaken, will inevitably cause some damage to the incredibly delicate roots. The challenge is to minimize that damage.

I have had the best luck with planting my seeds in a container at least as big as a Styrofoam coffee cup. This is generally twice the size of most planting trays that you can buy in the gardening stores, especially in terms of depth. My reasoning for starting out with larger containers goes like this: For most of the plants you grow in a greenhouse and many of those you grow in your garden, more than one transplanting before final setting is desirable. Two or three transplantings into successively larger containers creates a stronger root system and stem, among other advantages. These transplantings must be timed so that plants always have plenty of room to grow. A plant that is root-bound is set back in its growth and may never recover completely. If I use containers that are slightly larger than is usually necessary, then the timing for my transplanting is not quite so critical. I have a bit more flexibility. If I don't get to the task for a few days or even a week, it won't cause problems for the plants. The larger containers need watering less often, as well. I'm always trying to find ways to save time and still do the job effectively.

The beauty of learning about growing your own seedlings is that you don't have to wait a year to undo a mistake, as you sometimes have to do with mistakes in the main garden. You will be growing seedlings almost all year long if you use succession techniques and try to grow vegetables over the winter in a greenhouse or grow frame. Another satisfying aspect of growing your own seedlings that you can plant more carefully in a pot than you can when you're seeding an entire row or bed outdoors. If you plant just a few more seeds than the number of plants you want, there will be little thinning to do later on, and your seeds won't be wasted. A pack of seeds will last most families several years when husbanded in this manner.

Most gardening books give you some basics on starting your own seedlings. However, if you want an in-depth approach, the best book I've seen on the subject is Nancy Bubel's *The Seed-Starter's Handbook* (see the Bibliography).

Saving Your Own Seeds

When a package of 800 seeds cost only 25 cents, we didn't think so much about saving them. Now that a packet can cost $1.50 for half as many seeds, it seems a better idea to save them. Furthermore, knowing how to save your own seeds may be the only way to get certain varieties that you like in the future. **There are two ways to save your own seeds. You can save and store the unused seeds that you buy, to make them last as long as possible. Or, you can go all the way and collect your own seeds from some of your garden plants to be used next year. The first way is easy; the second takes more knowledge and skill and lots of commitment.** With each year of storage, the germination percentage is going to decrease a bit, but that just means you plant a few more seeds to get the number of plants you need.

Storing Seeds

The chart titled Important Facts about Seeds, in the Appendix, gives the approximate storage life in years for a wide range of seeds when stored under the proper conditions. Obviously, you will save some money if you save your unused seeds from this year's catalog order for planting in next year's garden. Some kinds, like onion seed, can be stored for only two years, while other kinds, like lettuce seed, will keep for over five years.

   Seeds are very vulnerable to moisture or humidity, so your primary concern when storing them is to minimize their contact with the air. I open my seed packets when I am ready to plant, and within an hour transfer the unused seeds into small glass pill bottles that I have collected over the years. I label each bottle with the variety and the year so I know how long I can store them. One of my friends, a real gardening expert, uses another approach. She keeps her excess seeds right in their packets and rolls them up tight. Then she places the packets in a glass jar with some powdered milk to absorb any moisture. Finally she stores that jar in the back of her refrigerator.

   Seeds must be stored in a cool, dry place. While my friend keeps hers in her refrigerator, I keep my assorted pill bottles and spice bottles of seeds down in the cool basement in an old spice rack. That way I can more easily spot the ones I need as I go through my succession planting schedule. I usually go through a packet of seeds within three years, so I don't press the limits of any seed's storage life very often.

Collecting Seeds from Your Own Plants

Saving seeds that you've grown yourself is a challenging but very satisfying activity. Why would anyone want to go to such trouble? In the first place, many of the older vegetable varieties are no longer available from seed companies; instead, they have to be passed around by gardeners who grow them and save the seeds. These older varieties very often have better flavor than newer, bigger varieties, and can also be perfectly suited for your specific climate and soil type.

Furthermore, the number of different varieties of vegetable seeds available from seed companies is being reduced every year as these companies are taken over by multi-national corporations that worry more about the profit margin than about maintaining a variety in their selections. In some ways these seed companies are geared toward the needs of commercial growers rather than home gardeners. Varieties are bred for large size, nice color, and shipping ability, while characteristics like special flavor and adaptation to various climates are left behind.

The procedures for saving your own seeds vary from vegetable to vegetable and can be somewhat complicated. For example, carrots must be allowed to grow two years before they produce seed. Most gardening books are a bit weak on this subject. The best information I've come across about saving seeds and who else is doing it comes from the Seed Savers' Exchange in Princeton, Missouri. A self-addressed, stamped envelope sent to the Exchange will get you the kind of information you need to get started. Write to Kent Whealy, R.F.D. 2, Box 92, Princeton, MO 64673. Saving your own seeds really doesn't save you a whole lot of money, but it does give you a very strong feeling of self-reliance. It is almost like beating the system, a satisfying activity for some of us.

Storing Vegetables in the Winter

Virtually every fruit and vegetable that you can grow in your backyard food production system can be stored in one way or another for a period of time. We've already discussed canning, freezing, and drying. Another storage method we'll get into now is called dry storage, and it's been a mainstay for food storage throughout history until just the last 50 years. **Dry storage is used for what are called the winter vegetables: beets, cabbages, carrots, potatoes, turnips, and others. There are three different dry storage methods to consider, depending on the needs of the vegetables or fruits to be stored. Some vegetables need a cold and very moist environment. Others keep best in a cool and very dry environment. You can also store a number of vegetables right in the ground, leaving them in the garden all winter.**

Cool, Moist Storage

The vegetables and fruits that prefer a cool, moist environment include apples, beets, broccoli, Brussels sprouts, cabbage, Chinese cabbage, carrots, cauliflower, celery, horseradish, kale, kohlrabi, leeks, parsnips, potatoes, white radishes, rutabagas, salsify, turnips, and watermelon.

Root crops can be stored during the winter in an unheated attic in wooden barrels or plastic garbage cans. Layer the vegetables with damp sand, and, as long as temperatures remain cool, the food will keep for many weeks.

One of the easiest ways to store some of these vegetables is in a container of damp sand in an unheated attic. Most attics are not heated and go down to 35 or 40 degrees during the winter. If you put carrots, beets, or parsnips in a plastic garbage can, alternating layers of vegetables with an inch or so of damp sand, you can keep them fresh all the way into March. The clamp-on top of a plastic garbage can keeps the dampness in, preventing the vegetables from drying out. We used this method in our first attempt at dry storage and it worked very well.

The ideal space for cold, moist storage is the traditional root cellar. We added one to our house under a newly built family room a number of years ago. Many people build what is called a cold room in the northeast or northwest corner of their basement, and use that for storage. Basically, what you need for a root cellar is a space that gets down to 32 to 40 degrees and maintains a humidity of at least 80 percent. Our root cellar has a foot of gravel over the dirt floor, and we periodically pour some water onto the gravel to keep the humidity up. Temperatures in the storage space should never go too much below freezing. Managing this kind

Our root cellar is small, but it works very well. Note the gravel floor, the insulated ceiling, and the air vent in the wall. These components allow me to maintain a humid, well-ventilated environment in the root cellar that has no effect on the rest of the house.

of environment does take some attention. Whether you have a root cellar or a cold room, you have to keep an eye on it almost every day, especially if the outside temperatures are way below freezing. This is really not all that difficult, since we must assume that you are taking vegetables out of storage to use at least once a week.

While there are many different designs for these cold storage areas, an absolutely critical requirement for all of them is sufficient ventilation. Stored vegetables and fruits produce gases which, if allowed to accumulate in stagnant air, promote spoilage. You need an intake and an exhaust vent of some sort to ensure proper air circulation in your root cellar. It doesn't have to be fancy—a single pipe to the outside will do. Natural convection will take care of moving the air around.

When you read seed catalogs you'll notice that certain varieties of these vegetables and fruits are said to store better than others. This is particularly true of apples and potatoes. **Be sure when you order your seeds or nursery stock that you select good-keeping varieties of the crops you wish to store.** It's tempting to buy apples in bulk when they are cheap in the fall, but unfortunately, most of the commercially grown varieties available today do not store very well. Using a root cellar successfully, then, requires some knowledge of the varieties best suited for such storage.

Dry Storage

Other vegetables require a dry storage environment and don't always need to be kept as cold as those vegetables stored in the root cellar. They include garlic, onions, sweet potatoes, pumpkins, shallots, green tomatoes, and winter squash. This group needs a storage area with temperatures of 35 to 45 degrees and a humidity below 70 percent (50 percent is great). This fits the description of most attics. It also could be a bedroom on the north side of the house that is closed off for the winter.

Storage in the Garden

Finally, some very hardy vegetables can be stored very easily right in the garden where they grow. They include carrots, horseradish, leeks, parsnips, white radishes, salsify, turnips, and rutabagas.

In order to keep the ground from freezing, so that you'll be able to dig the vegetables in the middle of January, you must cover them with a loose mulch of hay, straw, or shredded leaves that's about 2 feet deep. Many of these vegetables, including parsnips and salsify, actually taste better after they've been exposed to freezing temperatures. In-row storage is ideal for them. You will need to devise a marker system to remember where you have dug and where you still have stored vegetables, but that's really the only thing to worry about. Nature will take care of the rest, keeping these vegetables as fresh as if you had dug them in the fall.

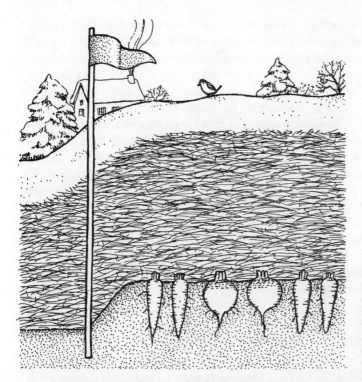

When storing root crops right in the garden, mulch them with at least a foot of loose straw or leaves, and mark their location with a flag or stake so you can find them later, when the garden is covered with snow.

An important point I want to emphasize here is that vegetables kept in dry storage provide the necessary complement to the greens you can produce over the winter in your grow frame or greenhouse. The combination gives you considerable variety in your diet while making a major nutritional contribution. Dry storage, like many of the other techniques we've discussed in this book, is not that complicated. It does, however, take some critical knowledge to do it properly. The Bubels have produced the best reference I've seen on the subject. Their book, *Root Cellaring,* contains the most complete discussion of dry storage on the market (see the Bibliography).

Buying in Bulk—Food Co-ops

Even if you make use of all the techniques that we've discussed to get maximum production from the backyard food system, it's very difficult to grow your year's supply of rice, grains, and dried beans. These sorts of crops would take up more space than even a good-size suburban backyard has to offer. Consequently, you will probably need to buy some food items simply because you don't have the space to grow them. You should consider buying some things in bulk, and you might find the best source to be a local food co-op.

A food co-op, no matter what size, is essentially a grocery store that is owned by its customers. Whether it be a little buying club of five or six families, or a full-size supermarket operation with a warehouse and transportation facilities, it can offer food of a quality and at a cost that's usually not available from the retail supermarket chains. There are over 550 co-ops in this country with over 1,500,000 members, so the idea is not as uncommon as you might think.

The primary reason I mention co-ops is that they often sell things like rice, grains, and dried beans in bulk quantities, and it's much cheaper than buying 1- or 2-pound packages in the supermarket. The only problem is that when you buy in bulk quantities, you must have the proper storage space available so the bulk product doesn't spoil. Usually you need a cool, dry space that is free of insects and rodents. Tightly covered containers are essential. (Clean metal or plastic trash cans with tightly fitting lids work very well.) If such a space is available in your home, then buying in bulk from a co-op can usually save you a considerable amount of money. If you can't find a co-op in your area, you may want to consider starting one on your own with some friends. In any case, the co-op is a valuable complement to a backyard food production system.

Cooking in the Winter Months

Winter is the best time for cooking as far as I'm concerned. With the wind whistling and the snow piling up outside, it seems absolutely appropriate to be making a stew or a soup that will simmer slowly on the back of the stove for a few hours. Also, the winter vegetables—cabbage, carrots, turnips, and the like—seem to lend themselves to stews and soups for some reason.

One of our mainstays in the wintertime is sprouts. Sprouts are easy to grow and provide a tasty and extremely nutritious addition to the greens from the greenhouse and the root vegetables from the root cellar. Sprouting takes little time and is very easy to do. Many different kinds of seeds lend themselves to sprouting. The most popular are alfalfa seeds, mung beans, and soybeans. Whether you use a commercial sprouting jar or a jar or bowl you've rigged yourself, first soak the seeds overnight. In the morning rinse the seeds and set the container in a cupboard, lightly covered with a towel or cloth that will let the air in. The seeds must be rinsed two or three times a day. They will sprout within a day or two, and the sprouts will be ready to eat in four to six days. We use the larger sprouts, like mung bean, in soups and cooked vegetable dishes. We use the small sprouts, like alfalfa, in place of lettuce in sandwiches and salads. Their taste and nutritional value truly enhance our winter diet.

Much is said about the great variety of fruits and vegetables available to Americans in their supermarkets in the winter. **While it's true that we backyard food producers in the northern United States can't grow avocados, pineapples, and or-**

anges, we can have available from our own production system a very respectable variety of vegetables and fruits for our tables during the winter months. The chart below gives some examples of the range of choices the cook will have to work with in January, even when the snow is up to the top step.

Choice of Winter Food Grown in Backyard Food System

Fresh	Frozen	Canned	Stored
Endive	Beans	Applesauce	Apples
Lettuce	Snap	Beets	Carrots
Oriental vegetables	Lima	Pickles	Horseradish
Parsley	Broccoli	Sauerkraut	Parsnips
Sprouts	Peas	Tomato juice	Squash, winter

Obviously, this is only a partial list of what could be available from a backyard food production system after a few years of experience. I still enjoy going to the supermarket in January and getting that avocado to add to a salad. But what is important to me is that I don't have to go to the supermarket for any of those things listed in the chart—I produce them myself.

The Economics of the Fourth Stage

At this point in the development of a backyard food production system, it is very difficult to predict exactly how much money can be saved from the vegetable garden. People have varying skills and levels of interest. Some people put in the minimum amount of time required to produce what they need, and other people will put in many, many hours, because they enjoy the activity, they have the time, and they want to get maximum production from their space. **I think a conservative estimate of the value of your garden after four years of experience, using at least some of the advanced growing techniques, is $1.10 per square foot.** Some experts have achieved values in excess of $2.00 a square foot, so such a goal is definitely attainable. Remember, inflation affects food costs every year, so that has to be factored in each year as you assess your efforts.

Obviously, the capital investment in a solar grow frame or a greenhouse is a substantial one, even if you do most of the work yourself. **The backyard food production system** *can* **give you your year's supply of vegetables, even in the winter, without a grow frame or greenhouse. What these structures offer you primarily is additional variety in the winter, especially with the green leafy vegetables. My root cellar and attic storage has allowed me to save more money on vegetables that**

I grew in the garden than I will save from the greenhouse. In the final analysis, we must return to my simple economic philosophy—if you can afford it, buy it and write off the total costs in the year that you pay for it. After that you can enjoy some real savings from your grow frame or greenhouse.

Dry storage of appropriate vegetables in a root cellar or attic definitely increases your total savings from your vegetable garden. However, those savings are difficult to compute. When you pick your carrots in the fall, when they are plentiful in the local farmers' markets, they may be worth 39 cents a bunch. But if you save them and use them in January, when the stores are charging 79 cents a bunch, then the value of your vegetable production has just gone up. It's like putting your vegetables in a savings bank. They gain value just sitting in the root cellar.

Once you learn how to save seeds, you can save a little money over the years with this practice. The actual monetary savings, about $5 to $20 each year, really are not as important as the security of knowing that you will have those seeds, no matter what happens to the seed industry. Furthermore, if you are collecting your seeds from just the best of your plants, you are gradually developing your own custom-bred variety of vegetable particularly suited to the conditions in your backyard. In the long run, it's the development of your own self-sufficiency rather than dollar savings that justifies the minimal effort it takes to save some of your own seeds.

Processing your own food, such as making your own tofu, pasta, or yogurt, doesn't always save you money over the cost of the same products in the stores. Sometimes home-processed foods actually cost you more; ice cream is a good example. **The justification, then, for purchasing food-processing equipment is often the desire to have the very highest quality and the best-tasting, additive-free food for your family, rather than saving lots of money.** While in some cases, you can save money with home-processed foods, these other reasons are just as strong a motivation to make any of these investments. By the way, home-processed foods make great bartering items with friends who are producing something that you do not have. Some homemade pasta may be the exchange for a jar of homemade jam.

Economics of the Fourth Stage

Item and Use in Food Production System	Initial Capital Investment	Operating Costs and Savings
Garden maintenance		
Seeds, plants, and natural fertilizers for garden of 800–1,000 sq. ft.	. . .	You'll spend $50–$100 for basic inputs, which will produce from $900–$1,100 in savings (assuming you produce $1.10 worth of food per sq. ft.).
Garden tools and equipment		
Solar grow frame	$400–$800	With this structure you can produce $30–$50 worth of food in a yr.
Solar greenhouse	$500–$3,000	Annual maintenance costs for a greenhouse can run $30–$50; however, you can produce from $50–$100 worth of food in a season.
Greenhouse tools and equipment	$20–$150	. . .
Fluorescent light fixtures (for seedlings)	$20–$40	Operating costs vary with cost of electricity. In 1982, a 40-watt, cool white 48-in. tube cost roughly $1 a mo. to operate for 12 hrs. a day.
Food processing equipment		
Sprouting jar	$4–$6	During the yr. you can pay $5–$10 for seeds for sprouting, which will produce $15–$30 worth of fresh sprouts for your salads and sandwiches.

Comments: When you add the production of a grow frame and/or a greenhouse to the components of the food production system previously described, you are approaching an annual food savings of over $1,200! Obviously not everyone is going to develop every single component, but each one does increase the savings after the capital investment has been written off.

7

FIFTH STAGE

The Ultimate Backyard Food Production System

THE GAME PLAN

The Goal: In this fifth, and final, stage, you'll increase your level of self-sufficiency by adding some small livestock and other creatures to your backyard food system.

The Strategy:

1. Learn what's involved in raising chickens and rabbits—how to shelter them, care for them, and "harvest" them. Investigate zoning laws. Carefully consider whether you're ready to make the commitment before plunging ahead.

2. Consider keeping a hive of bees to produce honey.

3. Investigate a backyard fish-farming setup, and assess the pros and cons.

4. Raise earthworms to improve your garden soil.

5. Encourage a permanent population of insect-eating wild bird species in your yard to assist in pest control.

6. Explore bartering as a way to trade excess produce for other goods and services.

39

Up to this point, in describing the first four stages of a backyard food production system, I haven't introduced any techniques that are not already found in many suburban backyards. Perhaps such an intensive approach is not found very often, but vegetable gardens, fruit trees, and greenhouses are not unique in the suburban communities across the country. In this, the fifth stage, I will introduce some components that are not commonly found in most suburban areas. Keeping animals has been viewed as almost the exclusive domain of the rural dweller. However, a number of demonstration projects around the country have shown conclusively that the suburban and urban homesteader can supply a significant portion of the family's meat needs.

If you have gotten to this point in your backyard system, you are now obviously serious enough about finding out how far you can go toward food self-sufficiency that you may be willing to make a fairly significant time commitment to the project. Consequently, you need to learn ways to integrate many of your activities so that they are more efficient both in terms of time requirements and in energy consumption. Finally, you will recognize that the time and energy you must spend in building and maintaining a truly comprehensive system is going to have some impact on the family—the roles of its members and their attitudes and values about the whole idea. This chapter is going to show how far a backyard food system can go in the suburban and urban areas. In the Conclusion we'll stand back and pull all the pieces together into a reasonable whole that is attainable by anyone intersted in decreasing dependence on this country's food production and distribution system.

Small Livestock and Other Animals in the Suburbs

Raising small livestock in the backyard—chickens and rabbits, for example—is not a new idea in this country. Fifty years ago many people had a few chickens in the backyard for some eggs and a little meat. The backyard chicken coop was not uncommon in small towns or even in the center of the cities. Small livestock, however, did not follow Americans into the suburbs. Zoning laws almost universally prohibited the raising of any farm animals, including chickens and rabbits. But even with the zoning laws still in place, all that is changing. Small livestock is coming to the suburbs.

Most people are watching the price of meat soaring with little hope that it will not continue to rise in the years ahead. Some of us are also getting more and more concerned about the chemical additives that the commercial producers put in meats to prevent animal disease, to give the meat color, and to increase storage time. These two issues are moving many suburbanites to consider raising their own meat. However, there are a few problems.

Considerations for Raising Animals

Raising small livestock takes quite a bit of knowledge and takes daily attention, unlike the garden which can be neglected for a week without any major damage. Many people underestimate the skills you must have and the demands on your time that raising small livestock imposes. As a result, many people try it and fail quickly. **Anyone seriously interested in raising some small livestock should prepare very carefully. You need to know what you really want; you must know how to properly care for the small livestock *before* you get them; and you must be prepared to make the time commitment necessary for successful production.** This means reading books, talking to people who already are doing it, and thinking the whole project through very carefully.

One of the biggest hurdles for many people is the fact that after you have nurtured your small livestock, fed them, watered them, cleaned them, and generally cared for them, you have to kill them. Many families have trouble with the idea of eating Charlie the chicken or Thumper the rabbit. **It is easy to enjoy the chicken from the grocery store with dispassion. It is another thing entirely to raise that chicken, get to know it and appreciate its habits and behavior, and then have to kill it for the dinner table.** Obviously, this issue must be resolved before embarking on any small livestock-raising project.

The zoning laws that exist in most communities to discourage the raising of farm animals are another real concern. Usually this does not have to be a problem. I believe that these laws will be revised in the future, and in the meantime there is a way to deal with them. Most zoning laws of this kind are in place because someone once complained. Furthermore, most of these zoning laws are only invoked if someone complains again. Towns do not send the police out on patrol to detect chicken coops. The secret then, is to involve your neighbors in the project so they do not complain. If they don't complain, the zoning law will not be a problem. For example, most towns today have numbers of people with beehives, which are usually prohibited by the zoning laws. When the beehives are properly maintained and are not a nuisance, no one complains, and the bees just keep on producing honey. If you let your neighbors in on your plans, and possibly bribe them a bit with offers of sharing the eggs, or honey, or whatever, then you can usually avoid any problems with zoning laws.

I believe that there are at least six small livestock projects which are feasible in most suburban backyards. They are chickens, rabbits, bees, fish, worms, and, from a point of view I'll explain later, wild birds. Rabbits and bees are not uncommon, even today. Chickens have been less common, because people don't know how to prevent the coop from smelling. Fish are a new item for the backyard, and I believe they will catch on increasingly in the coming years. Worms and birds are not food items, but they make major contributions to the food system as I will explain. I have personally had little experience with small livestock, so I can only report what I have learned from others. I intend to incorporate livestock into my own production system in the next few years. What follows then, is a brief summary of the issues we all need to consider if we are contemplating raising small livestock of any kind in our backyard.

Chickens

Chickens have a bad name in the suburbs. They are reputed to be noisy and smelly, but neither nuisance has to occur. **Chickens produce eggs, meat, and excellent manure for the garden.** Twelve chickens will produce about 60 eggs per week. Six chickens, then, will produce slightly more than 2 dozen eggs a week. You do not need a rooster for the hens to lay eggs. If you have no rooster you have less noise than the family dog produces. A proper shelter and proper management practices prevent any noxious odor.

The size of the chicken coop will be a function of how many chickens you intend to raise. **Twelve chickens need a coop that is about 5 by 10 feet with an outside exercise area or pen of about the same size—50 square feet. Six chickens would need about two-thirds that amount of space. You cannot afford to cheat on the minimum space or the nature of the shelter.** Inadequate space and shelter stunts the growth of the chickens, leads to cannibalism, and greatly increases their susceptibility to disease. The proper shelter will be odor-free, dry, light, and well ventilated. In order to ensure that it is odor-free, you must be able to clean it easily or be able to use the deep-bed method, which provides a deep layer of straw to absorb the manure and its odor.

Two important variables affecting the quality of your eggs and meat are heat and feed. A heated chicken coop will provide an environment for higher-quality eggs than one that is unheated in the winter in the northern parts of this country. Solar heating is an option which is being incorporated in some of the newer backyard systems. Skimping on your chickens' feed will directly reduce the quality of your eggs and meat. Some of their food can be produced in your household. They love all the vegetable scraps from your kitchen, and grass clippings also make good poultry food. However, this homegrown food can make up only about 30 to 40 percent of your chickens' diet. The rest should be a commercial feed designed for chickens. Commercial feeds have some essential nutrients and minerals that you cannot easily provide yourself. However, if you do give your chickens all your kitchen wastes and the weeds from the garden, you can cut your feed bill considerably.

Determining the cost of raising your own chickens is difficult, because there are so many variables, such as your own skill, how much you can supplement the diet, and the quality of the livestock. **Various reports of backyard chicken operations indicate that after you've had a bit of experience, your eggs will cost you between 50 and 95 cents a dozen, and you will get free meat from the chickens**

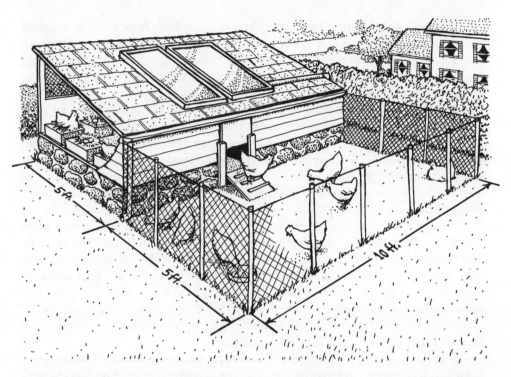

A dozen chickens can be comfortably housed in a 5 by 10-foot coop with 50 square feet of pen space attached. The coop can be attractively designed to fit into its surroundings in an unobtrusive way.

after they have given you eggs for about a year. If you have never tasted a fresh egg, you have not yet really tasted an egg. The difference is similar to eating an orange in New York City and then eating a fresh-picked, tree-ripened orange in Florida.

The capital costs of the coop will depend on your materials and how much of the building you can do for yourself. **Taking care of chickens does not take a great deal of time in total hours, but they do demand some attention every day. Ten to 15 minutes a day, or about two hours a week, will take care of the minimum maintenance chores.** *Chickens in Your Backyard,* by Rick and Gail Luttman (see the Bibliography), is a very helpful reference book for the beginning chicken grower.

Rabbits

I think rabbits are the most underrated member of the small livestock menagerie. Rabbits produce pelts, meat, and superior manure. Rabbit meat tastes similar to chicken and can be used in virtually any recipe that calls for chicken. It is higher in protein and lower in fat and calories than chicken, beef, pork, or veal. A rabbit is quiet, easy to raise, and very productive. I think the biggest disadvantage to raising rabbits, one that has prevented them from being commonly found in backyard food systems, is that they are so cute it is difficult to kill them. People identify the rabbit as a pet and not as a food source.

It takes only a few rabbits to provide plenty of meat and they take up little space. One male (buck) and two females (doe) will produce about 30 pounds of meat every three months. Rabbit meat freezes very well, so that 30 pounds represents about 2 to 3 pounds of rabbit meat per week. Those three rabbits need about 20 square feet of cage. The cages can be tucked away in a corner of your yard as long as they are somewhat protected from the weather. The young rabbits are slaughtered in eight to ten weeks, when they weigh 4 to 4½ pounds.

A female rabbit can produce young for two to three years. **In the first year, if you include your initial investment costs, the rabbit meat will cost you between $1 and $2 a pound. After that, if you can supplement the rabbit's diet of commercial food with greens and even alfalfa from your garden, the meat will cost under $1 a pound.** There are no meats in the market today that are as high in protein and as low in fat and calories and that cost less than $1 a pound. In addition, rabbit manure needs no aging at all. It can be placed directly on the garden, while chicken manure needs aging or it will burn young plants.

It really is a mystery why rabbit is so uncommon in our diet. It tastes good, is high in food value, and can be very inexpensive. Rabbits are easy to raise and the meat is easy to store. I will be surprised if Americans continue to pass up this gastronomic bargain for many more years, just because rabbits are so cute.

Rabbits are underestimated as small livestock. Three rabbits (a male and two females) need only about 20 square feet of cage space and can play an important role in a backyard food production system. If you wish, you can also place an earthworm box underneath the rabbit hutch.

A hive of bees will help pollination in the garden along with producing 50 pounds or more of honey for the gardener.

Bees

Bees are marvelous creatures. They produce honey, pollen, and wax. The honey is an excellent food and can be used to make mead, an alcoholic beverage similar to wine. For those people with serious allergy problems, especially problems related to grasses, trees, and flowers, several teaspoons of raw, unfiltered honey each day can almost eliminate the need for medication after a year or two of this pleasant routine.

While the bees collect their pollen, they are simultaneously pollinating your vegetable and fruit crops. A beehive in your backyard will improve the pollination of your vegetables so much that you will notice increases in yield just because of the bees. As I mentioned before, bees are not all that uncommon in the suburbs. When placed in an unobtrusive site, a beehive can easily go unnoticed.

A single beehive can usually produce far more honey than an average family can use. A hive will produce between 50 and 100 pounds of honey in the first year. As the beekeeper gains more experience, that production can exceed 200 pounds of honey from each mature hive! With honey costing over $1.25 a pound these days, that is not a bad return for very little effort expended on your part. And bees require relatively little attention. There are some maintenance chores every few months, but in some months you do nothing. Maybe 10 to 20 hours takes care of the duties for an entire year.

A new hive, the necessary equipment, and a colony of bees cost about $200. Again a good book and an opportunity to chat with someone who is already raising bees will give you all you need in terms of information to get started. A weekend short course on raising bees can save you many mistakes. The suburbs are particularly productive places to raise bees and produce honey, because of the higher concentration of flower gardens that can be found.

Fish

Raising fish in the backyard is a food production component which is still in its developmental stage. However, the question is not whether we can effectively raise fish, it is when we can begin. The feasibility of producing fish in the backyard in a cost-effective manner has been demonstrated at the Rodale Research Center. After a number of years of experimentation, the researchers developed a method for raising tilapia in a kid's 3 by 12-foot swimming pool in the backyard. The tilapia is an African fish that eats algae and grows very quickly. The experiments showed that you can produce 50 to 100 pounds of fish in such a setup in just five months.

Backyard fish farming is an idea with great potential for the future, and it's practical even now. A small tank like the one shown here can house enough fish to feed a family.

This developmental work has now been expanded to include community garden organizations in Philadelphia and in other cities to demonstrate that the average family can manage this fish production system. One problem that must be overcome is that while the fish are big enough to eat, they are too small to fillet. Consequently, they must be cooked whole. This method of cooking and eating fish is not commonly used in this country and will probably take some time to get used to. But with the cost of fish escalating each year, we will find it easier and easier to change our habits in order to have fresh fish that we have produced ourselves at a much lower cost than the fish found in the market.

Worms

You may not have considered earthworms as part of the family of livestock you might raise on your suburban homestead, but they may be among the most important of all of your animals. **Take a moment to consider the contributions earthworms can make to your backyard food production system:**

1. They fertilize your soil with their castings—a form needed by the plants for direct intake.
2. They aerate the soil, increasing its microbiotic health.
3. They improve the soil's water-holding capacity.
4. They improve the soil's structure and texture.
5. They bring mineral elements up from the subsoil, and make them available for plants.
6. They break up hardpans.
7. They neutralize soil that is too acid or too alkaline.
8. The total impact of the above contributions increases your crop yields.

It should be obvious that you should do what you can to have a maximum population of earthworms in your garden(s). How do you tell how many you have? Short of doing a scientific census, use the rule of thumb that says if you don't have two or three earthworms in each and every shovelful of soil you dig up, you could use some more.

There is mass confusion among gardeners and even in the literature about which species of earthworm we can raise. Let me try to clear up the issue. **There are two species of earthworms that you want to have in your garden in large numbers. They are night crawlers (*Lumbricus terrestris*) and field worms (*Allolobophora caliginosa*).** What you now have in your garden will most likely be one of or both of these worms. These worms are seldom available commercially. The worms that are available commercially will die in your garden! The three most common worms sold commercially are red worms, brandling worms, and African night crawlers. These worms are used for making compost and for fishing bait, but they will not survive in your vegetable garden. (Yes, the night crawlers left over from the fishing trip will die in your garden, because they most likely are the African type and live only in tropical areas.) The reason you can't get your garden variety of earthworm on the commercial market is that they do not reproduce as rapidly, so they are not economically feasible to raise for sale. They are, however, economically feasible for you to raise, because they take very little effort and their return in the long run to your production levels will be significant.

Raising earthworms is not a big deal. You need a box partially filled with the appropriate bedding material into which you introduce your breeding worms,

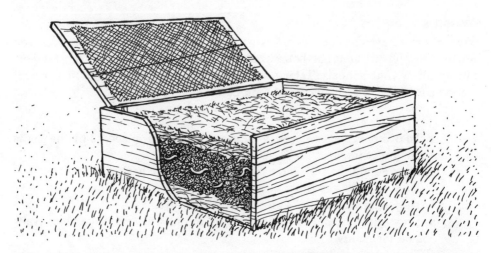

Earthworms can be raised in pits and boxes and later turned loose in the garden to work their magic with the soil. The ideal conditions in your earthworm box will encourage the creatures to reproduce and expand their population. Protect earthworms in pits and boxes from winter cold by "mulching" with a layer of loose straw. Insulate the lids of boxes with burlap.

which you dig out of your own garden. Then you simply add the kitchen waste and a bit more bedding material each week, and let the worms do their thing. Commercial growers use the rule of thumb that a cubic foot of bedding can handle 1,000 worms. Bedding can be a mixture of leaves, compost, and some garden soil. Once set up, your worms will consume your kitchen waste and reproduce more earthworms at no further cost to you. It is really as simple as that. There are several good books available on how to set up your box and how to avoid mistakes like freezing your stock or drowning them (see the Bibliography for one of them—Jerry Minnich's *Earthworm Book*). Actually, worm farming is almost foolproof.

If you are going to raise worms to increase their population in your garden, then you want to make sure you keep those already in the garden as happy and healthy as possible. While we really don't know exactly how long an earthworm lives, if it can avoid the birds, freezing in the winter, and fishermen looking for bait, it can live well over five years. You avoid freezing your worm stock by mulching your garden well during the winter months. This is good practice anyway. If you add lots of compost and mulch to your garden each year, then you are feeding your worm population, which in turn is feeding your vegetable plants.

Birds

Like worms, birds may not have been on your list of small livestock in your backyard food production system. But like worms, the birds make a direct contribution to your total yield. Therefore, if you can increase your bird population, especially those birds most beneficial to your garden, then it might be worth the relatively small effort it takes.

The argument for trying to manage your wild bird population is relatively simple. Birds represent the ultimate natural pesticide and herbicide. A tiny swallow will devour 1,000 leaf hoppers in 12 hours. A Baltimore oriole can eat 17 hairy caterpillars per minute! The diminutive house wren feeds 500 insects to its young in the course of just one afternoon! When you add the thousands of weed seeds that are consumed by other species, the contribution of birds to the maintenance of your garden should be obvious. Yet, on the other side of the coin, birds can eat your smallest seedlings and do a real number on your raspberries and strawberries. But you can take precautions to avoid these problems, an effort paid back many times by the pest management services provided by wild birds throughout the growing season.

Wild birds can be a real benefit to your garden—they eat insect pests and weed seeds. Installing some birdhouses and providing food and water year-round will help attract a permanent bird population to your yard.

The challenge in managing your bird population is to increase the number of desirable bird species as much as possible. The density of any bird species in your neighborhood is directly related to the nesting facilities that are available, the food that is available all year round, and access to water. **A vegetable gardener's wild bird management program will have five components:**

1. Selecting the Species You Want. This requires that you first familiarize yourself with the species of birds in your area. Find a friend who is a birder, and he/she will tell you all you need to know about what is around. Then you must learn which species like to eat seeds and which like to eat insects. Again your birder friends will be very helpful and probably fascinated with your project. As weed-seed eaters, goldfinches, redpolls, chickadees, titmouses, and cardinals are examples of desirable species. For insects, sparrows, juncos, purple finches, chickadees, and cardinals are good. Many birds, as you can see, eat both weed seeds and insects.

2. **Providing Housing.** Most bird species have very specific needs for nesting. Birdhouses must be designed to fit the desired bird's needs, which include the size of the hole, the dimensions of the box and how high you mount it, and in what kind of tree it is placed. This information is easy to obtain in your library and from groups like the Audubon Society and the National Wildlife Federation. By adding many different kinds of birdhouses as well as nesting boxes in your yard and even in your neighbor's yards, you will see an increase in your bird population in just one season.

3. **Supplementing Food Supply.** More and more people in this country are getting pleasure each winter by feeding the birds. Most everyone knows that if they start to feed the birds in the winter, they must not stop until spring or some of the birds who became dependent will die. This is because the density of each species that likes the seeds and suet has increased beyond the area's ability to support them if the backyard bird-feeding stations are closed down. The secret to increasing your bird population year round, then, is to supplement the birds' natural food year round as well. This means that you don't stop feeding in the spring as most people do. At the same time you do not feed as intensively in the spring, summer, and fall as you do in the winter. We put out bird seed about every two weeks and then throw out all our stale bread and fruit peelings so that something goes out for the birds almost every day. Again, various types of food are specific to various species of birds. What you want to do is put out food attractive to desirable species, and avoid putting out food attractive to undesirable species such as pigeons. See the chart titled Feeding the Birds, in the Appendix, for some additional information.

4. **Providing Water.** Birds need water just as we do, and it is often difficult for them to find it each day unless you do something to make sure water is always available in and around your garden. At least two birdbaths or some similar containers should be kept filled with water all year long. In the winter, the water supply is just as important as in the hot summer. You must be sure to break any ice that forms on your birdbath.

5. **Landscaping for the Birds.** A long-range method for supplementing the birds' food supply is to plant trees, shrubs, and bushes that have berries which can provide food to birds in the winter. Again, the library will have books identifying those shrubs and bushes that each species of bird likes as a winter food source. Bushes like bayberry, holly, pyracanthus, and autumn olive make very attractive material for landscaping, while giving food in the winter to desirable bird species you have enlisted into your food production system. If a tree or a bush does not provide food for you, it should provide food for your birds.

By following these five steps, you will have made a major contribution to the reduction of insect and weed pests in your garden, while having the pleasure of sharing your little ecosystem with a variety of beautiful and fascinating creatures. Simply by making sure all your efforts are specific to just the species that you consider desirable, your wild bird management program will be successful.

Selling Extra and Using Barter

A backyard food production system is not usually large enough to consider as a source of income from the sale of excess produce. Some people do have arrangements with a local grocery store to sell any excess fresh vegetables they may grow. This can generate a little cash but is not usually a major source of funds. Those folks with chickens and bees can usually have enough to sell extra eggs and excess honey without too much trouble. While it might be possible to sell some of your excess produce, I would like to make a case for using that excess in bartering rather than in selling.

Bartering has become a more common activity in this country, as the tax system has intruded further into our lives. Even large corporations are bartering millions of dollars' worth of goods with each other. There are bartering clubs popping up all over the country that give people interested in bartering all manner of goods and services access to people with the same interests.

People with a backyard food production system are in an excellent position to take advantage of the bartering phenomenon. They have goods that most other people will enjoy—that is, very fresh and tasty food. Everybody has a skill of some kind, everybody usually wants something or other, and most everybody has something to get rid of. Under those circumstances, it should not be too difficult to find someone with whom to barter your excess produce. Exchange raw food such as cabbages for processed food such as sauerkraut. Your strawberry jam can go in trade for their blueberry jam. You can keep your neighbor supplied with salad greens in return for his trimming your large tree. You can give your neighbor free eggs in return for his caring for your chickens when you are away.

One of the most interesting barter ideas is to plant your garden in cooperation with a neighbor who also has a garden. Everyone has different tastes and plants different kinds of vegetables. If you plant some extra kohlrabi and your neighbor plants an extra bit of okra, you can then share your crops, giving each of you much more variety than you have in your own garden alone. This can also be done with herb gardens. You have five herbs that your neighbor doesn't have, and he/she has four or five that you don't have. Together you each have ten herbs available fresh or later dried. It is a nice arrangement and is nothing more than a barter deal. The various barter arrangements that are possible with a backyard food production system are almost infinite, and besides being profitable to both parties, bartering is lots of fun.

The Economics of the Fifth Stage

Now all the parts of a comprehensive backyard food production system have been introduced. Each of you will pick and choose the components to fit your own interest, time, and resources. What is all this really worth, in dollars? While there is no precise answer, a conservative estimate can be made.

Economics of the Fifth Stage

Item and Use in Food Production System	Initial Capital Investment	Operating Costs and Savings
Garden maintenance Seeds, plants, and natural fertilizers for garden of 800–1,000 sq. ft.	. . .	As in the last stage, the $50–$100 annual costs produce a savings of $900–$1,100.
Livestock and supplies Bees and 1 hive	$150–$300	Bees may cost you $10 a yr. in maintenance. In the first yr. you can make $10–$40 by selling the extra honey from the 30–50 lb. you produce. That figure will double in a yr. or two.
Chickens and coop for 12 chickens	$200 and up	Commercial food and maintenance will cost you $200–$250 a yr. Production levels will net you $50–$100 a yr. over costs. Eggs are produced at a cost of about 85¢ a doz.
Rabbits and a hutch for 2 does and 1 buck	$100	Commercial food and maintenance will cost about $250 a yr. You will get about 130 lb. of meat at about $2 per lb. per year. Your savings accrue more from reduced consumption of more expensive meats like beef.
Fish, tank, and supplies	No good estimate is yet available.	
Bird feeders	$10–$50	

Comments: When the complete system is in place and has been worked for a few years, it is possible to enjoy a savings in the food budget in excess of $2,500! Most people will not do everything described in these five stages, and that is fine. The main point is that significant food self-sufficiency is now possible in a suburban backyard having about a quarter of an acre of space.

Someone who is very interested in developing the maximum possible backyard food production capacity must be willing to spend roughly 10 to 20 hours on the project each week. The garden has the best money return for energy spent, so let's assume we are talking about 1,000 square feet of garden. Along with the berries and fruit trees that are set around other parts of the yard, the garden might produce about $1,500 worth of food. The greenhouse might add about $100, and food storage and food processing efforts yield an additional savings of about $500. If our homesteader also keeps some bees, chickens, and rabbits, then we can add maybe another $200 in savings. That produces a total savings of $2,300! If the annual costs for setting up the garden and maintaining the greenhouse and for managing the small livestock are about $800, then we have almost tripled our cash outlay.

If this hypothetical household had four members, then a conservative estimate of how much of their total food consumed was produced by the setup we just described might be between 50 and 75 percent. This, of course, depends on how much this family eats out and how much meat and other processed products they buy from the store.

Looking Toward the Future

I have tried to make a number of key points in this book. The first one is that a vegetable garden is a very sound financial investment. I have also stressed that producing your own food takes considerable skill and knowledge. This skill and knowledge can only be gained over time. The estimated savings presented in this book will go up over the years for two reasons—inflation and increased ability on the part of the gardener to produce more food in the same space. Finally, I have tried to point out that your success is a direct function of your ability to plan ahead and your skill in managing time effectively. As planning and management skills increase, the time it takes to produce your food decreases.

These major points are not ideas that are static and frozen in concrete. There is constant change going on in our world, even in backyard food production. I would like to conclude this book by looking at three areas of change that we are now experiencing and that will have enormous impact on backyard food production in the coming decade. I want to discuss briefly a new tool for both planning and management—the home computer. Then I'll look at a more advanced planning process for backyard food systems that is still in the design stage. It's called permaculture. Finally, I'll discuss a much broader management approach that ties food production into the other aspects of the suburban life-style. I call this integrated living.

Home Computers and Backyard Food Production

I firmly believe that within the next five years, the home computer will become an integral component of serious backyard food production systems. The computer can solve many problems for the backyard food producer, but two of them stand out as most important: the need for more time and the need for more knowledge. The home computer will contribute to the solution of those two problems. I wrote this book on a personal computer using a word processing program. I expect to have the computer help me manage many of my food production activities in the next few years, as I learn how to develop my own computer programs and as I purchase commercial home computer programs as they become available.

There is already clear evidence that the application of a home computer to the backyard food production system is not far away. In California, fruit growers are now using home computers to manage many of the tasks formerly done by people or previously not even done at all. In one orchard I've read about, the computer automatically monitors the soil conditions throughout the property and then dictates a very accurate fertilizing procedure. The computer monitors weather conditions, including temperature and humidity, so that it can automatically control the drip irrigation system laid out throughout the orchards. This computerized system is now operating effectively, saving the farmer time and giving him much better control of his production system. He is also saving fertilizer and water, which means saving money. Since he uses the same computer that tens of thousands of people are buying for their homes, it is obvious that as soon as the programming can be developed, we backyard food producers can use our own computers to monitor our gardens, berry patches, and fruit trees in the same way.

Another project demonstrating the use of home computers is run by Control Data Corporation (CDC) in a project called Rural Venture. CDC has developed home computer programs for assisting small farmers with 100 to 200-acre farms in managing an integrated multi-crop farm. The farmer uses the computer not only as an information source, but also as a management tool telling him when to plant, when to water, when to fertilize, and even when to slaughter his geese for market. It also provides training programs for learning new methods and techniques. Again, it is not difficult to see that these same programs, scaled down of course, could be just as helpful to someone managing a comprehensive backyard food production system in the suburbs.

When we envison tying the home computer to the growing cable television systems in this country, all manner of supportive services can be anticipated for the backyard producer. The cable television can offer 24-hour weather information, while the computer will have access to all kinds of data services. Cable television and the home computer can be coupled to be used for comparative shopping, offering advertisements of the current food prices in the stores and farmers' markets. There will be agricultural reports updated daily which will warn of infestations of various garden pests as they show themselves throughout the season.

The computer can be used to manage succession planting in the garden and in the greenhouse. You can put all your many schedules into a single program so that each morning, or each week, the computer can tell you when it is time to turn the compost, when to clean the fish tank filter, when to water or feed the corn,

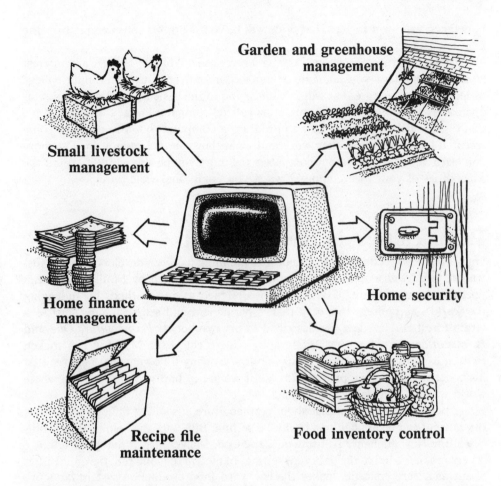

Garden and greenhouse management

Small livestock management

Home finance management

Home security

Recipe file maintenance

Food inventory control

Home computer applications for the suburban homestead. The home computer will become an increasingly important tool in coming years.

and when the pickles are ready to be put up in jars. Your whole food storage inventory can be easily managed on the computer, and your ever-expanding recipe file can be placed on one or two discs the size of a 45-RPM record. You can keep your homestead records on the computer, and it will be able to manage your finances. In short, it will become an essential tool to the busy suburbanite who is trying to grow as much of his own food as possible and still have time for other things in his life, such as having some fun and making a living.

I'm not suggesting that everybody run out and buy a home computer. They represent a major investment. A decent one that will serve the needs of a backyard food production system will cost from $2,000 to $5,000 (in 1982), depending on how fancy you want to get. That price will be coming down considerably over the next few years.

In the meantime, however, I strongly recommend that if you have any interest at all in computers, you take one or more courses from your community college or local computer store that will introduce you to the basic principles of computer operations and functions. These are often called "computer literacy" courses. They don't necessarily teach you how to program a computer, but you do learn some essential facts about how they work and what they can and cannot do. The more you learn ahead of time about computers the more you be able to fully exploit the capabilities of your own computer when you finally make the purchase.

Permaculture in the Backyard

One of the newest concepts in agricultural planning has been developed by an Australian, Bill Mollison. The term *permaculture* was coined by Mollison to mean "permanent agriculture." His concept is designed to find methods for managing the world's agriculture in a way that is permanent and self-sustaining, just as a virgin forest is. His ideas are described in his two books, *Permaculture One* and *Permaculture Two* (see the Bibliography). In recent years, Mollison has spoken to groups all over the world and has built a growing following that believes that his concept must be adopted worldwide if we are to find ways to feed the whole world with its increasing population.

Upon reading the material about permaculture, it's at first difficult to see how the concept can be applied to a backyard setting. But, with the help of John Quinney at the New Alchemy Institute on Cape Cod, I have learned that permaculture is very much related to the backyard setting. In fact, in the long run, the application of permaculture concepts makes the backyard food production system far more productive with much less investment of energy and time. Backyard permaculture is far more complex than the popular concept called edible landscaping. It is a model that can be integrated into your backyard food production system, giving you a new way of thinking about your long-range plan. Just as I discussed in chapter 2, you look at your total three-dimensional space incorporated by your suburban property. You consider the entire ecosystem of your whole property when you begin to think in terms of permaculture. You consider the species of your trees and shrubs in terms of their food production capability and/or their relationship to birds, insects, bees, and/or energy conservation. You plan the location of fruit trees, asparagus patches, and other permanent crops, keeping in mind how your property will look in ten years as everything matures. A permaculture plan takes years to understand and develop. It requires a very long view of a food production system but provides many short-range benefits as well. A backyard permaculture plan involves thinking through the interrelationships of at least six basic principles:

(1) permaculture is self-sustaining; (2) it is diverse; (3) it is intensive; (4) it takes less maintenance; (5) it serves as a microclimate control; and (6) it's beautiful.

Permaculture Is Self-Sustaining

A backyard permaculture system combines perennial food-producing plants with the more traditional annual vegetables into a food system that is low on energy use and that over the years takes less and less time to manage. Nut trees, fruit trees, and berries (discussed in chapter 5) join the asparagus, rhubarb, and Jerusalem artichokes as examples of permanent food producers. These plants bring up minerals from the deep soil and make them available through the leaves that are collected each autumn ultimately to become compost. In turn, these plants need nitrogen which comes from annual nitrogen-fixing plants such as peas, beans, and alfalfa. The peas and beans feed you, while the alfalfa feeds your rabbits or chickens. Their manure in turn fertilizes both the perennial and annual plants in your system. The birds live and multiply in the trees, and the bees pollinate the fruit trees, berry bushes, and vegetable flowers, creating higher yields. Your property can be designed over the years to take advantage of each interrelationship among the various components of your food production system, so that you have to use less and less outside energy, and you have to take less and less time to manage the system. It moves from being self-sustaining in many ways to being restorative, in that, by virtue of its design and your practices, the land becomes more fertile and more productive with each year of use.

Permaculture Is Diverse

By planning your backyard permaculture system to become as diverse as possible, you increase the number of possible positive interrelationships among the various components. If you were to make a list of all the perennial plants that could be grown in your area that also produce food, you'd be amazed to find that they number in the hundreds!

A good example of a perennial food plant that is available but not yet common is bamboo. There are over 80 species of bamboo available in this country, and many of them will grow well in northern areas. Bamboo is handled much like asparagus in that some of the shoots are harvested for food while they are young, and others are left to grow out so the plant will be sustained from year to year. Bamboo out-produces asparagus and, as a side benefit, produces attractive garden stakes that are six to eight feet long. Bamboo is attractive and easy to grow; it also grows well in the shade that is a problem in many backyards. All things considered, bamboo is an excellent candidate for any backyard food production system, and it fits naturally into the diversity of a permaculture plan.

The greater the diversity of your backyard system, the more positive links are made between components in the system. A great variety of bushes, shrubs, plants,

and grasses create an environment for the same extensive variety of insect populations. By encouraging a healthy mix of predators and prey among the insects in
your system, you will have less chance of a serious infestation of any one species
of harmful insect pest. As discussed in chapter 5, interplanting and companion
planting often repel or confuse insects, a function of the diversity of the planting
scheme.

Permaculture Is Intensive

A permaculture plan looks at every cubic foot on and around your property to
determine its production potential. We talk about production per square foot in
our vegetable garden. In permaculture we can talk about production per cubic foot.
A border of your backyard can have a row of nut trees and fruit trees making up
the fence line. Under the trees can be lines of raspberries or blackberries. Under
or beside the berries can be herbs or annual vegetables or flowers. Here we have
at least a three-story production system. The trees produce nuts and leaves and
reduce air pollution; they cool with their shade, reduce the impact of wind, protect
your bird population, pull minerals from the soil, and add beauty to your property.
The berries offer food for you and/or the birds, offer cover for friendly insects and
birds, and serve as a fence to keep out unwanted guests. The flowers offer pollen
to the bees for honey, offer a different cover for friendly insects, and give beauty
to the property. All this on one strip of your property. That is intensive use of the
land.

Permaculture Takes Less Maintenance

One of the main points of this book is that planning your food production system
now will save you time and work in the long run. Permaculture manifests that same
benefit. In chapter 2 I introduced the idea of raised beds. I said that they took a
bit of time to establish, but then after a few years of maintenance, you could virtually stop all digging in your garden each spring forever. In chapter 3 I talked about
a backyard pest management system that was based on the principle of prevention
and planning ahead so that you would not have to spend much time spraying for
insects. The diverse and carefully planned permaculture design will have contributed to a balanced insect population that almost takes care of itself.

Permaculture Serves as a Microclimate Control

As I mentioned, if you plan your permaculture system properly, you will not only
be producing food but you will also be influencing the microclimate of your property. A proper windbreak on the north will directly reduce your energy costs for keeping your house warm in the winter. Food-producing bushes and shrubs up close
to the house create a natural insulation for the house that also reduces energy costs.
Proper layout of trees and bushes in relation to the garden will reduce frost damage

to your vegetables and fruits. Trees and shrubs around the house cool it in the summer, again reducing or eliminating any need for air conditioning.

Permaculture Is Beautiful

While a backyard permaculture food system can be designed to produce a large percentage of your family's food needs, as well as reduce your energy consumption, it can also be quite beautiful. The aesthetics of your property can be the most challenging component of any permaculture plan. It can also be the most satisfying. You must be able to visualize how a tree is going to look ten years from now when it reaches its full 40-foot height. Right now it is a little whip of a thing. You must look for a variety of plants, bushes, and trees that give you different textures and colors in a balanced and pleasing fashion. These decisions, the aesthetic ones, take years to make, and the process of making those decisions is truly enjoyable in its own right.

These six principles of backyard permaculture give you a way to think about your plans for your backyard food production system. They offer a perspective that takes many years to understand fully and to incorporate into your suburban or urban homestead. Developing the various components of a food production system takes time, knowledge, and skill. Understanding and using the benefits of the interrelationships among all those components takes imagination and a philosophy of life that appreciates and supports nature's way of doing things as much as possible. We have much to learn about permaculture and how it relates to the backyard, but I believe that even now in its embryonic stage it is an extremely helpful tool for teaching us how to see and understand how nature works for us and against us in our own little backyard ecosystem.

Integrated Living in the Suburbs

In the final analysis, producing and processing your own food are only two components of homestead life, whether you live in the country, the city, or the suburbs. Other components can include recycling resources, conserving energy, and even producing energy. A truly challenging life-style is finding ways to integrate all five of these components into your day-to-day life in ways which give you the benefits of saving money while giving you the satisfaction of what you feel is a good life.

Recycling has been discussed in a number of sections of this book. We recycle garbage into our compost pile or into the chickens' food tray. We recycle leaves and grass into the compost or onto the garden for mulch. There are many other areas of home life where recycling can be introduced to the benefit of our pocketbooks as well as to the benefit of a world with diminishing resources. Recycling bottles, cans, and paper are obvious examples. Ashes from the wood stove go into the garden or compost. Scrap lumber from a trash pile becomes flats in the greenhouse. Recycling requires an attitude that despises throwing anything away. There is almost always another use for most of the things we throw into our trash in this country.

Conserving energy has now become a major preoccupation in the United States. Unfortunately, it took an energy crisis to get us interested, but I think most of us have been sensitized to the need to conserve energy. In our backyard food production system, we save energy by avoiding commercial fertilizers and pesticides that require great amounts of energy to make and to deliver. We save energy by growing much of our food so that it does not have to be trucked 3,000 miles from the farm to our tables.

There are many other areas in our lives where energy can be saved. Insulating and winterizing our homes can save enormous amounts of fossil fuel. Attic fans reduce the need for air conditioners. Smaller cars and altered driving habits are another area where great savings have occurred in recent years. Again, just as with recycling, energy conservation must become an integral part of our day-to-day thinking and behavior.

Energy production within the individual home is still a fairly unusual activity in this country. However, it is predictable that in the next decade, more and more of us will be producing at least some of our own energy right within our own homes. Wood stoves are common examples in the northern parts of this nation. Solar hot water heaters are becoming more common. People are designing their new homes or retrofitting their existing homes to make use of some form of solar heating device to supplement their home heating needs. In a few years, we will see people using photovoltaic cells on their roofs to transform solar energy directly into electric energy. Windmills and hydroelectric generators are also coming back in some areas where the climate and the geography are appropriate.

Some of this energy production is directly related to the food production and processing system. The wood stove is used to cook our food. The solar greenhouse can sometimes produce excess heat to supplement the home's heating system. The windmill can pump water from a well.

When you put all these activities together—food production and processing, resources recycling, and energy conservation and production—you have created a life-style which is much less destructive to our world's environment, which generally costs less to manage, and which can be truly self-fulfilling and satisfying. You don't have to try to escape complexity in life to find enjoyment and peace. If we choose to live in the suburbs of the United States, as many of us do, then we've already bought into considerable complexity and rapid change in our lives. By moving toward this integrated life-style which I have described, I believe you can have a life that is challenging, exciting, and truly enjoyable without having the stress and the pressure that seem to accompany suburban living for so many Americans.

By beginning this process of moving toward a more integrated and self-reliant way of life with a backyard food production system, almost immediate benefits can be experienced with relatively little initial investment either in time or in money. There's something about growing some of your own vegetables that gives you a pleasure that borders on the spiritual. As you proceed toward a more comprehensive food production effort, the accompanying sense of satisfaction and feeling of self-worth are benefits difficult to describe but so valuable when experienced.

As my final observation, I wish to report that as I have moved each year toward a more self-reliant and integrated suburban life-style, I have found myself becoming less depressed about the future of the world we live in. In fact, I've overcome much of my cynicism and depression about the future and have become a bonafide optimist! I can't prove scientifically that my life-style change on my quarter of an acre is the direct cause of the change in my world view, but I am certain the two are intimately related. I'm excited about the future of this world. I believe it will be ultimately a good one. I'm also excited about what is going to happen in my own backyard in the next few years. I hope you can join me in that excitement as you take another look at your own backyard—it is a potentially very productive little piece of the earth.

Gardening Data for Beginners and Experts Alike

The charts and tables on the following pages contain data culled from many books, magazines, and newspapers, and from personal experience. The information should be used as a guide, rather than as scientifically based figures that allow no variation. It is said often that gardening is as much an art as it is a science. The variables of soil, climate, weather, and your own skills make it impossible to give you precise information that will always be correct for your needs. Many of the charts use the words *approximate* or *average* and some charts give ranges (such as 50–95 days) instead of finite figures. Nevertheless, the charts can serve as useful guides as you embark on your trip into the world of backyard food production. You can use these charts for:

- Planning the garden and determining how much seed to buy
- Planting the garden—large or small
- Tending the growing garden
- Protecting the garden from bugs and diseases
- Harvesting and storing the garden's bounty.

Rather than arranging the charts alphabetically, I've grouped them according to the season in which you'll be most likely to use them, beginning with your garden planning in late winter. To locate a particular chart, just turn to the table of contents to find out what page it's on.

APPENDIX

Conversion Table: From Garden to Canning Jar or Freezer

This chart will help you figure how many quarts of canned and frozen vegetables and fruits you can expect to get from a certain amount of fresh produce. In addition, it will help you figure how much produce your garden should yield in order to satisfy your family's food needs. First, you must figure out how many quarts of canned and frozen produce your family will eat in a year's time. Then, figure out how many pounds of each particular vegetable or fruit you should harvest from your garden in order to have enough to can or freeze. Refer to the following chart, How Much to Plant, to see how many feet of row or area of bed you'll need to plant in order to harvest the desired amount of vegetables and fruits.

Crop	Volume vs. Weight	Number of Quarts Canned from One Bushel	Weight in One Quart Canning Jar	Number of Quarts Frozen from One Bushel
Apples	1 bu. = 48 lb. 1 bu. = 120 apples	16–20 qt.	Not available	16–19 qt.
Asparagus	1 bu. = 40 lb.	9–16 qt.	2–3 lb.	14–18 qt.
Beans				
Snap	1 bu. = 30 lb.	12–20 qt.	1½–2 lb.	15–22 qt.
Lima	1 bu. = 32 lb.	6–10 qt.	3–5 lb.	6–8 qt.
Beets				
(without tops)	1 bu. = 52 lb.	16–25 qt.	2–3 lb.	17–22 qt.
Broccoli	1 crate = 25 lb.	10–12 qt.	2–3 lb.	12 qt.
Brussels sprouts	4-qt. box = 6 lb.	1–1½ qt.	2 lb.	3 qt.
Cabbage	Not available	2–3 lb. = 1 qt.	. . .	2–3 lb. = 1 qt
Carrots				
(without tops)	1 bu. = 50 lb.	16–25 qt.	2–3 lb.	16–20 qt.
Cauliflower	1 bu. = 12 lb. 2 med. heads = 4 lb.	4–6 qt.	2–3 lb.	2 qt.
Corn	1 bu. = 35 lb. (in husks)	6–12 qt. (kernels)	4–5 lb. (kernels)	7–9 qt.
Cucumbers	Not available	*	. . .	†
Eggplant	Not available	*	. . .	†
Kale	1 bu. = 18 lb.	6–9 qt.	2–3 lb.	6–9 qt.
Mustard	1 bu. = 12 lb.	4–6 qt.	2–3 lb.	6–9 qt.

*Not recommended for canning.
†Not recommended for freezing.

Conversion Table: From Garden to Canning Jar or Freezer—*Continued*

Crop	Volume vs. Weight	Number of Quarts Canned from One Brushel	Weight in One Quart Canning Jar	Number of Quarts Frozen from One Bushel
Onions	1 bu. = 50 lb.	18 qt.	Not available	4–6 whole onions make 1 qt.
Parsnips	1 bu. = 50 lb.	*	. . .	†
Peaches	1 bu. = 48 lb.	16–24 qt.	Not available	19 qt.
Pears	1 bu. = 50 lb. 1 bu. = 125 pears	17–25 qt.	Not available	†
Peas (garden)	1 bu. = 30 lb.	12–15 qt.	2–3 lb.	6–8 qt.
Peppers	1 bu. = 25 lb.	12 qt.	Not available	18 qt.
Potatoes	1 bu. = 50 lb. 1 bu. = 150 potatoes	20 qt.	3–4 lb.	. . .
Pumpkins	1 bu. = 40 lb.	15 qt.	1½–3 lb.	30 qt.
Spinach	1 bu. = 18 lb.	6–9 qt.	2–3 lb.	9–12 qt.
Squash				
Summer	1 bu. = 40 lb.	16–20 qt.	2–4 lb.	16–20 qt.
Winter	1 bu. = 11 lb.	16–20 qt.	1½–3 lb.	4 qt.
Strawberries	16 qt. = 25 lb.	*	. . .	16 qt.
Sweet potatoes	1 bu. = 50 lb.	18–22 qt.	2–3 lb.	37 qt.
Swiss chard	1 bu. = 12 lb.	4–6 qt.	2–3 lb.	4–6 qt.
Tomatoes (whole)	1 bu. = 53 lb.	15–21 qt.	2–4 lb.	32–42 qt.

How Much to Plant

This chart will give you a rough idea of how much area to plant in order to harvest the amount you need to feed your family throughout the year. Amounts given are total pounds harvested over the course of a growing season unless otherwise indicated.

Crop	Approximate Yield from 24-Sq.-Ft. Bed (3 by 8 ft.)	Approximate Yield from 25-Ft. Row
Asparagus	15–20	7–12
Beans		
Snap	20–30	20–30
Lima	6–8	6–8
Soybeans	Not available	12–15
Beets	30–40	25–35
Broccoli	15–25	15–25
Brussels sprouts	18–25	12–20
Cabbage	24–50	30–50
Carrots	25–40	20–25
Cauliflower	11–25	12–16
Celery	20–40	12–20
Chinese cabbage	20–30	15–25
Corn	12–20	12–20
Cucumbers	40–70	25–40
Eggplant	40–80	30–70
Kale	15–30	5–12
Kohlrabi	20–40	15–20
Lettuce		
Head	25–30	12–25
Leaf	25–30	12
Muskmelons	15–20 fruits	12–15
Mustard	25–30	10–20

How Much to Plant—*Continued*

Crop	Approximate Yield from 24-Sq.-Ft. Bed (3 by 8 ft.)	Approximate Yield from 25-Ft. Row
Onions		
Bulb	25–50	15–20
Garlic	13–25	10–15
Leeks	80–100 plants	13–25
Shallots	60–80 plants	10
Parsley	Not available	1–25
Parsnips	180 roots	25
Peas, garden	5–15	4–10
Peppers		
Hot	120 fruits	Not available
Sweet	75 fruits	12–15
Potatoes		
Sweet	Not available	30–40
White	Not available	30–50
Pumpkins	Not available	30–40
Radishes	Not available	8–12
Rhubarb	Not available	15–25
Rutabagas	Not available	25
Salsify	Not available	20–25
Spinach	Not available	10–15
Squash		
Summer	Not available	20–40
Winter	Not available	30–40
Strawberries	Not available	5–10
Sunflowers	Not available	5–10
Swiss chard	Not available	15–25
Tomatoes	Not available	30–50
Turnips	Not available	25
Watermelon	Not available	20–50

Important Facts about Seeds

Whenever you have leftover seeds, store them carefully so you can use them in next season's garden. It is important to keep seeds cool and dry. Place seed packets in a container with a secure lid such as a coffee can with plastic lid or a screw-top jar. Add a bundle of powdered milk to the container to absorb any moisture. Spread 2 tablespoons of powdered milk on four layers of facial tissue, roll into a bundle, and secure with a rubber band. Add a fresh bundle every few months to make sure the seeds stay as dry as possible. Store container in the refrigerator.

Crop	Approximate Life Span in Storage (in yrs.)	How Many Feet of Row Will One Packet Plant?
Asparagus	3	One packet produces 60 roots; need 15 to 20 roots to plant 25-ft. row.
Beans		
Snap (bush)	3	2 oz. packet contains 130 to 150 seeds, enough to sow 25-ft. row.
Snap (pole)	3	2 oz. packet contains 100 seeds, enough to sow 16 poles or 25-ft. row.
Lima (bush)	3	2 oz. packet contains 115 to 130 of small-seeded variety, 45 to 50 of large-seeded variety; large-seeded packet will sow 15-ft. row, small-seeded packet will sow longer row.
Lima (pole)	3	One packet will plant 10 poles or 10-ft. row.
Fava	2	2 oz. packet contains 35 to 40 seeds, enough to plant a 20-ft. row.
Kidney	2	2½ oz. packet contains 120 to 220 seeds, enough to sow 15-ft. row.
Mung	2	Not available
Soybean	2	2 oz. packet contains 200 to 400 seeds; depending on variety, enough to plant 33 to 66-ft. row.
Beets	4–6	½ oz. packet contains 600 seeds, enough to sow 50-ft. row.
Broccoli	4–5	1½ g. packet contains 375 seeds, enough to sow 30-ft. row; 1 oz. packet produces 2,500 to 3,500 plants.
Brussels sprouts	4–5	1 g. packet contains 250 seeds, enough to plant 25-ft. row; 1 oz. packet produces 2,500 to 3,000 plants.
Cabbage	4–5	see Brussels sprouts
Carrots	3–5	2 g. packet contains 960 seeds, enough to sow 20-ft. row; 1 oz. packet contains 6,000 to 9,000 seeds, enough to sow 250 to 300-ft. row.

Important Facts about Seeds—*Continued*

Crop	Approximate Life Span in Storage (in yrs.)	How Many Feet of Row Will One Packet Plant?
Cauliflower	4–5	0.75 g. packet contains 225 seeds, enough to transplant 20-ft. row.
Celery	3–5	0.5 g. packet contains 900 seeds.
Chinese cabbage	3–5	1 g. packet contains 500 seeds, enough to plant 30-ft. row.
Corn	1–2	2 oz. packet contains 200 seeds, enough to plant 50 to 100-ft. row.
Cress, garden	5	¼ oz. packet contains 250 to 300 seeds, enough to plant 25-ft. row.
Cucumbers	5	2.5 g. packet contains 83 seeds, enough to plant 12-ft. row.
Eggplant	4–5	0.25 g. packet contains 50 seeds, enough to transplant 100-ft. row.
Garlic	1	1 lb. of sets plants 20-ft. row.
Kale	4–5	2 g. packet contains 500 seeds, enough to sow 45 to 50-ft. row.
Kohlrabi	3–5	2 g. packet contains 400 seeds, enough to sow 40 to 60-ft. row.
Leeks	2–3	2 g. packet contains 750 seeds, enough to transplant 100-ft. row.
Lettuce		
Bibb	5–6	1 g. packet contains 670 seeds, enough to sow 30-ft. row.
Leaf	5–6	see Bibb lettuce
Romaine	5–6	see Bibb lettuce
Muskmelons	5	4 g. packet contains 140 seeds, enough to transplant 30-ft. row or 12 hills.
Mustard	4	1 g. packet contains 500 seeds, enough to plant 30-ft. row.
Onions		
Plants	. . .	75 plants will cover 18-ft. row.
Seeds	1–2	5 g. packet contains 1,700 seeds, enough to sow 50-ft. row.
Sets	Overwinter in cool, dry location	1 lb. will plant 50-ft. row.
Parsley	1–2	1.2 g. packet contains 600 seeds, enough to plant 20-ft. row.
Parsnips	1	4 g. packet contains 1,400 seeds, enough to sow 50-ft. row.

[*Continued on next page*]

Important Facts about Seeds—*Continued*

Crop	Approximate Life Span in Storage (in yrs.)	How Many Feet of Row Will One Packet Plant?
Peas		
Edible-podded	3	4 oz. packet contains 500 seeds, enough to sow 25-ft. row.
Garden	3	see Edible-podded peas
Snap	3	see Edible-podded peas
Peppers		
Hot	4	0.5 g. packet contains 50 seeds, enough to transplant 30-ft. row.
Sweet	2–4	see Hot peppers
Pumpkins	4	Packet containing 30 seeds will sow 10 to 15-ft. row.
Radishes	4–5	5 g. packet contains 350 seeds, enough to sow 25 to 30-ft. row.
Rhubarb	1	8 roots are enough to plant 25-ft. row.
Rutabagas	4	2 g. packet contains 570 seeds, enough to plant 50-ft. row.
Salsify	1–2	¼ oz. packet will sow 25-ft. row.
Spinach	3–5	5 g. packet contains enough seed to plant 20-ft. row.
Squash		
Summer	4–5	4 g. packet contains 35 seeds, enough to plant 10 to 15-ft. row.
Winter	4–5	Packet containing 30 seeds will plant 10 to 15-ft. row.
Sunflowers	2	Packet containing 50 to 75 seeds will plant 25-ft. row.
Swiss chard	4	5 g. packet will plant 30-ft. row.
Tomatoes	4	0.5 g. packet contains 150 seeds; 8 to 10 plants needed to transplant 25-ft. row.
Turnips	4–5	2.5 g. packet contains 938 seeds, enough to plant 20-ft. row.
Watermelon	4–5	2.5 g. packet contains 50 seeds, enough to transplant 15-ft. row.

Seed and Plant Sources

W. F. Allen Co.
Box 1577
Salisbury, MD 21801

Bishop Seeds Ltd.
Box 338
Belleville, ON K8N 5A5
Canada

Brittingham Plant Farms
Box 2538
Ocean City Rd.
Salisbury, MD 21801

Burgess Seed and Plant Co.
905 Four Seasons Rd.
Bloomington, IL 61701

Di Giorgi Company, Inc.
Box 413
Council Bluffs, IA 51502

Farmer Seed and
Nursery Co.
818 Northwest 4th St.
Faribault, MN 55021

Grace's Garden
10 Bay St.
Westport, CT 06880

Gurney Seed and
Nursery Co.
Yankton, SD 57079

Joseph Harris Company, Inc.
Moreton Farm
Rochester, NY 14624

Herbst Brothers
Seedsmen, Inc.
1000 N. Main St.
Brewster, NY 10509

Johnny's Selected Seeds
Albion, ME 04910

J. W. Jung Seed Co.
Randolph, WI 53956

Kitazawa Seed Co.
356 W. Taylor St.
San Jose, CA 95110

J. Labonte et Fils
250 Chemin Chembly
Longeuil, PQ J4H 3L8
Canada

Le Jardin du Gourmet
Box 248
West Danville, VT 05873

Earl May Seed and
Nursery Co.
100 N. Elm St.
Shenandoah, IA 51603

J. E. Miller Nurseries, Inc.
5060 W. Lake Rd.
Canandaigua, NY 14424

L. L. Olds Seed Co.
Box 7790
Madison, WI 53707

George W. Park Seed Co.
Box 31
Greenwood, SC 29647

Redwood City Seed Co.
Box 361
Redwood City, CA 94064

Seedway, Inc.
Box 250
Hall, NY 14463

R. H. Shumway
Seedsman, Inc.
628 Cedar St.
Box 777
Rockford, IL 61101

Stark Brothers
Louisiana, MO 63353

Stokes Seeds, Inc.
Box 548
737 Main St.
Buffalo, NY 14240

Thompson and Morgan, Inc.
Box 100
Farmingdale, NY 07727

Tsang and Ma International
1556 Laurel St.
San Carlos, CA 94070

Otis S. Twilley
Box 65
Trevose, PA 19047

Vermont Bean Seed Co.
Garden Lane
Bomoseen, VT 05732

Wilhite Seed Co.
Poolville, TX 76076

Seed-Starting Tips (to use indoors or in the greenhouse)

Crop	Germination Temperature*	Growing Temperature*	Weeks to Transplant Size†	Provide Individual Container‡	Transplant at Least Once§	Growing Tips
Beans, lima	Room	Room	3–5	X	. . .	Any root disturbance will hinder growth; handle seedlings as little as possible; when thinning, cut rather than pull seedlings.
Broccoli	Room	Cool	4–6	. . .	X	Start fall transplants 18 wks. before first expected frost.
Brussels sprouts	Room	Cool	4–6	. . .	X	Short-season gardeners should always use transplants.
Cabbage	Room	Cool	6–8	. . .	X	Early varieties usually started indoors; midseason and late varieties are sown right in garden.
Cauliflower	Room	Cool	4–6	. . .	X	Only use seedlings with tiny bud in the center; no bud means no head will form.
Celery	Cool	Cool	10–12	X	X	Soak seed overnight before sowing.
Chinese cabbage	Room	Cool	4–6	. . .	. . .	Fall crops are less likely to bolt to seed.
Cucumbers	Warm	Room	3–4	X	. . .	Roots are very sensitive to any disturbance.
Eggplant	Warm	Warm	6–8	X	X	Make sure seedlings are never chilled.
Kale	Room	Cool	4–6	. . .	X	Seedlings are very hardy and can be set out even before the last expected frost.

*Cool: 55–65°F. Room: 65–75°F. Warm: 75–80°F.

†Figure the date for starting seeds indoors by simply subtracting the number of weeks given in this column from the date you plan to put the plants outside in the garden.

‡Use biodegradable containers such as peat pots or paper cartons that can be planted directly into the garden; tear sides a bit to make it easy for roots to grow out.

§Certain vegetables should be transplanted at least once prior to the final move into the garden. Each transplanting stimulates root growth, making a stronger plant.

Seed-Starting Tips—*Continued*

Crop	Germination Temperature*	Growing Temperature*	Weeks to Transplant Size†	Provide Individual Container‡	Transplant at Least Once§	Growing Tips
Kohlrabi	Room	Cool	4–6	. . .	X	Long-season gardeners should start a second group of transplants for succession planting.
Leeks	Room	Cool	10–12	. . .	X	Best transplants are at least 4 in. tall.
Lettuce	Room	Cool	3–5	. . .	X	Start fall transplants about 8 wks. before first expected frost.
Muskmelons	Warm	Room	3–4	X	. . .	Growth is slowed by any disturbance to roots while transplanting.
Onions	Room	Cool	8–12	. . .	X	Keep seedling tops trimmed to ½ to 1 in. until a week before planting outdoors.
Parsley	Room	Cool	8–10	. . .	X	Soak seeds overnight in warm water before planting.
Peppers	Warm	Warm	6–8	. . .	X	The warmer the germination temperature, the quicker the seeds will sprout.
Squash	Warm	Room	4–6	X	. . .	Be careful not to disturb roots when planting in the garden.
Sweet potatoes	Warm	Warm	6–8	X	. . .	Detach sprouts from potato when 4 to 8 in. tall with 4 to 5 leaves and roots; plant in individual pot.
Tomatoes	Warm	Cool	6–8	. . .	X	Too much warmth and too little light will result in straggly seedlings.
Watermelon	Warm	Room	3–5	X	. . .	Be careful not to disturb roots when planting in the garden.

Planting Guide

All distances given are in inches unless otherwise indicated.

Crop	Planting Depth	Intensive Planting Distance for Beds	Distance between Plants in Rows	Distance between Rows
Asparagus	6–8 (roots)	12–18	12–18	24–36
Beans				
Snap (bush)	1–2 (deeper in hotter, drier weather)	4	3–6	15–18
Snap (pole)	1–1½	6	4–6	30
Lima (bush)	1½–2	4–6	3–6	24–30
Lima (pole)	1½–2	6–8	8–10	30–36
Fava	2½	8	3–4	18–24
Kidney	1–2	4	2–3	18–30
Mung	1–2	4	2–3	18–30
Soybeans	1	10	3–4	24
Beets	1½–2	6	2–6	12–18
Broccoli	¼–½	12–14	14–24	24–30
Brussels sprouts	½	16–18	12–18	24–30
Cabbage	½	12–16	12–20	24–30
Carrots	¼	3	1–2	14–24
Cauliflower	¼	12–15	18	30–36
Celery	½	6–8	6	12–24
Chinese cabbage	½	10	10–12	18–24
Corn	2	12–18	10–14	30–36
Cress, garden	¼	3	2–3	12–16
Cucumbers	1	12 (when trellised)	12	48–72
Eggplant	¼–½	18–24	18	36
Garlic	1	2–3	2–4	12–18
Horseradish	Set top of root cutting 3 in. below surface.	12–15	10–18	12
Kale	½	15–18	8–12	18–24
Kohlrabi	½	4–5	3–4	18–24
Leeks	½–1	6	2–4	12–18
Lettuce				
Head	¼–½	10–12	12–14	14
Leaf	¼–½	6–8	4–6	12–18

Planting Guide—*Continued*

Crop	Planting Depth	Intensive Planting Distance for Beds	Distance between Plants in Rows	Distance between Rows
Lettuce–*continued*				
Romaine	¼–½	10	12–14	14
Muskmelons	½–1	24 (when trellised)	48–72	48–72
Mustard	½	6–9	6–9	12
Onions				
Seeds	½	2–3	2	10–12
Sets	Plant so that tip of bulb is exposed.	3	3–4	14–16
Parsley	¼	4	3–6	12–15
Parsnips	½	3	4–6	16–24
Peas				
Edible-podded	2	3–4	2–3	18–30
Garden	2	3–4	2–3	18–30
Snap	2	3–4	2–3	18–30
Peppers	¼	12–15	18–24	24–36
Potatoes	4	12–18	12–15	24–36
Pumpkins	1	24–30	Hills 4–6 ft. apart	. . .
Radishes	½	1	1–2	6–12
Rhubarb	2–3	24	3 ft.	4 ft.
Rutabagas	¼	6–9	8–12	18
Salsify	½	6	4	18
Shallots	1	2–3	2–6	12–18
Spinach	½	6	6	12–14
Squash				
Summer	1	12–18	Hills 6–8 ft. apart	. . .
Winter	1	24–30	Hills 8–12 ft. apart	. . .
Strawberries	. . .	24	24–36	24
Sunflowers	1	24	16–24	36–48
Sweet potatoes	4–5	12	12	36–40
Swiss chard	½–1	9	9	18
Tomatoes	½	18–24	18–36	36–60
Turnips	½	6	4–6	15–18
Watermelon	½	18–24	Hills 6–8 ft. apart	. . .

APPENDIX

Interplanting Guide

Certain plants make especially good neighbors in the garden when paired up and planted on virtually the same space. This closeness increases the productivity of your garden, and when the pairing is done correctly, in no way hinders the growth of the interplanted crops. Always interplant with an eye toward avoiding competition; good interplanting partners never compete with each other for light, nutrients, water, or growing room underground and aboveground. This chart gives you some successful pairings; for each crop listed, you'll find an assortment of others that are compatible interplanting partners.

Crop	Shade Tolerance	Plants with Compatible Shade/Light Needs	Plants with Compatible Root Systems	Plants with Compatible Aboveground Growth
Beans				
Snap (bush)	Poor	Celery, lettuce, spinach	Carrots, celery, corn, cucumbers, onions, radishes, squash (summer)	Celery, corn, melons, radishes, squash (summer or winter), tomatoes
Snap (pole)	Poor	Lettuce, spinach	Carrots, celery, corn, cucumbers, onions, radishes, squash (summer)	Celery, corn, cucumbers, radishes, tomatoes
Beets	Slight	None	Kohlrabi	Kohlrabi
Broccoli	Slight	Celery, lettuce, spinach	None	None
Brussels sprouts	Poor	Celery, lettuce, spinach	None	None
Cabbage	Slight	Celery, lettuce, spinach	Onions	Carrots, corn, cucumbers, onions, peppers, tomatoes
Carrots	Slight	Onions	Leeks, lettuce, onions, snap beans (bush or pole)	Cabbage, leeks, lettuce, onions
Cauliflower	Poor	Celery, lettuce, spinach	None	None
Celery	Good	Broccoli, Brussels sprouts, cabbage, cauliflower, cucumbers, eggplant, snap beans (bush)	Snap beans (bush or pole)	Snap beans (bush or pole)
Chinese cabbage	Poor	None	Corn	Corn
Corn	Poor	Lettuce	Chinese cabbage, lettuce, potatoes,	Cabbage, Chinese cabbage, lettuce,

Interplanting Guide—*Continued*

Crop	Shade Tolerance	Plants with Compatible Shade/Light Needs	Plants with Compatible Root Systems	Plants with Compatible Aboveground Growth
Corn— *continued*			snap beans (bush or pole)	melons, potatoes, snap beans (bush or pole), squash (summer or winter)
Cucumbers	Slight	Celery, lettuce, sunflowers	Snap beans (bush or pole), Swiss chard	Cabbage, snap beans (pole), sunflowers
Eggplant	Poor	Celery	Onions	Onions
Lettuce	Good	Broccoli, Brussels sprouts, cabbage, cauliflower, corn, cucumbers, onions, peas, radishes, snap beans (bush or pole), tomatoes	Carrots, corn, onions, parsnips, radishes	Carrots, corn, onions, radishes
Melons	Poor	None	Radishes	Corn, radishes, snap beans (bush)
Onions	Good	Carrots, lettuce	Cabbage, carrots, eggplant, lettuce, peppers, radishes, snap beans, (bush or pole), spinach	Cabbage, carrots, eggplant, lettuce, peppers, spinach
Parsley	Good	None	None	Leeks
Parsnips	Poor	None	Lettuce	None
Peas (all)	Good	Lettuce, spinach	Radishes, turnips	None
Peppers	Poor	None	Onions	Cabbage, onions
Potatoes	Poor	None	Corn	Corn
Pumpkins	Good	None	None	Sweet potatoes
Radishes	Slight	Lettuce, Swiss chard	Lettuce, melons, onions, peas, snap beans (bush or pole)	Lettuce, melons, snap beans (bush or pole)
Spinach	Good	Broccoli, Brussels sprouts, cabbage, cauliflower, peas, snap beans (bush or pole)	Onions	Onions

[*Continued on next page*]

Interplanting Guide—*Continued*

Crop	Shade Tolerance	Plants with Compatible Shade/Light Needs	Plants with Compatible Root Systems	Plants with Compatible Aboveground Growth
Squash				
Summer	Poor	None	Snap beans (bush or pole)	Corn, snap beans (bush)
Winter	Poor	None	None	Corn, snap beans (bush)
Sunflowers	Poor	Cucumbers	None	Cucumbers
Sweet potatoes	Good	None	None	Pumpkins
Swiss chard	Good	Radishes	Cucumbers	None
Tomatoes	Poor	Lettuce	None	Cabbage, snap beans (bush or pole)
Turnips	Slight	None	Peas	None

Companion Planting Guide

Crop	Friends (enhance growth)	Enemies (hinder growth)
Asparagus	Tomatoes repel asparagus beetles; parsley and basil help growth.	Onion family
Beans	Potatoes repel Mexican bean beetles; corn improves growth; rosemary repels insects; catnip repels flea beetles; celery helps growth.	Fennel, gladiolus, onion family
Beets	Onion family repels insects.	Beans (pole)
Cabbage family (broccoli, Brussels sprouts, cabbage, cauliflower, collards, kale, kohlrabi)	Celery repels cabbage worms; onion family deters maggots; rosemary, sage, and thyme repel insects.	Beans, (pole), strawberries, tomatoes
Carrots	Peas add nutrients; onion family repels carrot flies; rosemary and sage repel insects.	Dill
Celery	Cabbage repels insects.	Carrots, parsnips
Corn	Beans and peas add nutrients; potatoes repel insects; soybeans deter chinch bugs.	Tomatoes
Cucumbers	Radishes deter cucumber beetles; beans add nutrients.	Potatoes, sage
Eggplant	Green beans deter Colorado potato beetles; potatoes can be used as trap plant.	None
Lettuce	Carrots, radishes	None
Muskmelons	Corn	None
Onion family (bulb onions, garlic, leeks, scallions, shallots)	Beets, carrots	Beans, peas
Peas	Carrots help growth; turnips	Gladiolus, onion family
Peppers	Carrots	Fennel, kohlrabi
Potatoes	Beans and corn repel insects; use eggplant as trap plant.	Apples, pumpkins, raspberries, tomatoes
Pumpkins	Corn	Potatoes
Radishes	Cucumbers repel insects; lettuce	Hyssop
Spinach	Strawberries	Potatoes

[Continued on next page]

Companion Planting Guide—*Continued*

Crop	Friends (enhance growth)	Enemies (hinder growth)
Squash	Corn	Potatoes
Swiss chard	Onion family	Beans (pole)
Tomatoes	Asparagus and basil repel insects; parsley helps growth.	Corn, dill, kohlrabi, potatoes
Turnips	Peas help growth.	Potatoes

Succession Planting Guide

In addition to the information given here, refer to Feeding and Watering Guidelines as you plan your successions. You don't want to follow a crop with heavy feeding needs with another heavy feeder or one that needs the same nutrients. Alternate light with heavy feeders, and be sure to replenish the soil's nutrient reserves after each succession.

Crop	Temperature Preference	Timing for Succession Plantings	Days before First Frost to Make Last Succession Planting	Average Days to Maturity*
Beans				
Snap	Warm	Once a wk. for bush beans; for pole beans only one planting is necessary.	85	50–65
Lima	Warm	Once a wk. for bush beans; for pole beans only one planting is necessary	85	75–80
Fava	Cool	One planting	. . .	85–90
Kidney	Warm	One planting	. . .	100
Soybean	Warm	One planting	. . .	75–100
Beets	Cool	Every 2 to 3 wks. until midsummer	74	50–70
Broccoli	Cool	2 mos. after first planting	70–84	60–80T
Brussels sprouts	Cool	2½ mos. after first planting	120	80–90T

*T indicates average days to maturity from date of transplanting.

Succession Planting Guide—*Continued*

Crop	Temperature Preference	Timing for Succession Plantings	Days before First Frost to Make Last Succession Planting	Average Days to Maturity*
Cabbage	Cool	2 mos. after first planting and again in late summer	99	65–95T
Carrots	Cool	Every 2 to 3 wks.	85	55–90
Cauliflower	Cool	2½ mos. after first planting	90	50–95T
Celery	Cool	2 mos. after first planting	130	80–135T
Chinese cabbage	Cool	Early spring and late summer	94	80–90T
Collards	Cool	2 mos. after first planting	94	70–80
Corn	Warm	Second planting 3 wks. after first, third planting 4 wks. later	97	70–100
Cress, garden	Cool	Every 4 wks. until midsummer	50	25–45
Cucumbers	Warm	Every 2 wks. until midsummer	86	60–80
Eggplant	Warm	One planting	. . .	75–95T
Endive	Cool	1 mo. after first planting and again in late summer	113	80–100
Garlic	Cool	Early spring and early fall	. . .	90–110
Horseradish	Cool	One planting	. . .	6–8 mos.
Kale	Cool	Midsummer planting for fall harvest	95	55–75
Kohlrabi	Cool	Early spring and late summer	63	55–70
Leeks	Cool	2 wks. after first planting	. . .	80–130T
Lettuce Head	Cool	Early spring and late summer	96	60–95

[*Continued on next page*]

Succession Planting Guide—*Continued*

Crop	Temperature Preference	Timing for Succession Plantings	Days before First Frost to Make Last Succession Planting	Average Days to Maturity*
Lettuce—*continued*				
Leaf	Cool	Every 3 wks. until midsummer; start again in late summer	35	45–65
Romaine	Cool	Early spring, early summer, and midsummer	76	55–80
Muskmelons	Warm	One planting	. . .	80–120
Mustard	Cool	1 mo. after first planting and again in late summer	60	30–50
Onions (sets)	Cool	2½ mos. after first planting for crop of scallions	. . .	60–80
Parsley	Cool	One planting	. . .	70–90
Parsnips	Cool	7 wks. after first planting	120	85–110
Peas (all)	Cool	Every 3 wks. until late spring and again in late summer	70	55–85
Peppers	Warm	One planting	. . .	60–75T
Potatoes	Cool	6 wks. after first planting	120	90–140
Pumpkins	Warm	One planting	. . .	90–110
Radishes	Cool	Every 10 days until warm weather and again in late summer	35	25–35
Rhubarb	Cool	One planting	. . .	2–3 yrs.
Rutabagas	Cool	Early spring and summer	100	90–100
Salsify	Cool	2 mos. after first planting	130	130–150
Shallots	Cool	Early spring and early fall	. . .	100

Succession Planting Guide—*Continued*

Crop	Temperature Preference	Timing for Succession Plantings	Days before First Frost to Make Last Succession Planting	Average Days to Maturity*
Spinach	Cool	Every 2 wks. until temperatures rise and days lengthen; again in late summer		
Squash				
Summer	Warm	One planting	. . .	50–80
Winter	Warm	2 wks. after first planting	110	90–110
Strawberries	Cool	One planting	. . .	. . .
Sunflowers	Warm	1 mo. after first planting	85	80–90
Sweet potatoes	Warm	One planting	. . .	100–125T
Swiss chard	Cool	Early spring and late fall	69	50–60
Tomatoes	Warm	1 mo. after first planting	110	52–80T
Turnips	Cool	Every 3 wks. until midsummer	51	50–80
Watermelon	Warm	One planting	. . .	70–90T

Vegetables and Fruits to Grow in Containers

As a general rule of thumb, compact, bushy, or shallow-rooted vegetables do the best in container gardens. Full-size vining crops take up too much space and tend to become unmanageable. Fortunately, many dwarf or bush varieties of melons, cucumbers, and squash are widely available. Even that most popular of garden crops, the tomato, comes in compact sizes perfect for growing in planters or hanging baskets. Vining crops such as pole beans and peas aren't off limits as long as they're located next to a railing, trellis, or other support. Fruit trees come in a range of scaled-down sizes: semidwarf (four-fifths standard size), dwarf (one-half standard size), and extradwarf (less than half standard size). These dwarfs start bearing at an earlier age than standard trees and produce full-size fruit. One caution about semidwarfs; they're the least expensive, but after eight to ten years they'll need to be transplanted to an in-ground location. Better to start out with the smaller-growing dwarfs or extradwarfs. Also, be sure to provide self-unfruitful varieties with a variety suitable for cross-pollination. Listed below are some vegetable and fruit varieties especially suited to container gardening.

Crop	Recommended Varieties	Comments
Apples	Any variety grafted or budded onto MMIX or EM26 dwarfing rootstocks; "spur type" apples are also good for containers	A vast array of dwarf varieties are available; use recommended rootstocks as a general guide in your selection.
Bush beans, snap	Bush Romano, Contender, Provider, Tendercrop Stringless	Bush beans produce a crop all at once, as opposed to pole beans, which have a more dispersed harvest.
Bush beans, lima	Fordhook Bush Lima, Fordhook 242, Henderson Bush Baby	see Bush beans, snap
Beets	Baby Canning, Spinel Baby Beets	Golf-ball-size roots are handy for pickling or canning whole.
Broccoli	Crusader Hybrid	Any variety is suitable; Crusader tends to be smaller and more compact than most.
Cabbage	Baby Head, Dwarf Morden	These dwarf varieties take up half the space of standard-size heads.
Carrots	Baby Finger Nantes, Gold Nugget, Oxheart, Short N' Sweet, Tiny Sweet	Short-rooted or round varieties are the best; avoid long, slender varieties.
Chinese cabbage	Bok choy, michihli, wong bok	Most varieties are compact enough to thrive in containers; both heading and nonheading types are available.
Cress, garden	. . .	Quick to mature—only 10 days from seeding to harvest.

Vegetables and Fruits to Grow in Containers—*Continued*

Crop	Recommended Varieties	Comments
Cucumbers	Bush Crop, Patio Pic, Pot Luck, Spacemaster	These bushy varieties produce full-size cucumbers.
Eggplant	Dusky, Morden Midget	Besides being dwarf, these varieties are early to mature.
Lettuce, leaf	Oakleaf	Any variety will do well; Oakleaf is heat-resistant.
Muskmelons	Ha-Ogen, Minnesota Midget, Short N' Sweet	These dwarf plants produce roughly 3-ft.-long vines.
Onions	Beltsville Bunching, Japanese Bunching, White Pearl	Bunching onions are more productive in small spaces than bulbing onions.
Parsley	Any variety	Either the curly- or flat-leaved variety will do fine.
Pears	Duchess (self-fruitful), Dwarf Bartlett (will need pollinator variety)	Most dwarf varieties are grafted onto quince rootstocks.
Peas	Laxton's Progress, Little Marvel, SugarBon, SugarMel, SugarRae	Dwarf peas still require low trellis or support to keep air circulating through vines; last 3 varieties are dwarf snap peas.
Peppers	Canape, Gypsy Hybrid, Italian Sweet, Pepper Pot	These sweet peppers exhibit compact growth; any hot pepper variety is suitable for container growing.
Radishes	Cherry Belle, Early Scarlet Globe, French Breakfast, Sparkler	Round red and white-tipped varieties do well; stay away from large winter radishes like Daikon.
Spinach	Any variety	Good hot-weather substitutes include New Zealand spinach and vegetable amaranth.
Squash, summer	Early Yellow Summer Crookneck, Goldbar Straightneck, Park's Creamy, Scallopine	Avoid winter squash, which are too clumsy and heavy to fare well in containers.
Swiss chard	Any variety	Red-stalked varieties are especially eye-catching.
Tomatoes	Patio VF, Pixie, Small Fry VFN, Sweet 100, Toy Boy, Tumblin' Tom, Yellow Pear	These small-fruited varieties bear an abundant early crop.

Container Planting Guide

Crop	Size of Pot	Number of Plants per Pot	Comments on Care
Apples	12–18 in. deep; minimum of 3–4 gal. soil	1	As tree matures it will need larger container; 5-yr.-old dwarf will need 24-in. container with 10–15 gal. of soil.
Beans, bush (snap and lima)	8 in. deep; 1½–2 qt. soil	1	Treat seed with legume inoculant before planting.
Beans, pole (snap and lima)	12 in. deep; ½ gal. soil	1	Must provide trellis; take longer to mature than bush beans.
Beets	6 in. for dwarf varieties; 8–10 in. for larger types	As many as pot can accommodate	Don't let roots grow too large; roots larger than 3 in. are tough and woody.
Broccoli	20 in. deep; 3 gal. soil	1	Provide good drainage and keep plants cool and moist.
Cabbage	12 in. deep; 1–2 gal. soil	1	Hot, dry weather prompts bitter flavor; keep cool and moist.
Carrots	8 in. deep	As many as pot can accommodate	Be sure container is deep enough; even shortest varieties do best with plenty of space.
Chinese cabbage	20 in. deep; 3 gal. soil	1	Does best when grown as fall crop.
Cress, garden	4 in. deep	As many as pot can accommodate	Prefers cool temperatures; can also be grown indoors.
Cucumbers	8–10 in. deep; 1–2 gal. soil	1	Keep soil moist, especially while fruit is setting.
Eggplant	12 in. deep; 5–6 gal. soil	1	Needs full sun, lots of water, and weekly fertilizing.
Lettuce, leaf	6 in. deep, ½ qt. soil	1	Partial shade and constant moisture are keys to success.

Container Planting Guide—*Continued*

Crop	Size of Pot	Number of Plants per Pot	Comments on Care
Muskmelons	24 in. deep; 3–5 gal. soil	1	Full sun, warm temperatures, lavish amounts of water, and weekly fertilizing are critical.
Onions	6 in. deep; 1 gal. soil	12	Easy to grow; aside from watering, almost maintenance-free.
Parsley	6 in. deep	As many as pot can accommodate	Soak seeds overnight to improve germination rate.
Pears—see Apples			
Peas	12 in. deep; 1 qt. soil	1	Keep soil moist once flowers appear; keep picking to encourage production.
Peppers	12 in. deep; 1–2 gal. soil	1	Full sun, warm temperatures, and lots of water during fruit set are important.
Radishes	4–6 in. deep	As many as pot can accommodate	Underwatering leads to cracked pithy roots.
Spinach	4–6 in. deep; 2–4 qt. soil	1	Absolutely needs cool, moist conditions to grow.
Squash, summer	24 in. deep; 3–5 gal. soil	1	Provide rich soil, full sun, and weekly feedings for best production.
Swiss chard	8 in. deep; 1–2 gal. soil	1	Versatile vegetable, growing well in both cool and hot weather.
Tomatoes	8 in. deep; 3 qts. soil for midget varieties—12–14 in. deep; 1 gal. soil for 2–3-ft.-tall plants	1	Full sun, warmth, steady moisture, and weekly feedings guarantee a bumper crop.

Growing Guide

Crop	pH Range	Soil Temperature for Best Germination (°F)	Days to Germination	Air Temperature for Best Growth (°F)	Frost Tolerance	Average Days to Maturity*	Harvest Period
Asparagus	6.0–7.5	60–85°	. . .	. . .	Hardy	3 yrs.	4–5 wks.
Beans							
Snap	5.8–6.5	65–85°	4–10	60–79°	None	48–95	4–5 wks.
Lima	6.0–7.0	65–85°	7–12	60–70°	None	60–80	3–4 wks.
Fava	6.0–7.5	. . .	7–14	60–65°	Good	80–90	At 5-day intervals
Kidney	5.7–6.5	65–85°	7–14	60–70°	None	65–100	Once at end of season for dry use
Mung	. . .	65–85°	7–14	60–70°	None	65–100	Once at end of season for dry use
Soybean	6.0–7.0	65–85°	5–8	60–70°	None	70–96	As needed for fresh use; once at end of season for dry use
Beets	6.0–7.5	50–85°	7–10	60–65°	Good	56–80	4–6 wks.
Broccoli	6.0–7.5	45–90°	3–10	60–65°	Very good	60–80T	8–10 wks.
Brussels sprouts	6.0–7.5	45–85°	3–10	60–65°	Very good	80–90T	8–10 wks.
Cabbage	6.0–7.5	45–95°	4–10	45–95°	Good	65–95T	4–6 wks.
Carrots	5.5–6.5	45–85°	10–17	60–65°	Good	65–76	6–8 wks.
Cauliflower	6.0–7.5	45–85°	4–10	60–65°	Some	50–95T	1–2 wks.
Celery	6.0–7.5	60–70°	10–21	60–65°	Light	80–135T	6–8 wks.
Chinese cabbage	6.0–7.0	45–95°	4–10	60–65°	Very good	80–90T	4–6 wks.
Collards	6.7	45–95°	10–14	60–65°	Very good	80	As needed all season long into late fall
Corn	5.5–7.5	60–95°	6–10	60–75°	Light	65–100	1–2 wks.
Cress, garden	. . .	65°	4–10	60–65°	Light	35–45	1–2 wks.
Cucumbers	6.0–7.5	60–95°	6–10	65–75°	None	50–70	4–6 wks.
Eggplant	5.5–6.5	75–90°	7–14	70–85°	None	75–95T	Until frost
Garlic	5.5–6.5	. . .	6–10	55–75°	Good	90 (sets)	Once at end of season
Horseradish	6.0–7.0	. . .	. . .	60–65°	Hardy	6–8 mos.	In fall for storage

*T indicates average days to maturity from date of transplanting.

Growing Guide—*Continued*

Crop	pH Range	Soil Temperature for Best Germination (°F)	Days to Germination	Air Temperature for Best Growth (°F)	Frost Tolerance	Average Days to Maturity*	Harvest Period
Kale	6.0–7.0	45–95°	3–10	60–65°	Very good	55–80	As needed all season long into late fall
Kohlrabi	6.0–7.0	45–95°	3–10	60–65°	Good	55–70	2–3 wks.
Leeks	6.5–7.5	50–95°	6–14	55–75°	Very good	80–130T	As needed all season long throughout fall and winter
Lettuce							
Head	6.0–7.5	40–80°	4–10	60–65°	Some	55–80	Once and done
Leaf	6.0–7.5	40–80°	4–10	60–65°	Some	45–60	4–6 wks.
Romaine	6.0–7.5	40–80°	4–10	60–65°	Some	55–80	Once and done
Muskmelons	6.0–7.5	75–95°	4–10	65–75°	None	80–120	3–4 wks.
Mustard	6.0–7.0	50–70°	3–7	60–65°	Light	33–50	As needed all season long into late fall
Onions and scallions	6.0–7.5	50–95°	7–12	55–75°	Good	100–165	As needed all season long
Parsley	6.0–7.0	50–85°	11–28	60–65°	Very good	70–90	As needed all season long into fall
Parsnips	6.0–8.0	50–70°	15–25	60–65°	Very good	100–120	At end of season, after roots touched by frost
Peas							
Edible-podded	6.5–7.0	40–75°	6–15	60–65°	Some	70	1–2 wks.
Garden	6.75	40–75°	6–15	60–65°	Some	55–85	1–2 wks.
Snap	. . .	40–75°	6–15	60–65°	Some	70	1–2 wks.
Peppers	6.0–7.0	65–95°	10–20	70–75°	None	60–75T	Until frost
Potatoes	5.0–6.5	64–72°	10–15	60–65°	None	90–120	New potatoes 1 wk. after flowering as needed; storage potatoes in fall
Pumpkins	6.0–7.0	70–90°	4–6	65–75°	None	100–120	Until frost

[Continued on next page]

Growing Guide—*Continued*

Crop	pH Range	Soil Temperature for Best Germination (°F)	Days to Germination	Air Temperature for Best Growth (°F)	Frost Tolerance	Average Days to Maturity*	Harvest Period
Radishes							
Red	5.0–6.0	45–90°	3–6	60–65°	Good	20–25	1–2 wks.
White	5.0–6.0	45–90°	3–6	60–65°	Very good	25–28	1–2 wks.
Rhubarb	6.0–7.0	. . .	7–21	. . .	Hardy	1–2 yrs.	4 wks.
Rutabagas	6.0–8.0	50–75°	3–14	60–65°	Very good	90–100	In late fall for storage
Salsify	7.0	50–75°	. . .	55–75°	Good	130–150	In late fall for storage
Shallots	6.0–7.5	. . .	6–14	55–75°	Good	60–75	As needed all season long for green onion use; once at end of season for dry bulbs
Spinach	6.5–7.5	45–75°	6–14	60–65°	Good	42–65	1–2 wks.
Squash							
Summer	6.0–8.0	70–95°	3–12	65–75°	None	50–60	Until frost
Winter	6.0–8.0	70–95°	6–10	65–75°	None	80–120	Late in season for storage
Strawberries	5.0–6.0	55°	30	. . .	Good	. . .	2 wks. in June (everbearing plants again 6–8 wks. later through to frost)
Sunflowers	6.0–7.5	. . .	7–12	. . .	None	80–90	Once at end of season for storage
Sweet potatoes	5.0–6.0	. . .	8–12	70–85°	None	100–200T	At first frost
Swiss chard	6.0–7.5	50–85°	3–14	60–65°	Good	50–60	As needed all season long
Tomatoes	5.5–7.0	60–85°	6–14	70–75°	None	52–80T	Until frost
Turnips	6.0–8.0	60–105°	3–10	60–65°	Very good	30–60	4 wks.
Watermelon	5.5–6.5	70–95°	5–10	70–85°	None	70–90T	3–4 wks.

Feeding and Watering Guidelines

Crop	Feeding Needs	Specific Nutrient Needs			Watering Needs
		Nitrogen (N)	Phosphorus (P)	Potassium (K)	
Asparagus	H	EH	H	EH	H
Beans					
Snap	L	L	M	M	M
Lima	L	L	M	M	H
Soybean	L	L	M	M	L
Beets	H	L	EH	H	M
Broccoli	H	H	H	H	M to H
Brussels sprouts	H	H	H	H	M
Cabbage	H	H	H	H	H then M later in season
Carrots	L	H	H	H	M
Cauliflower	H	H	H	EH	M
Celery	H	H	H	H	H
Corn	H	M	M	M	M to H
Cucumbers	H	H	H	H	H
Eggplant	H	H	H	H	H

[Continued on next page]

L = light   M = medium   H = heavy   EH = extra heavy

Key to Feeding Needs: amounts given are per 100 sq. ft.; organic fertilizers are generally used only once or twice a season—once before planting as the soil is being worked, and again at midseason for a nutrient boost.

Light   For N—0.75 lb. blood meal or 2 lb. cottonseed meal
         For P—1 lb. bone meal or 2 lb. phosphate rock
         For K—1 lb. wood ashes or 3 lb. granite dust

Medium   For N—2.25 lb. blood meal or 6 lb. cottonseed meal
         For P—2 lb. bone meal or 4 lb. phosphate rock
         For K—1.5 lb. wood ashes or 6 lb. granite dust

Heavy   For N—4 lb. blood meal or 10 lb. cottonseed meal
         For P—3 lb. bone meal or 6 lb. phosphate rock
         For K—2 lb. wood ashes or 10 lb. granite dust

Extra heavy   Above and beyond amounts listed under Heavy.

Key to Watering Needs
Light   ½ to ¾ gal. per sq. ft. per week or 0.8 in. rain
Medium   ¾ gal. per sq. ft. per week or 1.2 in. rain
Heavy   1 gal. per sq. ft. per week or 1.6 in. rain

Feeding and Watering Guidelines—*Continued*

| Crop | Feeding Needs | Specific Nutrient Needs | | | Watering Needs |
		Nitrogen (N)	Phosphorus (P)	Potassium (K)	
Garlic	M	M	M	M	M
Horseradish	H	L	H	L	H
Kale	H	L	L	H	H
Kohlrabi	H	H	H	H	H
Leeks	H	H	H	H	H
Lettuce					
Head	H	H	EH	EH	L to M
Leaf	H	H	EH	EH	L to M
Muskmelons	H	H	H	H	M to H
Mustard	L	M	L	M	H
Onions	M	H	H	H	M
Parsley	H	H	H	H	L
Parsnips	L	L	M	M	M
Peas					
Garden	L	L	H	H	L to M
Snap	L	L	H	H	L to M
Peppers	M	L	L	L	M to H
Potatoes	L	EH	EH	EH	H
Pumpkins	H	M	M	M	H
Radishes	L	H	EH	EH	M
Rhubarb	H	M	H	H	M
Rutabagas	L	M	H	M	M
Spinach	H	EH	EH	EH	L to M
Squash					
Summer	H	H	H	H	H
Winter	H	M	M	M	H
Strawberries	H	M	M	L	M
Sunflowers	H	. . .	. . .	. . .	. . .
Sweet potatoes	L	L	M	H	M to H
Swiss chard	H	H	H	H	H
Tomatoes	H	M	H	H	H
Turnips	L	L	H	M	M
Watermelon	H	H	H	H	M

Approximate Nutrient Composition (%) of Organic Materials

Material	Nitrogen* (N)	Phosphorus† (P)	Potassium‡ (K)	Carbon/Nitrogen Ratio§
Alfalfa hay	2.5	0.5	2.0	12:1
Blood meal	15.0	1.3	0.7	. . .
Bone meal (steamed)	4.0	22.0	0.2	. . .
Coffee grounds	2.08	0.32	0.28	. . .
Cottonseed meal	6.0	3.0	1.0	. . .
Cow manure				
Dried	1.3	0.9	0.8	20:1
Fresh	0.5	0.2	0.5	. . .
Crabgrass	0.66	0.19	0.71	. . .
Eggshells	1.1	0.38	0.14	. . .
Feathers	15.3	. . .	. . .	. . .
Fish meal	10.0	6.0	. . .	. . .
Fish scrap	5.0	3.0	. . .	. . .
Garbage	3.4–3.7	0.1–1.47	2.25–4.25	. . .
Grain straw	0.6	0.2	1.0	80:1
Grass clippings	. . .	. . .	. . .	19:1
Greensand	. . .	1.4	9.5–40.0	. . .
Hair	12.0–16.0	. . .	. . .	. . .
Hen manure (dried)	2.8	2.8	1.5	. . .
Horse manure (fresh)	1.1	0.9	0.5	. . .
Leaves				
Apple	1.0	0.15	0.35	Range of
Cherry	0.6	0.11	0.74	80:1 to
Grape	0.45	0.1	0.35	40:1
Oak	0.8	0.35	0.15	
Peach	0.9	0.15	0.6	
Pear	0.7	0.12	0.4	
Peanut shells	0.8	0.15	0.5	. . .
Peat	2.3	0.4	0.8	. . .
Phosphate rock	. . .	38.0–40.0	4.5	. . .
Pine needles	0.46	0.12	0.03	. . .
Sawdust	0.2	. . .	0.2	500:1
Seaweed	1.68	0.75	4.93	. . .
Sewage sludge (digested)	2.0–6.0	1.5–3.0	1.0–0.5	16:1
Timothy hay	1.0	0.2	1.5	80:1
Wood ashes	. . .	1.8	5.0	. . .

*Promotes rapid growth; gives healthy dark green color to plants.
†Stimulates early root formation and growth; promotes flowering.
‡Gives increased vigor and disease resistance; aids plants in protein production.
§For a fast-acting, efficient compost pile, try to maintain a carbon/nitrogen ratio of 25:1. Mix materials with different ratios in the pile to average out to 25:1.

Dealing with Common Garden Pests

Pests	Crops Infested	Controls
Aphids (plant lice)	Many vegetables and fruits; general feeders	Spray foliage with soapy water, then clear water. Or, use garlic oil spray. Use rotenone for serious problems. Plant companion crops of garlic, chives, nasturtiums, mint. Strips of aluminum foil around plant bases confuse these pests.
Cabbage worms and cabbage loopers	Broccoli, cabbage, cauliflower, celery, collards, kale, lettuce, parsley, peas, potatoes, radishes, spinach, tomatoes, turnips	Use *Bacillus thuringiensis* or rotenone. Plant natural repellent herbs such as thyme. Trichogramma wasps are natural predators.
Colorado potato beetles	Eggplant, peppers, potatoes, tomatoes	Use rotenone. Spread wheat bran in early morning when the garden is moist. Beetles eat the bran and die.
Corn earworms and corn borers	Beans, corn, peas, peppers, potatoes, squash, tomatoes	Add a few drops of mineral oil on the tassels for infested corn. Use ryania for sweet corn. Make successive sowings. Tachinid fly is natural predator.
Cutworms	General feeders, but prefer cabbage family and young seedlings and transplants	Push paper or tin collars into soil around transplants. Use *Bacillus thuringiensis.*
Hornworms	Eggplant, peppers, potatoes, tomatoes	Use *Bacillus thuringiensis.* A diluted hot pepper spray should help. If any of the worms have cocoons on their backs, leave them alone. They're carrying the eggs of the parasitic braconid wasp, a natural predator.
Leafhoppers	Many vegetables and fruits; general feeders	Use diatomaceous earth or pyrethrum. Plantings of marigolds, nasturtiums, and chrysanthemums repel these insects.

Dealing with Common Garden Pests—*Continued*

Pests	Crops Infested	Controls
Mexican bean beetles	Beans, especially snap and lima	Use rotenone or pyrethrum. Marigolds and rosemary repel these pests. Handpicking and crushing these bugs wards off other bean beetles.
Root maggots	Broccoli, cabbage, carrots, celery, onions, radishes, turnips	Natural repellents include rosemary, mint, sage, and wood ashes. Small squares of tar paper slit and placed around stems prevent maggots from entering the soil.
Slugs	Many vegetables and fruits; general feeders	Coarse material such as sand ringing plants will discourage slugs. A saucer of beer set at soil level will lure slugs to their death. Use diatomaceous earth for serious problems.
Spider mites	Many vegetables and fruits; general feeders	Use pyrethrum. Lacewings and lady beetles are natural predators. Spray cold water on leaves or use mixture of wheat flour, buttermilk, and water.
Spotted and striped cucumber beetles	Cabbage, corn, cucumbers, eggplant, melons, peas, squash	Use rotenone. Marigolds deter these pests. Apply a mixture of water, wood ashes, and hydrated lime. Make mid-late planting. Cover plants with cheesecloth to prevent egg laying.
Squash bugs	All cucurbits, especially squash and pumpkins	Nasturtiums ward off these pests. Crushing these bugs gives off an odor unpleasant to other bugs. Make mid-late plantings. Tachinid fly is natural predator.
Squash vine borers	Cucumbers, melons, pumpkins, squash	If vine wilts, slit stem, remove borer, and bury stem area. Successive planting also helps.
Whiteflies	Many vegetables and fruits; general feeders	Use pyrethrum. Plant marigolds as a companion crop.

When to Pick Your Crops

Asparagus: Start harvesting third year after planting; look for green, thick spears 6 to 8 inches tall; heads should still be tight and spears brittle; snap spears off at ground level or at tenderest part; first harvest season is 2 weeks long, second harvest season 4 weeks long, and subsequent harvests can run 6 to 8 weeks.

Beans, Snap (bush): Ready 2 to 3 weeks after first bloom when pods snap readily but the tips are still pliable; pick before seeds fill out pods; wax beans are slower than snap beans to mature.

Beans, Snap (pole): Same as for bush beans, but snap pods off just below stem end and another bean will form in same spot for a second harvest.

Beans, Lima: For green shell use, pick when pods are well filled and plump, but still bright colored; end of pod should feel spongy when squeezed between fingers; for dry use, let pods pass mature stage, and pick when pods are dry and papery.

Beans, Kidney: Pick when pods are dry and papery and foliage has yellowed and withered.

Beets: Best when fairly small, 1 to 2 inches in diameter; larger roots are sweeter, but also tougher and woodier.

Broccoli: Cut central head while buds are still compact and not showing any yellow color; more side shoots will form after main head is cut.

Brussels Sprouts: Sprouts should be bright green, firm, compact, at least the size of your thumb; sprouts larger than 1 inch in diameter have passed their prime; pick lowest sprouts first; frost vastly improves flavor; after picking lower stem clean, mound dirt around base of stem to keep top-heavy plant from toppling over.

Cabbage: Pick any time heads are heavy for their size and firm when squeezed; splitting heads have passed their prime.

Carrots: Even though sugar content is greater in mature roots, pick while small, no more than 1 to 1½ inches in diameter; roots should be firm but tender, and well colored.

Cauliflower: To blanch, tie outer leaves over head when curd is 2 to 3 inches in diameter; check head every couple days; pick when head is firm and white; pick as soon as ready, since head deteriorates quickly.

When to Pick Your Crops—*Continued*

Celery: A few stalks can be harvested from the outside of the plant as needed, once they reach usable size; or, entire plant can be taken by lifting it and cutting off roots right below the crown.

Chinese Cabbage: Cut heading types as soon as they reach usable size; for nonheading types, harvest a few outer leaves at a time, or cut entire plant for single harvest.

Corn: Ears are ripe when silks look dry and brown, kernels spurt forth with milky liquid when pressed; corn past its prime has starchy, doughy kernels; best when picked in late afternoon; keep ears cool and cook within an hour.

Cucumbers: At their best when dark green, firm, and of moderate size; overripe fruit is yellow and tough; picking increases vines' production.

Eggplant: Bigger is not better; pick whenever fruit reaches usable size, 3 to 5 inches long; look for shiny, deep purple skin; dull skin and brown seeds are signs of overripe fruit.

Garlic: Bulbs are ready when tops yellow and droop; cure before storing.

Horseradish: Wait to harvest until several frosts have hit for best flavor.

Kohlrabi: Bulb should never be allowed to grow larger than golf ball or tennis ball, depending on variety; bulb should be tender and easily marked with a fingernail; if too large, bulb will be woody.

Leeks: Ready whenever stem reaches usable size, about 1 inch in diameter; at maturity, stem will measure up to 2½ inches around.

Lettuce, Head: Ready as soon as heads have formed and are firm when squeezed; pick before seed stalk breaks through top of head.

Lettuce, Leaf: Start harvesting a few outer leaves as soon as they reach usable size, about 2 inches long; keep picking outer leaves for ongoing harvest until seed stalk appears.

Muskmelons: Netting should be coarse, cordlike, grayish, and prominent; there should be a crack all around the stem and melon should separate easily from the stem.

Onions: For use as scallions, harvest when bulbs are ¼ to ⅝-inch in diameter; for boiling or pickling, harvest when 1 to 1½ inches in diameter; for storage, harvest when tops fall over and turn brown; cure before storing.

[*Continued on next page*]

When to Pick Your Crops—*Continued*

Parsley: Snip off leaves when fully formed; pick middle stem in triple-stemmed bunches to encourage full, bushy growth.

Parsnips: For best flavor, harvest after a few hard frosts; overwintered roots must be dug before new growth starts in spring.

Peas, Edible-Podded: Pick before peas grow too large; peas should barely be discernible in pods; pods should be tender and no bigger than 1½ to 2½ inches.

Peas, Garden: Pods should be fairly well filled but still bright green; raw peas should taste sweet; harvest lower pods first; picking increases vines' production.

Peas, Snap: The older the sweeter—up to a point; harvest before peas touch each other in pod for sweetest flavor and crunchiest texture.

Peppers, Hot: Ready when fruit is shiny with uniformly colored skin; peppers do not get hotter the longer they're left on the plant.

Peppers, Sweet: Skin should be firm and shiny; fruit is green at early stage, red when mature; the bigger the pepper, the thicker the skin.

Potatoes: A week or two after blooming, dig for new potatoes; for storage crop, wait to harvest until tops have died down; don't delay harvest too long—once tubers freeze they become watery and unusable; discard any green tubers.

Pumpkins: Wait until color is good all over; ripe fruit gives a sharp thud when rapped with knuckles; pumpkins for storage should have tough shells that resist denting.

Radishes: Harvest once roots reach usable size, about 1 inch around; large, overgrown roots split or turn spongy.

Rhubarb: Start harvesting third year after planting; pick stalks 12 to 24 inches long with developed leaves; twist off stalks at base of plant; both roots and leaves are toxic and should never be eaten.

Rutabagas: Dig whenever roots reach usable size; never let roots get bigger than 5 to 7 inches in diameter; best flavor comes with a touch of frost.

Salsify: Harvest whenever roots reach usable size; for best flavor, wait to dig until several frosts have hit.

When to Pick Your Crops—*Continued*

Shallots: see Garlic

Soybeans: For green shell use, pick when seeds are mature, before pods wither and yellow; harvest period lasts 1 week; for dry use, harvest when pods are dry but plant stems are still green; waiting too long gives pods chance to shatter.

Spinach: Pick a few outer leaves at a time once they're large enough to use, before they become tired and tattered.

Squash, Summer: Best when young and tender, about 8 inches long; rind can be dented readily with thumbnail.

Squash, Winter: Ready when stem begins to shrivel and takes on grayish color; rind should resist denting from thumbnail; pick before first hard frost; cure before storing.

Strawberries: Pick when completely red and still firm; gently pinch fruit off its stem.

Sweet Potatoes: Harvest after frost kills the vines; cure before storing.

Swiss Chard: Pick a few outer leaves at a time once they are 6 to 10 inches long.

Tomatoes: Ripe fruit will have rich color and feel firm; size of ripened tomato is governed by variety; will ripen after picking, but vine-ripened fruit taste the best.

Turnips: Pull up when no larger than 2 to 3 inches in diameter; larger roots have woody texture.

Watermelon: Pick when a rap on side gives a dull thud; a metallic ring means melon isn't quite ripe (a better indicator on large rather than midget-size melons); watch for the white underside to turn yellow.

Food Storage Options

Numbers in parentheses give months food can remain in storage under ideal conditions.

Crop	Freeze	Can	Dry
Asparagus	Excellent (12)	Good (12+)	Fair (12+)
Beans			
Snap	Good (12)	Fair (12+)	Fair (12+)
Lima	Excellent (12)	Fair (12+)	Excellent (12+)
Fava	Excellent (12)	Fair (12+)	Fair (12+)
Kidney	. . .	Fair (12+)	Excellent (12+)
Mung	. . .	. . .	Excellent (12+)
Soybean	Good (12)	Fair (12+)	Excellent (12+)
Beets	Fair (8)	Good (12+)	Fair (12+)
Broccoli	Excellent (12)	Fair (12+)	Fair (12+)
Brussels sprouts	Good (12)	Fair (12+)	. . .
Cabbage	Fair (8)	. . .	Fair (12+)
Carrots	Fair (8)	Fair (12+)	Fair (12+)
Cauliflower	Excellent (12)	Fair (12+)	. . .
Celery	Good (5)	Fair (12+)	Good (12+)
Chinese cabbage	Fair (8)	. . .	. . .
Corn	Good (8)	Excellent (12+)	Good (12+)
Cucumbers	. . .	. . .	. . .

Dry Root Cellar* (40–50°F, 60–70% humidity)	Humid Root Cellar† (32–40°F, 80–90% humidity)	Mulched in Ground	Other
. . .	. . .	. . .	. . .
. . .	. . .	. . .	Pickled (12+)
. . .	. . .	. . .	. . .
. . .	. . .	. . .	. . .
. . .	. . .	. . .	. . .
. . .	. . .	. . .	Sprouts
. . .	. . .	. . .	Sprouts
. . .	Excellent (5)	Excellent (4)	Pickled (12+)
. . .	Fair (1)	. . .	Pickled (12+)
. . .	Fair (1)	Good (2)	Pickled (12+)
. . .	Excellent (4)	. . .	Pickled (sauerkraut)
. . .	Excellent (8)	Excellent (4)	Pickled
. . .	Good (2)	. . .	Pickled
. . .	Good (3)	. . .	. . .
. . .	Good (4)	. . .	In cold frame
. . .	. . .	. . .	Pickled
. . .	. . .	. . .	Pickled

[Continued on next page]

*An attic is suitable.
†A basement or closed container is suitable.

Food Storage Options—*Continued*

Crop	Freeze	Can	Dry
Eggplant	Fair (8)	Fair (12+)	Fair (12+)
Garlic	. . .	. . .	Excellent (12)
Horseradish	. . .	. . .	. . .
Kale	Good (12)	Good (12+)	Fair (12+)
Kohlrabi	Fair (8)	. . .	. . .
Leeks	Fair (3)	. . .	. . .
Lettuce (all)	. . .	. . .	. . .
Muskmelons	Good (3)	. . .	. . .
Mustard	Good	. . .	. . .
Onions	Fair (3)	Good (12+)	Good (12)
Parsley	Good	. . .	Good
Parsnips	Fair (8)	Good (12+)	Good (12+)
Peas (all)	Excellent (12)	Good (12+)	Good (12+)
Peppers			
Hot	Fair (3)	Good (12+)	Excellent (12+)
Sweet	Fair (3)	Good (12+)	Excellent (12+)
Potatoes	Good (8)	Good (12+)	. . .
Pumpkins	Good (8)	Good (12+)	Good (12+)

Dry Root Cellar* (40–50°F, 60–70% humidity)	Humid Root Cellar† (32–40°F, 80–90% humidity)	Mulched in Ground	Other
. . .	Excellent (6)	Excellent (4)	Pickled
Excellent (5)	. . .	. . .	. . .
. . .	Excellent (6)	Excellent (4)	Pickled
. . .	Fair (10)	Good (2)	. . .
. . .	Good (3)	. . .	. . .
. . .	Good (3)	Excellent (5)	. . .
. . .	Fair (1)	. . .	. . .
. . .	Fair (1)	. . .	Pickled
. . .	. . .	Good (2)	In cold frame
Excellent 56°F (5)	. . .	. . .	Pickled
. . .	. . .	. . .	Indoors in pot
. . .	Excellent (5)	Excellent (4)	. . .
. . .	. . .	. . .	. . .
. . .	. . .	. . .	Pickled
. . .	. . .	. . .	Pickled
. . .	Excellent (6)	. . .	. . .
Excellent (5)	. . .	. . .	. . .

[Continued on next page]

Food Storage Options—*Continued*

Crop	Freeze	Can	Dry
Radishes, white	. . .	. . .	. . .
Rhubarb	Excellent (12)	Good (12+)	Good (12+)
Rutabagas	Fair (8)	Good (12+)	. . .
Salsify	. . .	. . .	. . .
Shallots	. . .	. . .	Excellent (12)
Spinach	Excellent (12)	Good (12+)	. . .
Squash			
Summer	Fair (8)	Good (12+)	Good (12+)
Winter	Good (8)	Good (12+)	Good (12+)
Strawberries	Excellent (12)	. . .	Good as fruit leather
Sunflowers	. . .	. . .	Excellent (12+)
Sweet potatoes	Good (8)	Good (12+)	Good (12+)
Swiss chard	Good (12)	Good (12+)	. . .
Tomatoes	Good (8)	Excellent (12+)	Good (12+)
Turnips	Fair (8)	Good (12+)	. . .
Watermelon	Fair (3)	. . .	. . .

Dry Root Cellar* (40–50°F, 60–70% humidity)	Humid Root Cellar† (32–40°F, 80–90% humidity)	Mulched in Ground	Other
. . .	Excellent (4)	Good (2)	Pickled
. . .	. . .	. . .	. . .
. . .	Excellent (6)	Excellent (4)	. . .
. . .	Good (6)	Excellent (4)	. . .
Excellent (5)	. . .	. . .	. . .
. . .	. . .	. . .	In cold frame
. . .	. . .	. . .	Pickled
Excellent (5)	. . .	. . .	. . .
. . .	. . .	. . .	. . .
. . .	. . .	. . .	. . .
Excellent 56°F (4)	. . .	. . .	. . .
. . .	. . .	. . .	In cold frame
Green, to ripen	. . .	. . .	Pickled
. . .	Excellent (4)	Excellent (4)	Pickled
. . .	Fair (2)	. . .	Pickled

Vegetables Commonly Grown
in Solar Grow Frames and Greenhouses

Crop	Comments
Basil	Transplants easily from outside or can be started in greenhouse.
Beets	Grow for greens only.
Chinese cabbage	Does very well; all varieties seem to be prolific growers.
Chinese mustard	Does well; most varieties slow to bolt.
Chives	Transplant from outside.
Cucumbers	Difficult for the beginner; long-fruited European varieties are best suited to greenhouse conditions. Not recommended at all for grow frames.
Endive and escarole	Grow well in pots, just like leaf lettuce.
Kale	Good, reliable producer of fresh greens that thrives in cold temperatures. Also try collards, which are closely related.
Lettuce, leaf	Head lettuce will not head; leaf lettuce is easy to grow in beds or in pots, and almost all varieties work well.
Parsley	Easy to grow in beds or pots.
Radishes	White winter radishes do best; round-rooted varieties are recommended instead of the long-rooted types.
Spinach	Difficult to grow; New Zealand spinach is more successful in the solar greenhouse.
Swiss chard	Produces an abundance of fresh greens; transplant two-thirds-mature-size plants from outside garden into greenhouse in the fall.
Tomatoes	Difficult for beginners; special varieties are available for greenhouse growing; whiteflies are a serious problem with tomatoes in the greenhouse. Not recommended for grow frames.
Turnips	Oriental varieties of turnips seem to work the best.

Sprouting: Everything You Need to Know

Seed	Rinses per Day	Length at Harvest (in.)	Sprouting Time (days)	Approximate Yield (seeds to sprouts)	Characteristics	Stays Fresh in Refrigerator (days)
Alfalfa	2	1–2	3–5	3 tbs. = 4 cups	Easy to sprout; pleasant, light taste.	10
Lentil	2–4	¼–1	3	1 cup = 6 cups	Chewy bean texture; can be eaten raw or steamed lightly.	10
Mung bean	3–4	1½–2	3–5	1 cup = 6–8 cups	Easy to sprout; popular in oriental dishes.	7
Radish	2	¼–1	2–4	1 tbs. = 1 cup	Sprouts taste just like the vegetable.	9
Soybean	4–6	1–2	4–6	1 cup = 4–6 cups	Difficult to sprout because they ferment easily; need frequent, thorough rinses; should be cooked before eating for optimum protein availability.	7
Sunflower	2	Sprout is length of seed.	1–3	½ cup = 1½ cups	Good snacks, especially if lightly roasted; become bitter if grown too long.	11
Wheat	2–3	Sprout is length of seed.	2–4	1 cup = 3½–4 cups	Simple to sprout; very sweet taste.	9

Nutritional Content of Foods (in 100-g./3½-oz. serving)
Note: All the figures are based on foods in their raw form.

Food	Grams Protein	Energy in Calories	Grams Carbohydrates
Asparagus	2.5	26	5.0
Beans			
Snap	1.9	32	7.1
Lima		345	64.0
	20.4		
Mung	3.8	35	6.6
Soybean	. . .	46	5.3
Beets (with greens)	1.9	34	7.3
Broccoli	3.6	32	5.9
Brussels sprouts	4.9	45	8.3
Cabbage	1.3	24	5.4
Carrots	1.1	42	9.7
Cauliflower	2.7	27	5.2
Celery	0.9	17	3.9
Chinese cabbage	1.2	14	3.0
Collards	4.8	45	7.5
Corn	3.5	96	22.1
Cress, garden	. . .	22	3.9
Cucumbers	0.9	15	3.4
Eggplant	1.2	25	5.6
Garlic (1 oz.)	1.7	39	8.7
Horseradish (1 oz.)	3.2	25	5.6
Kale	6.0	53	9.0
Kohlrabi	. . .	29	6.6
Leeks	2.2	52	11.1
Lettuce			
Head	0.0	13	2.0
Leaf	1.3	18	3.5
Muskmelons	0.7	30	7.5
Mustard	3.0	31	5.6

Grams Fiber Content	Good Source of These Vitamins and Minerals*
. . .	*Thiamine; riboflavin; iron; niacin; vitamins A and C;* magnesium
1.0	Calcium, magnesium, zinc
. . .	*Iron, thiamine, niacin, calcium,* copper, magnesium, zinc, *potassium, riboflavin,* vitamin C, phosphorus
0.7	Phosphorus
. . .	Calcium, magnesium
. . .	Manganese, calcium, riboflavin
. . .	*Calcium, vitamin C,* iron, *potassium, riboflavin,* 2,500 I.U. *vitamin A, niacin, thiamine*
1.6	*Vitamin C, iron, riboflavin, niacin, potassium, calcium, thiamine*
0.8	Zinc
1.0	*Vitamin A,* zinc, *potassium, calcium*
. . .	*Vitamin C, iron, thiamine, riboflavin*
0.6	†
0.6	†
1.2	†
. . .	Thiamine, *niacin,* copper, manganese, zinc, *phosphorus,* magnesium
1.1	Potassium, vitamin A, riboflavin
0.6	†
. . .	†
1.5	Thiamine
2.4	†
1.3	Calcium, iron, vitamins A and C, copper, thiamine, riboflavin, niacin
. . .	†
1.3	†
0.5	Manganese
0.7	†
3.0	†
1.1	Calcium, iron, vitamins A and C, riboflavin

[*Continued on next page*]

*Based on author's research among several different sources; italicized vitamins and minerals are present in especially significant amounts in relation to other foods.
†Vitamins and minerals not present in significant amounts.

Nutritional Content of Foods—*Continued*

Food	Grams Protein	Energy in Calories	Grams Carbohydrates
Onions			
Sets	1.5	38	8.7
Shallots (1 oz.)	. . .	20	4.8
Parsley	3.6	43	8.4
Parsnips	1.7	76	17.5
Peas			
Edible-podded	. . .	. . .	. . .
Garden	3.4	53	12.0
Peppers			
Hot	1.3	37	9.0
Sweet	1.2	22	4.8
Potatoes	2.1	76	17.1
Pumpkins	1.0	26	6.5
Radishes	1.0	17	3.6
Rhubarb (sweetened)	. . .	141	36.0
Rutabagas	1.1	46	11.0
Salsify	2.0	69	18.0
Spinach	3.2	26	4.3
Squash			
Summer	1.1	19	4.2
Winter	1.4	50	15.4
Strawberries	. . .	36	8.3
Sunflowers (hulled)	. . .	556	19.6
Sweet potatoes	1.7	114	26.0
Swiss chard	. . .	24	4.5
Tomatoes	1.1	22	4.7
Turnip greens	1.0	30	6.6
Watermelon	0.5	26	6.4

Grams Fiber Content	Good Source of These Vitamins and Minerals*
0.6	†
. . .	†
1.5	Calcium, vitamin A
2.0	†
. . .	†
. . .	*Thiamine*, calcium, copper, magnesium, zinc, *vitamin B, iron, niacin, riboflavin, phosphorus*
1.8	†
1.4	Vitamin C
. . .	Niacin, potassium
1.1	Vitamin A
0.7	†
. . .	†
1.1	
1.8	
0.6	*Calcium, iron, vitamin A, potassium, riboflavin,* manganese
0.6	Niacin
. . .	†
1.3	†
. . .	†
. . .	*Vitamin A, thiamine*
. . .	Iron, potassium, vitamin A, magnesium
0.5	†
. . .	Vitamins A and C, calcium, thiamine, riboflavin
0.3	*Potassium*

Feeding the Birds

Bird	Feeding Area	Natural Food	Favorite Substitute	Acceptable Substitute
Sparrow, junco, towhee	On or close to ground	Grass, weed seed, small fruit, insects	Wild bird seed mix	None
Goldfinch, redpoll, pine siskin	On ground or thistle seed feeder	Pine and alder seed, weed seed	Thistle seed	Sunflower seed, wild bird seed mix
Purple finch, evening grosbeak, house finch	Feeder at least 4 ft. off ground	Insects, maple seed	Sunflower seed	Wild bird seed mix
Chickadee, titmouse, nuthatch	Raised or hanging feeder	Insects, moth eggs, spiders, pine seed, small seed	Sunflower seed	Wild bird seed mix
Woodpecker	Hanging net or bag	Insects, small berries and fruit	Suet cakes	None
Cardinal	On ground or low tray	Insects, small fruit, weed seed	Sunflower seed	Cracked corn
Mockingbird	Aboveground	Insects, small fruit	Raisins, chopped fruit	None
Blue jay	Anywhere	Insects, small fruit, acorns, grain	Chopped fruit, suet cakes, all seeds except thistle seed	None
Brown-headed cowbird, redwing blackbird	On ground or feeder	Grain, weed seed	Wild bird seed mix	None

Directory of Research Centers

This list includes demonstration projects and research centers in both the United States and Canada that are either operational or in development. They have publications or information available, and several publish newsletters. These centers are the focus of a great deal of exciting research in the areas of food production, energy conservation, and self-sufficiency for populated areas.

Conserver House
180 St. John St.
Fredericton, NB E3B 4A9
Canada

Ecology House
12 Madison Ave.
Toronto, ON M5R 2S1
Canada
Infiltration system, solar hot water system, insulating shutters and curtains, graywater system, composting toilet, hydroponics, trombe wall, winterization and insulation demonstration, wood stove, and an organic vegetable garden. Newsletter available.

Energy House
Responsible Urban Neighborhood Technology
3116 North Williams Ave.
Portland, OR 97227
Organic vegetable garden, root storage, energy-efficient kitchen, recycling bins, solar greenhouse, passive solar water preheat, insulated shutters, vapor barriers, porch airlocks, wood stove, winterization and insulation, fruits and berries. Planning composting toilet, graywater system. Newsletter available.

Energy Information Center of SPEC
The Canadian Society Promoting Environmental Conservation
2150 Maple St.
Vancouver, BC V6J 3T3
Canada
An office-demonstration building including energy conservation, solar greenhouse, solar hot water system, solar heating, winterization/insulation, and computer. Planning organic vegetable garden. Newsletter available.

E.R.I.F. Center
Energy Research and Information Foundation
3500 Kingman Blvd.
Des Moines, IA 50311
Winterization and insulation demonstration, insulating window treatments, solar hot water heater, graywater system, solar greenhouse.

Integral Urban House
The Farallones Institute
1516 Fifth St.
Berkeley, CA 94710

> Organic vegetable garden, fruits, berries, chickens, rabbits, fish, bees, composting toilet, graywater system, solar greenhouse, solar hot water system, solar heating, winterization and insulation, windmill, food storage system, hydroponics, wood stove. Planning photovoltaics.

Kalamazoo Nature Center
7000 North Westnedge Ave.
Kalamazoo, MI 49007

> Weatherization, wood stove, thermosiphoning air panels, solar greenhouse, graywater filtration system, solar hot water system, composting toilet, organic garden.

Long Branch Environmental Education Center
Big Sandy Mush Creek
Route 2, Box 132
Leicester, NC 28748

> Organic vegetable garden, solar heat, composting toilet, solar greenhouse, fish, fruit and berries.

The New Alchemy Institute
237 Hatchville Rd.
East Falmouth, MA 02536

> Now developing a demonstration single-family attached bioshelter, installation of a low-cost "bread box" solar hot water heater, vertical wall solar air panels, and expansion of southern windows.

Resource Management, Inc.
Route 2, Norman Dr.
Fletcher, NC 28732

> Organic vegetable garden, solar greenhouse, chickens, food storage system, wood stove, winterization/insulation. Planning fruits and berries, bees, composting toilet, graywater system, solar hot water, solar heating, photovoltaics, energy load management system, and a home computer.

Rodale Research Center
Box 323, R.D.1
Kutztown, PA 19530

> Part of Rodale Press, Inc., the Research Center carries on work with organic farming methods, solar greenhouses and grow frames, cold frames, amaranth and other new crops, fish farming, and nutritional analysis of crops and soils. Several demonstration gardens are maintained, and a self-guided tour is available.

Suburban Homesteaders, Inc.
17 Greenhill Rd.
Springfield, PA 19064
Organic vegetable garden, fruit, berries, root cellar, graywater system, solar greenhouse, wood stove, and home computer.

TERAD House
West Virginia University
Technology Education Program
2945 University Ave.
Morgantown, WV 26506
Attached solar greenhouse, window box solar collector, vertical solar wall collector, solar hot water system, direct gain solar wall collector, winterization and insulation demonstration, passive solar cooling system, wood stove, organic vegetable garden, solar cold frame, solar food dryer, composting toilet, chickens and rabbits. Planning fruits and berries, fish, food storage, and photovoltaics. Newsletter available.

Upland Hills Ecological Awareness Center
2575 Indian Lake Rd.
Oxford, MI 48051
Solar heating, solar cooling, wind-generated electricity, organic vegetable garden. Newsletter available.

The Urban Environmental Laboratory
Brown University
Center for Environmental Studies
Box 1943
Providence, RI 02912
Now developing a project that includes passive and active solar technologies, a solar greenhouse, thermosiphon air panels, domestic hot water panels, and photovoltaic cells. The greenhouse will be used both for growing vegetables and for aquaculture. Graywater systems are planned. Also planned is a vegetable garden, fruits and berries, bees, food storage system, composting toilet, wood stove, winterization and insulation, and a windmill. They are developing a building performance monitoring system.

Urban Options Energy House
135 Linden St.
East Lansing, MI 48823
Vegetable garden, solar greenhouse, solar hot water, solar heating, wood stove, winterization/insulation, food dryer, recycling. Material and newsletter available.

An Annotated Bibliography

This is not an exhaustive bibliography on the subject of backyard food production, but a listing of resources I've found helpful, and that may prove valuable to you as sources of further information. I have read most of the books in this list, so I feel confident in recommending them to someone else. The few I have not read come strongly recommended by friends who probably know more than I do about this subject.

General Readings and Inspirations

Diet for a Small Planet, by Frances Moore Lappé, Ballantine Books, 1975 (revised edition). This book—a landmark vegetarian cookbook when first published in 1971—sets forth a meatless diet based on the theory of protein complementarity. It also examines the waste of protein caused by the inefficiency of the U.S. food production and distribution system.

Future Shock, by Alvin Toffler, Bantam Books, 1971. A pivotal book in my life, it deals with how we can cope with change in our lives.

The Integral Urban House, by Helga Olkowski et al., Sierra Club Books, 1979. Based on the work of the Farallones Institute, this is one of the best and most complete descriptions of what can be done with food production, recycling, and energy production in an urban setting. Somewhat technical but very valuable.

Living the Good Life, by Helen Nearing and Scott Nearing, Schocken, 1971. A "must" book for anyone interested in moving toward more self-sufficiency. It is as much motivational as informative.

Never Kiss a Goat on the Lips, by Vic Sussman, Rodale Press, 1981. A hilarious and informative account of the trials and happy times of a suburban homesteader.

The Next Whole Earth Catalog, edited by Stewart Brand, Random House, 1980. A compendium of information and resources, it's as much fun as it is informative. The book is a catalog of all manner of tools, books, gadgets, and resources, and it also contains very interesting and helpful discussions of topics like gardening and homesteading.

The One-Straw Revolution, by Masanobu Fukuoka, Rodale Press, 1978. A delightful and inspirational book about pure organic farming.

Permaculture One and *Permaculture Two,* by Bill Mollison, Tagari Community Books, 1978 and 1979. Two books about a system of agriculture that combines landscaping with perennial plants and animals. While it does not deal directly with backyard applications, I believe that permaculture will be practiced in American backyards by 1990.

Small Is Beautiful, by E. F. Schumacher, Harper & Row, 1976. This book helped me sort out some confusion about my power equipment and my hand equipment. The book deals with the issue of making technology relevant to people.

The Supermarket Handbook, by Nikki Goldbeck and David Goldbeck, New American Library, 1976 (expanded edition). A guide to choosing whole, natural foods from supermarket shelves. This book surveys a wide variety of foods, pointing out which ones contain lots of additives and which are less processed and healthier for you. It was a real eye-opener for me.

The Third Wave, by Alvin Toffler, Bantam Books, 1981. This is one of the clearest explanations of what is happening to our world in the 1980s that I have encountered.

Books about Gardening

Better Vegetable Gardens the Chinese Way, by Peter Chan and Spencer Gill, Graphic Arts Center Publishing Co., 1980. This is pleasant and informative reading about an approach that emphasizes the value of raised beds. The beautiful color photographs are a special treat.

The Encyclopedia of Organic Gardening, by the staff of *Organic Gardening* magazine, Rodale Press, 1978. A basic reference for any serious gardener—defines and explains gardening concepts and practices.

Getting the Most from Your Garden, by the editors of *Organic Gardening* magazine, Rodale Press, 1980. A comprehensive guide to raised-bed and intensive gardening methods, including succession and relay planting.

How to Grow More Vegetables, by John Jeavons, Ten Speed Press, 1979. An excellent primer on intensive planting and raised-bed gardening.

The Organic Gardener's Complete Guide to Vegetables and Fruits, by the editors of Rodale Press, 1982. A very current, detailed reference on all aspects of fruit and vegetable culture.

The Seed-Starter's Handbook, by Nancy Bubel, Rodale Press, 1978. A very complete discussion about saving seeds and starting your own seedlings.

Square Foot Gardening, by Mel Bartholomew, Rodale Press, 1981. A really good book for beginning gardeners, it gives no-nonsense information on a carefully designed system of growing vegetables in limited spaces.

Books about Fruits and Berries

All about Growing Fruits and Berries, edited by Will Kirkman, Ortho Books, 1976. Although it espouses the use of chemical fertilizers and pesticides, this book contains my favorite description of the espalier process, and for that I recommend it. It also contains excellent photos and illustrations.

The Complete Book of Edible Landscaping, by Rosalind Creasy, Sierra Club Books, 1982. This is a most thorough and useful reference on edible landscaping, with much information on fruit and berry bushes and trees.

Books about Soil and Compost

Easy Composting, by Vic Sussman, Rodale Press, 1982. An excellent guide for beginners on making and using compost.

The Gardener's Guide to Better Soil, by Gene Logsdon, Rodale Press, 1976. All you need to know about soil management—how to build and maintain healthy soil.

The Rodale Guide to Composting, by Jerry Minnich et al., Rodale Press, 1979. A detailed guide for the most experienced compost producer, covering methods, structures, and uses for compost.

Books about Bugs

The Bug Book: Harmless Insect Controls, by John Philbrick and Helen Philbrick, Garden Way Publishing, 1974. An excellent little book for when the bugs are getting you down.

Insect Pests, by George S. Fichter, Golden Press, 1966. Basically a field guide, but it often gives more behavioral information about some of the common pests than you find in books on pest control.

AN ANNOTATED BIBLIOGRAPHY

Organic Plant Protection, edited by Roger B. Yepsen, Rodale Press, 1976. A detailed review of all the garden pests and the many organic approaches to their control—a classic reference.

Rodale's Color Handbook of Garden Insects, by Anna Carr, Rodale Press, 1979. My favorite basic reference, this book has color photos of the most common garden pests. I keep it in the kitchen so it's handy when I spot a new bug.

Books about Greenhouses and Grow Frames

Growing Food in Solar Greenhouses, by Delores Wolfe, Dolphin Books, 1981. A useful book on growing vegetables in a solar greenhouse, this one is organized around a month-by-month schedule of activities.

Horticultural Management of Solar Greenhouses in the Northeast, by Miriam Klein, The Memphremagog Group, 1980. An excellent book about how actually to grow things in a solar greenhouse, excellent for gardeners in the northeastern states.

The Solar Greenhouse Book, edited by James C. McCullagh, Rodale Press, 1978. An outstanding book for anyone planning a greenhouse, it covers everything you need to think about in terms of designing the best greenhouse for your needs.

Solar Growing Frame, edited by Ray Wolf, Rodale Plans, Rodale Press, 1980. A complete manual on how to build and use a solar grow frame designed at the Rodale Research Center. Includes specific instructions and ten pages of blueprints.

Books about Food Processing and Storing

The Blue Book, published by the Ball Jar Corp., Muncie, IN 47302. An old standby through many decades of canning and freezing. A good basic reference, with lots of recipes.

The Garden-to-Table Cookbook, by James Beard et al., McGraw Hill, 1976. A good collection of vegetable recipes, although not all using natural foods.

The Green Thumb Cookbook, by the editors of *Organic Gardening and Farming* magazine, Rodale Press, 1977. A good collection of natural vegetable recipes.

Putting Food By, by Ruth Hertzberg et al., Stephen Greene Press, 1975 (2d edition). A good general reference on food storage and additive-free preservation.

Root Cellaring, by Mike Bubel and Nancy Bubel, Rodale Press, 1979. A complete discussion, from the design to the building to the management of a root cellar—an excellent book with good recipes as well.

Simple Food for the Good Life, by Helen Nearing, Delacorte Press, 1980. A wonderful collection of recipes from a lifetime of living on a self-sufficient homestead.

Stocking Up, edited by Carol H. Stoner, Rodale Press, 1977 (revised edition). Another excellent general reference on canning, freezing, and storing your produce. Contains numerous all-natural recipes.

Books about Small Livestock

Chickens in Your Backyard, by Rick Luttmann and Gail Luttmann, Rodale Press, 1976. A good review for someone thinking about getting into raising chickens.

The Earthworm Book, by Jerry Minnich et al., Rodale Press, 1977. An excellent general reference on the subject, with plenty of information on raising your own earthworms and putting them to work in your garden.

First Lessons in Beekeeping, by C. P. Dadant, Dadant and Sons, 1976. A very good first book for a person planning on getting into raising bees.

Raising Rabbits, by Ann Kanable, Rodale Press, 1977. A guide to raising a small herd of rabbits, including information on building housing, selecting stock, and caring for rabbits.

Magazines for the Backyard Food Producer

The Avant Gardener, published by Horticultural Data Processing, Box 489, New York, NY 10028. This newsletter covers the entire spectrum of horticulture, but contains information on new developments in vegetable gardening in almost every issue.

Country Journal, published monthly by Country Journal Publishing, 205 Main St., Brattleboro, VT 05301, also available on newsstands.

Gardens for All News, published monthly by Gardens for All, 180 Flynn Ave., Burlington, VT 05401. A clearinghouse of information for and from vegetable gardeners across the country.

The Mother Earth News, published bimonthly by the Mother Earth News, Inc., Hendersonville, NC 28739, also available on newsstands.

Organic Gardening, published monthly by Rodale Press, Emmaus, PA 18049, available at newsstands as well as by subscription.

Index

Page numbers in **boldface** indicate table entry.